*"I consider this completely valid. It requires immediate action."*

—VICTOR KOVDA
Former President, Scientific Committee for Environmental Problems, International Council of Scientific Unions

*"This deserves the most urgent attention."*

—WALTER CORSON
Global Tomorrow Coalition

*"An ice age is coming, and I welcome it as a much needed cleansing. I see no possible solution to our ruination of Earth except for a drastic reduction of the human population."*

—DAVE FOREMAN,
Founder of Earth First!

*"This is very important."*

—PIERRE LEHMAN
Atmospheric Physicist, *Société de l'étude de l'environment,* Switzerland

*"This book is must reading."*

—C. BERTRAND SCHULTZ
Director, Institute for Tertiary-Quaternary Studies and Nebraska Academy of Sciences

*"This seems very important to me."*

—WIBJÖRN KARLÉN
Climatologist, University of Stockholm

*"The significance and timeliness of this material cannot be overstated. We have absolutely no time to lose."*

—GREG WATSON
Office of Science and Technology, Commonwealth of Massachusetts and science adviser to Governor Michael Dukakis

*Larry Ephron, Ph.D.*

# THE
# END

## *The Imminent Ice Age & How We Can Stop It*

An Institute for a Future book

**Celestial Arts**
*Berkeley, California*

CELESTIAL ARTS
P.O. Box 7327
Berkeley, California 94707

Front cover photo by Gordon Wiltsie/Alpenimage © 1988
Cover photo of author by Elliot Khuner
Cover design by Ken Scott

Recycled paper was not available for this printing process.

Library of Congress Cataloging-in-Publication Data

Ephron, Larry.
    The end: the imminent ice age & how we can stop it.

Bibliography: p.
    1. Man—Influence on nature. 2. Climatic changes.
3. Greenhouse effect, Atmospheric. 4. Air—Pollution.
I. Title.
GF75.E59   1988            304.2'5            88-6118
ISBN 0-89087-507-3

# Contents

*"The magical mystery tour
is coming to take you away."*

—THE BEATLES

*Chapter One*

# WILL WE HAVE TO STOP EATING SOON?

*"Come hear Uncle John's Band
By the riverside.
Got some things to talk about
Here beside the rising tide ..."*

—ROBERT HUNTER, JERRY GARCIA
AND THE GRATEFUL DEAD

**M**any of us take our food for granted these days, like so much else in our lives. If we live in cities, we may even have little awareness of where our food really comes from: from agriculture. Many things must be present for a successful agriculture, one of the most important being a favorable climate. Without warm, sunny weather during several months of the year, the huge amounts of food we all need for our survival would not grow at all.

There is some very ominous news. It has been widely accepted that the earth will enter another ice age sometime "soon," meaning sometime in the next few hundred, or perhaps thousand years. The news is that there is now considerable evidence that the first stages of the next ice age may really begin *soon*, within the next few years—and that the transitional stage of extreme and increasingly inhospitable climate may have already begun.

*1*

# The cycle of ice ages

Ask the average person when the last ice age was and they may think of mastodons and saber-tooth tigers and tell you it was probably a few million years ago. The fact is that the last ice age ended only 10,000 years ago, a few seconds in geological time; and everything we think of as civilization—agriculture, cities, pottery, weaving cloth, the wheel, writing, history itself—has taken place only in that brief span of time since the earth last warmed up.

Though glaciers covered only about 40% of the earth's surface during the height of the last ice age, most of the temperate zones had freezing night-time temperatures the year round, destroying most sources of food. Moreover, rainfall was minimal in the tropics during the last ice age, and much of the regions which remained warm enough for food to grow became deserts. Only small pockets of life could exist on the earth during those hundreds of centuries of cold. Most living things died.

But what could be the significance of these ancient events to us, living in our warm, sunny climates thousands of years later? Simply this: The major ice ages are now known to occur with great regularity, on an awesome 100,000-year cycle. Each ice age lasts some 90,000 years of that cycle, with the warmer interglacial periods, such as the one we're now living in, averaging only about 10,000 years (Figure 1). And *it has now been some 10,800 years since the end of the last ice age*. We're due for another one any time now.[1]/*

**FIGURE 1**

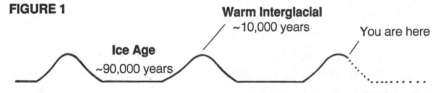

* Numbered notes containing further discussion of certain topics are found at the end of each chapter. A section of additional endnotes is found at the end of the book, keyed to page numbers in the text.

But who can say exactly when it will occur? Although the warm interglacial periods have averaged about 10,000 years, they have occasionally lasted as long as 12,000 years. How long is ours going to last—before most of the earth gets too cold or too dried out to grow food, and we stop eating?

Most scientists seem to be noncommittal at this point—they're taking a wait-and-see attitude. They believe the whole field of climatology is in its infancy. A few have begun to express some concern and point to signs that we may be much closer to the beginning of the next ice age than anybody would like to think.

One scientist, however, has presented evidence that we are *already* moving rapidly toward ice age conditions on the planet, conditions which could lead to massive worldwide starvation without regard for national boundaries or standards of living—*within five to seven years,* from 1988. Though John Hamaker is rare in his extreme pessimism at this point, his reading of the evidence seems to gain credibility from the fact that he alone has developed a plausible theory of what causes the ice ages to reappear, almost on schedule, every hundred thousand years.

If all this sounds like more bad news than we can possibly stand, there may yet be one bright ray of hope here: if Hamaker is right, and we act very quickly, wc may be able to pull off the incredible feat of stopping the cycle of ice ages completely.

## *Record cold*

There is no doubt that Northern Hemisphere winters have been cooling for several decades now, and increasingly so: eight of the past ten winters have been severely cold. Climatologists know that the world's weather and temperature fluctuate all the time, however, in cycles lasting years, decades, and centuries—cycles which are usually recognized only after the fact. Perhaps this is only a temporary fluctuation? What, if anything, is significant about *this* long cold spell?

The most obvious thing is that it has been colder at times during the past few years *than ever before in recorded history* for those times of year. World temperature extremes began in 1972, with record cold in scores of places. The Soviet Union, situated at a high latitude, lost much of its grain harvest and began buying large quantities of wheat abroad. Satellite photographs showed that the Northern Hemisphere's total snow cover had increased by an enormous one-and-a-half million square miles over the previous year. It was estimated that only seven such winters consecutively could establish an ice cover the equivalent in area (not yet in depth) of the last ice age.

The dramatic increase of snow and ice cover in the Canadian arctic in just a few years is shown graphically in Figure 2.

**FIGURE 2**

## Incease in Canadian Snow and Ice Cover from 1967-1970 to 1971-1975

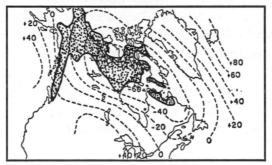

Source: Williams (1978)

Shaded area indicates the difference in median October 1st snow/ice cover boundary from 1967-70 to 1971-75, as mapped by NOAA National Environmental Satellite Service.

In 1977 the first snow in recorded history fell on Miami, Florida. In the United States the winters of 1977–78 and 1978–79 were both unprecedented. By 1979 record cold to 60 degrees below normal was being recorded in some places, and the spring snow cover was greater in area than it had ever been before, as late storms battered much of the country. On June 25, almost mid-summer, a cold wave came from the north and killed frost-sensitive vegetables from Minnesota to Michigan.

The total Northern Hemisphere snow cover had increased by another million square miles since 1972. Snow fell on the Sahara Desert for the first time in recorded history.

The next five years saw the temperature drop to 50° below zero in Maine, 41 inches of snow fall on Norfolk, Virginia, crops freeze in Texas and Florida (three southern states), and 60 to 120 MPH winds in many parts of the United States drive hailstones the size of golfballs in some areas, softballs in others. Severe crop damage spread from Nebraska to Texas, Oregon to South Carolina. The snow cover on North America in mid-April 1982 was once again the largest ever recorded for that time of year.

In recent springs the mercury has again fallen to new all-time lows. Never in history has snow fallen so late in the season in some areas. Tens of millions of young peaches, apples, strawberries, and tomatoes were turned into ice cubes. Parts of Canada once rich in wheat no longer had the necessary 41 frost-free days to grow it at all.

And the roof of the Minneapolis Metrodome collapsed under an unexpected load of snow—in the middle of April.

A cold snap in December 1983 damaged almost one-third of Florida's citrus trees so badly they would not bear fruit the next year. And in January 1985 this newspaper story appeared:

> For the fourth time in five years, Florida citrus grove owners this week awoke to icicles hanging from their oranges.... Grove owners, some in tears, fought through the night to keep their groves warm.... Some were talking about the annihilation of the citrus industry throughout many Florida counties, where oranges and grapefruits had been growing for generations.

One grove owner said "It used to be that these freezes came along once a decade. But now they're coming every year. It makes you wonder if another ice age isn't upon us."

On January 28 of that year the space shuttle Challenger exploded in flight soon after it left the launching pad. The tragedy was finally traced to rubbery seals on the booster rockets, which had lost their resiliency when south Florida temperatures dropped to 22 degrees below freezing the night before (there was ice on the fuel tank), and had apparently not recovered by the time the launching took place in temperatures 6 degrees above freezing. It was 13 degrees colder than any previous shuttle launching.

The extreme cold continued. In February 1986 the North Sea froze off the coast of Belgium. In May, Charles Bentley, director of the University of Wisconsin's polar research center, said that field observations during the last decade indicate that both the Antarctic and Greenland ice sheets are growing, not declining as many scientists had reasoned because of the greenhouse effect. By fall the Hubbard Glacier in Alaska made headlines by closing off a fresh water inlet and trapping dozens of seals and porpoises. Scientists noted that it was only one of some fifty Alaskan glaciers in some state of fast motion. "Usually we have only ten in any given year."

In January 1987 new all-time low temperatures were recorded in many regions, including the East Coast of the United States, the Soviet Union, and parts of Europe. In the Caucasus Mountains, snow fell continuously for an entire month. In late March a 23°F freeze damaged hundreds of thousands of acres of early wheat in Texas and Oklahoma; an agronomist said, "We have never before seen what happened last night. . . ." The following month brought the first April snow in recorded history to parts of Mississippi and Alabama.

The growing season in the temperate region of the Northern Hemisphere became noticeably shorter as early as 1976—27 days shorter than it was in 1946—squeezed at both ends by colder winters. Another 22% decrease would begin to threaten the growing of hybrid corn at all, whose minimum growing season is 100 to 130 days.

Is all this extreme cold just a temporary aberration? Analysis of temperature data provided by the U.S. National Climatic Data Center suggests otherwise. The extreme winters which have occurred so frequently during the past 15 years are clearly the extension of a trend that began at least half a century ago. January in New England averages some 6°F colder than it was only five decades ago, when systematic data first began to be collected; in the west south central states it is some 8° colder now.[2] Data on February temperatures in central England, available since 1860, show that the long-term cooling trend began at least a hundred years ago.[3]

Extremely cold winters are not the only weather anomaly of recent decades. The climate seems to be getting extreme in many different ways.

# Hurricanes, tornados

The incidence of major storms and tornados has been increasing for many years now, and at an accelerating rate. Several decades ago the United States was hit with an average of a hundred or so tornados each year. Now there are close to a thousand per year, and the number is steadily rising (Figure 3, see next page).[4] The average number of Atlantic hurricanes has increased from 4.1 a year (1886 to 1939) to 6.3 a year (since 1940)—an increase of more than 50%.

It appears to be no coincidence that all these extremes of weather are happening simultaneously. The fierce winds that propel storms, hurricanes, and tornados are caused by the extreme temperature differentials between the poles and the equatorial regions, differentials which have been increasing steadily in recent years. The warm air of the tropics creates low-pressure systems (warm air is lighter, so it rises), which are quickly filled by the heavy, cold, high-pressure systems coming down from the polar regions.[5]

# Drought

While the temperature differential between the poles and tropics is being widened by the almost steadily refrigerating trend of higher latitude winters, it is being widened still further by the tropical regions becoming hotter and hotter. This sounds paradoxical, but it appears to make perfect sense meteorologically. As higher latitude winters become colder and wind conditions increase in range and

**FIGURE 3**

## Average Number of Tornados per Year
## in the United States, 1916 to 1986*

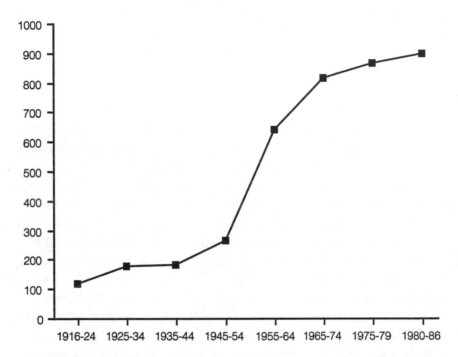

| 1916-24 | 1925-34 | 1935-44 | 1945-54 | 1955-64 | 1965-74 | 1975-79 | 1980-86 |

Source:  The World Almanac, 1972, 1980; U. S. Department of Commerce, National Oceanic and
Atmospheric Administration, Technical Report, 1986

*There is probably some error factor due to more complete reporting, but it is probably significantly less
than the 900% increase shown from 1920 to 1986, and the 350% increase shown between 1950 and
1986.  One assumes more complete reporting is a function primarily of population increase, but U. S.
population increased only 124% from 1920-86.  Even the square of the population increase is
substantially less than the increases shown here.

magnitude, evaporated moisture which normally would have fallen
back on the tropics as rain now falls farther away, as rain or snow.
Thus the tropics tend to get hotter and drier, the higher latitudes
colder and wetter.

Drought has been increasing, somewhat erratically, since the
1960s. Since 1972—the same year northern winters began to get
much colder—a million people have died of starvation in the tropical
regions of Africa and Asia.[6]

In 1983, for the first time since the dust bowl of the 1930s, severe drought destroyed a huge part of America's food supply—one-third of the entire soybean crop and *half of all the corn*. In late summer 1986 the whole of the southeastern United States was again devastated by a long drought, which reportedly destroyed some *90%* of all its crops. As one newspaper report put it, "chickens die in their sheds, fish in their ponds, cattle in their fields, ancient oaks in their woods and people in their homes." The drought of the tropics is moving into the temperate zones. (Like the song says, we *are* the world—all of us.) In India, the summer monsoon rains failed to come until the end of August, resulting in the worst drought in this century. (Northern India is the same latitude as Texas.) Massive starvation was averted only because sufficient food reserves were on hand and were quickly distributed.

Summer in the Northern Hemisphere is winter in the Southern Hemisphere. The increasing pole-to-tropics temperature differential in the Southern Hemisphere carries off some of the north's summer showers to fall as winter rain and snow on South America, Australia, the southern oceans, and Antarctica.

Over a period of time, drought creates deserts. The spreading of drought as the tropics heat up can be graphically seen in the exponentially increasing desertification of the earth's usable agricultural lands (Figure 4, see next page).

# Flooding

The moisture-laden clouds carried poleward from the tropics by the increasing wind systems often release part of their burden over the temperate zones in the form of rain or snow, primarily in the fall, winter, and spring. The result is increased flooding.

In the United States, 1985 and 1986 saw heavy flooding in many areas. During one period parts of Kansas, Missouri, Illinois, Ohio, Michigan, Arkansas, and Oklahoma were all battling floodwaters. Heavy rains ruined much of the winter wheat crop in several states; almost two-thirds of Missouri's 1987 winter wheat was lost. The

**FIGURE 4**

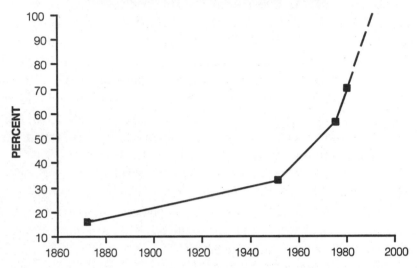

### Percentage of Usable Agricultural Land on the Planet that has Become Desert*

Source: *RAIN* magazine, December 1982

*Excludes treeless tundra, polar, and high mountain regions.

Sacramento River in California's agricultural Central Valley broke levees and flooded a wide area in February 1986. One official said "the highest volume of water in history" was coming through the river system.

The Great Salt Lake rose 11 feet in four years, inundating interstate highways and railroad tracks and making maps obsolete. The Great Lakes rose to record levels in 1985 and then continued to rise, lapping at the doors of the Chicago luxury hotels once set back from the shore of Lake Michigan and making one wonder if the city itself would soon be covered with water. Some Chicago suburbs were flooded in August 1987 as a result of the heaviest 24-hour rainfall ever recorded in the area. In September Bangladesh experienced the worst floods in its history, leaving 24 million people homeless or without food.

If present climatic trends continue, the United States, along with Europe, the Soviet Union, Japan, much of China, India, and the other temperate agricultural zones of the world, will be increasingly caught in a huge pincer—longer, wetter, and colder winters and shorter, hotter, and drier summers. The temperate zones themselves will begin to disappear, reducing the growing season to the point where we will not be able to grow enough food to live.

# What causes the ice ages?

What could cause the major ice ages to recur approximately every hundred thousand years?

Until recently, most scientists have believed that the cycle of ice ages could be explained by something called the Milankovitch theory. Milutin Milankovitch was a Yugoslavian mathematician who, around the turn of the century, was looking for "a cosmic problem" to solve. Deciding to try to develop a mathematical theory capable of describing the long-term climatic changes of the earth, he began to refine some ideas which had been gaining credence during the latter part of the nineteenth century, that ice ages are caused by changes in the earth's orbit around the sun.

Three separate factors were involved in Milankovitch's refinement of the theory: the size of the orbit itself, which changes very slightly over a 100,000-year cycle; the tilt of the earth's axis, which varies by about one-and-a-half degrees in a cycle of some 41,000 years; and the slight "wobble" of the axis around its center (like a top just beginning to slow down), which has approximately a 22,000-year cycle. Each of these changes was calculated for its effect on the amount of sunlight falling on the earth in different areas, which would presumably affect its climate.

Milankovitch believed that he had succeeded in explaining the cause of the ice ages. Others, however, pointed out that the slight,

100,000-year variation in the size of the earth's orbit was so small that it changed the amount of sunlight falling on the earth by no more than one-half of 1%, surely not enough to explain the enormous temperature change of major ice ages.[7] These very regular orbital cycles also appear to be inconsistent with the very skewed ice age pattern of 90,000 years cold, 10,000 warm. But the battle has continued to rage in scientific circles for more than half a century.[8]

Recent computer modeling—by a man who has been the foremost modern exponent of the Milankovitch theory, John Imbrie at Brown University—has finally cast serious doubt on the validity of much of Milankovitch's ice age hypothesis. In a paper published in *Science* in February 1980, Imbrie reports that the most sophisticated recent version of the Milankovitch theory (Imbrie's) is capable of explaining only the smaller climatic changes associated with minor fluctuations in glaciation, and only for the past 150,000 years or so. It seems to do least well on the 100,000 year cycle. And beyond about 350,000 years ago, it seems to have little value in predicting any of the climatic changes we now know about. (The 100,000-year ice age cycle is now known to have occurred over at least the last 2.5 million years.)[9]

With astronomical causes more or less ruled out at least for the present, could the great ice age cycle be caused by something here on earth? This is where John Hamaker comes in.

Hamaker was trained in mechanical engineering at Purdue. He became interested in climatology after thinking about the environment for many years and watching it deteriorate from neglect and abuse. He got first-hand information on the dangers of toxic chemicals while working as an engineer for Monsanto in 1940, long before the rest of us got the bad news from *Silent Spring*. After serving in the army for five years during the war and coming out a captain in the reserve, he went to work designing oil refinery machinery in Texas. But he began to feel sicker and sicker and realized that he had to get out of the toxic environments he had been working in.

Hamaker bought a farm in East Texas and "learned about really worn-out soil—and the mess that chemicals make on farmland." He noted that his cows kept as far away from agricultural chemicals as they could, and he wondered whether they were smarter than people. Later he moved to Michigan, where for many years he did experimental work on a ten-acre farm outside of Lansing.

During the mid-1970s, while thinking about big questions like the health of the soil and man's relationship to the earth, Hamaker began reading earnestly in the *Encyclopedia Brittanica*. Each article seemed to lead to another, and after a few years of thinking and reading every book and scientific article he could get his hands on about climate and soil and the health of plant life, he believed he understood what causes the ice ages to come and go with such predictability.

Why, he had wondered, are winters now getting colder, summers hotter and drier, storms and tornados increasingly frequent with every decade? What forces on earth are large enough to cause such global changes?

When he looked at these rising curves, another came to mind: the exponentially rising curve of carbon dioxide ($CO_2$) in the earth's atmosphere (Figure 5, see next page).

The $CO_2$ curve is well known. Most scientists believe it is caused by the ever-increasing burning of fossil fuels—coal, oil, natural gas—since the industrial revolution began early in the last century. And many of them presume the increased $CO_2$ will eventually create a "greenhouse effect," trapping additional warmth radiated off the earth from the sun and increasing the temperature all over the globe. Supposedly, if the climate gets warm enough, the ice caps at the poles would melt, raising the height of sea level by 200 feet or more and inundating most of the major cities of the world.

But there is no consensus as to when this global greenhouse effect might be large enough to cause such changes. In spite of the huge increase of $CO_2$ that has already occurred during the past century (more than 38%), there is no consensus as to whether the earth's climate has been affected yet. Climatologists are still debating whether the earth's average temperature may have increased by as much as ½ of 1° Celsius in the last hundred years, and whether this is attributable to the greenhouse effect. Some argue that this may just be random fluctuation; others point out that the greenhouse effect was large and increasing even during the period 1940 to 1965, when it is pretty generally agreed that the earth as a whole was getting colder.

Hamaker saw what no one else seems to have seen: that the greenhouse effect is not equal over the globe, but occurs *differentially*—primarily in the tropics and lower latitudes, because they get the most sunlight. (The poles get almost no sunlight six months out of the year, and very indirect rays the rest of the time.) He recognized that the tropics have *already* been heating up and drying out for the past few decades (witness the extreme drought and famine in Africa), which might be directly attributable to increasing carbon dioxide and the greenhouse effect.

Are there any climatic effects from $CO_2$ in the higher latitudes? These regions seem to be getting colder, at least in the winter, and

**FIGURE 5**

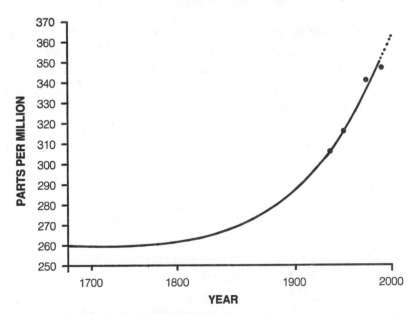

## Atmospheric Carbon Dioxide
## as Recorded at Mauna Loa Observatory

Source: National Oceanic and Atmospheric Administration, U. S. Dept. of Commerce; historical value from research cited by Schneider and Londer (1984)

with increased precipitation rather than drought. Hamaker reasoned that as the greenhouse effect produced by increasing carbon dioxide warms up the tropics primarily, the temperature difference between the tropics and the poles increases. This warming tropical air then rises more quickly, and cold, heavy polar air rushes in more rapidly to fill the vacuum. The result is increasingly high winds, including more hurricanes and tornados.

As the tropics are increasingly warmed by the greenhouse effect, warm tropical ocean water evaporates faster, forming additional moisture-laden clouds. Most of these tropical clouds are then moved by the increasing wind systems toward higher latitudes. In the mid-latitudes they tend to precipitate out as rainfall, resulting in increased flooding. In the higher latitudes and polar regions their moisture tends to fall as snow and ice—building up the polar glaciers and ice sheets.

Hamaker's insights seem to be borne out by recent studies, both theoretical and empirical. At Princeton University, Wetherald and Manabe (1986) used computer modeling to predict the hypothetical results of increased atmospheric $CO_2$. They found that the amount of moisture-laden clouds would be expected to decrease in tropical and lower latitudes, and to increase greatly in the middle and higher latitudes. In Germany, Roeckner and others (1987) added cloud cover to their modeling (a variable that is usually left out of atmospheric circulation models) and calculated that the cooling effects of the increased cloudiness caused by a doubling of atmospheric carbon dioxide would result, paradoxically, in a very substantial *net cooling* from the greenhouse effect. In its subsequent summary of this research, *New Scientist* titled their article, "Towards a cold greenhouse."

These theoretical conclusions are borne out by recent empirical research. Bradley and others (1987) recently found "marked increases" in Northern Hemisphere mid-latitude precipitation over the last 30 to 40 years. The heaviest precipitation was found to have occurred in winter. Since their mid-latitude zone extends northward to the middle of Baffin Island in northern Canada, we can assume that much of this markedly increased winter precipitation of the past 30 to 40 years was snowfall.

Bradley and his colleagues also found that in the lower latitudes, "a pronounced downward trend" in precipitation began in the early 1950s and has continued to the present. The increasing drought in this region "is mainly a characteristic of summer and fall months. . . ." In Europe, despite steadily increasing fall, winter, and spring precipitation for the past 130 years, summer rainfall has declined during the same period. All these recent findings are consistent with Hamaker's theory.[10]

Hamaker suggests that a sustained greenhouse effect brought on by increased carbon dioxide could, paradoxically, be the trigger for an ice age. Sir George Simpson, former head of Britain's Royal Meteorological Office, was the first to point out that the glaciation characteristic of an ice age cannot come about by a general cooling of the earth's atmosphere. Why? Because some source of *increased energy* is required to transport poleward the huge amounts of moisture which make up the glaciers. Many climatologists now agree. But until Hamaker's explanation of a differential greenhouse effect mediated by atmospheric carbon dioxide, no one had been able to figure out what the source of such an enormous amount of energy could be.[11]

The greenhouse effect resulting from increased carbon dioxide may well have warmed the earth's average temperature about ½° Celsius in the last hundred years. But the warming has been far from uniform, and to speak of averages at all can be very misleading. The warming seems to have resulted in increasingly erratic weather, in climatic extremes of every kind, including record cold winters again and again and increasing rain and snowfall in the higher latitudes, hardly what one expects when one hears of global warming.

The potential or actual buildup of polar ice as a result of lower latitude and oceanic warming has become increasingly recognized by climatologists, including W. F. Ruddiman and A. McIntyre of Columbia University's Lamont-Doherty Geological Observatory; Lester Machta, head of the National Oceanic and Atmospheric Administration's Air Resources Laboratory; David P. Adam of the U.S. Geological Survey; Jay Harmon, Roger G. Barry, Sir H. H. Lamb, John Gribbin,

Dominique Raynaud, Ian Whillans, Wibjörn Karlén, Pierre Lehman, Kenneth E. F. Watt, Victor Kovda, N. A. Volkov, V. F. Zhakarov, and Kirill Kondrat'ev.

Lamb, often thought of as the grand old man of climatology, points out that the increased cloud cover likely to be generated by any warming resulting from $CO_2$ would at least be likely to cancel out such warming and would probably produce lower temperatures and increased precipitation in the middle latitudes. James Coakley at the National Center for Atmospheric Research says that an increase of only 4 to 7% in certain types of cloud cover could offset a *doubling* of carbon dioxide. Stephen Schneider, director of NCAR, writes, "It is conceivable . . . that about a 10 percent sustained change in cloud cover . . . could bring on . . . an ice age."

The increasing temperature differential between the tropics and the poles caused by a greenhouse effect also leads to increasing circulation of ocean currents. Colder, heavier polar waters flow south along the ocean bottom, warmer, lighter tropical currents flow northward. As a result, surface ocean waters in the middle to higher latitudes may be warmer than usual even while nearby land surfaces are becoming colder due to increasing cloud cover and snowfall. The warmer surface waters evaporate faster, and the colder land surfaces condense the evaporated moisture faster, to increase rain and snowfall. Ruddiman and McIntyre (1979) go so far as to say that a warm ocean next to a cold land mass, such as is currently found in the middle north latitudes and was present during the first half of the last two 10,000-year periods of major ice sheet growth (during the last ice age), is "an *optimal* configuration for delivering moisture to the growing ice sheets" (emphasis added).

Ray Bradley and Gifford Miller (1972), studying the climate of Baffin Island in northern Canada from 1960 to 1969, found that snow and ice increased substantiallly while the average yearly temperature remained unchanged. Old glaciers grew bigger and two new ones were born. Summer temperatures were slightly below normal but fall-winter-spring temperatures were actually above normal. They noted that "the landscape seems to be moving toward more glacial conditions" though the overall climate had not cooled at all.

It is widely believed that the exponential rise of $CO_2$ in the last century, and the resultant greenhouse effect, is directly attributable primarily to our burning of fossil fuels. Yet the cycle of major ice ages has been going on for some 2.5 million years, and every previous ice age occurred before human beings ever existed. What on earth could possibly have triggered a global greenhouse effect every hundred thousand years or so before we came along?

# Why are the earth's forests dying?

Another crucial observation Hamaker made started from the well-known fact that the earth's vegetation, especially its millions of square miles of trees, plays a key role in regulating atmospheric carbon dioxide. Since trees consume $CO_2$ (while giving off oxygen), the more $CO_2$ in the atmosphere, the more plant life should thrive and spread, thus taking in more $CO_2$ and in effect regulating the atmosphere.

But that doesn't appear to be what is happening. Why not? Is it just that all our fossil fuel burning has overwhelmed the trees' ability to absorb carbon dioxide? Or are the earth's trees themselves under so much stress that they are no longer able to act as guardians of the earth's climate?

The answer is frightening: a large proportion of the world's trees are *dying.* Many forestry scientists are aware that this has been going on for almost a century, at a rate that again seems to be increasing exponentially in the last few decades. One forester in Europe's Black Forest says his job has changed "from forester to undertaker. All we do now all day every day is to cut down sick and dying trees while their timber is still worth anything ... the young trees ... usually die before they are two years old." They have an ominous name for it in Germany: *waldsterben,* forest-death.

A chart showing the accelerating death of the Black Forest—which may present graphic evidence of what will be happening to many other temperate forests within a few years—is presented in

Figure 6. More than half the trees in the Swiss Alps are reported to be damaged, and some major tree species in Britain are showing signs of dying off.

Arthur H. Johnson, a soil scientist at the University of Pennsylvania, has found "alarming incidences of decline and mortality in several species" of trees from Maine to Alabama. Robert I. Bruck, a plant pathologist at North Carolina State University, says "Something very dramatic is happening very quickly to the forests of the Eastern United States." Hans Enghardt, a forestry expert in Karlsruhe, West Germany, told the *New York Times* in 1983, "It's not five minutes before midnight, it's five seconds before midnight."

The blights that have killed off millions of America's trees—Dutch Elm disease, Chestnut blight, and so on—began to take their heavy toll only in the past 50 to 100 years. Insect populations that formerly lived in ecological balance with the forests—borers, budworms, gypsy moths, bark beetles, and so on (and fungi similar to Ireland's infamous "potato blight," which led to massive starvation)—have

**FIGURE 6**

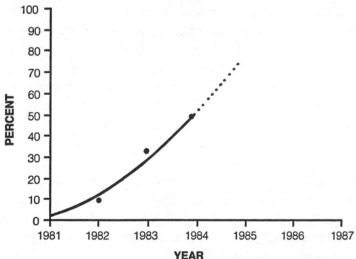

Dead or Dying Trees in
West Germany's Black Forest

Source: Embassy of the Federal Republic of Germany, Washington, D. C., 1985

*Dead trees in the southern Appalachian mountains of the United States.*

been exploding in number lately to all-time record levels, and destroying millions of acres of trees. Chemical poisons do not stop them.

Similar blights are already beginning to threaten our food supply, in spite of the massive application of chemicals that characterizes our agriculture (and in part because of it). In 1984 a mysterious citrus canker appeared on Florida's orange and grapefruit trees, resulting in the destruction of *ten million* trees. In 1985 a new citrus infestation *never before seen in the United States* appeared on Florida trees, a black scale that sucks the leaves and twigs dry. It can't be washed off, and it has a hard, waxy shell that protects it from pesticides.

The forests of the world are also being increasingly consumed by fires. Many forest fires are started by lightning rather than by humans, and the condition of the forests themselves—including things like unusually cold weather, drought, and insects and disease— seems to be the key factor in whether fires spread. In April 1986 a Tennessee forester said "the woods are drier than they've ever been—freakishly dry. Large logs that are usually spongy with water are dry as kindling, and that means they will burn like a match."

Figure 7 charts some recent forest fire statistics. Among other fires worldwide in recent years was the vast fire that began in Indonesia in 1983, eventually burning 13,000 square miles of forest—an area the size of Massachusetts and Connecticut combined. The area had just suffered two years of the most extreme drought in a century. Underlying deposits of soft coal and peat kept the fires

**FIGURE 7**

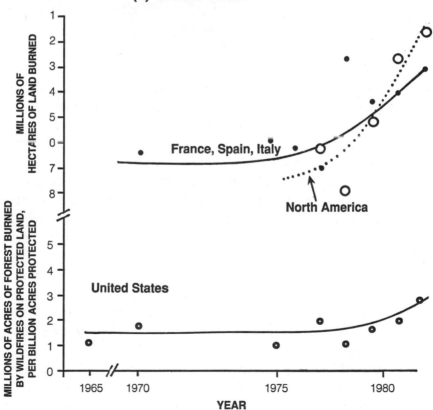

**Area Burned by Forest Fires:**
**(1) France, Spain, and Italy;  (2) North America;**
**(3) United States**

Source:  France, Spain, Italy, North America:  UN Publications; United States: U. S. Forest Service, Dept. of Agriculture

burning for months. It was said that "the earth literally caught fire." Countless animals died, and many species were extinguished forever.

Forest fires, diseases, and insects have been around for centuries, but the forests survived nicely during most of that time because trees (and other organisms, including people) that are basically healthy do not succumb readily to disease or stress. Why are the world's forests dying now? Drought, cold, acid rain, and pollution are factors; but they do not explain why the world's forests are dying so widely and so fast.

# The role of minerals in the soil

A little-noticed article in the *Harvard Forest Bulletin* (1947) suggests the answer. Studying the gypsy moth, the authors found that the most susceptible forests were growing on *calcium-depleted soils*— and that the forests growing on calcium-rich soils were *highly resistant to insect damage.*

In fact, forest ecologists have been aware for half a century that healthy trees seldom succumb to parasites of any kind. As early as 1929 Professor W. R. Day of Oxford University was pointing out that it is the trees *that are already weakened and diseased* which make an attractive target for blights and insects. And that trees become weakened and diseased primarily because of adverse soil conditions, especially the presence or absence of nutrients in the soil, such as minerals. Soil minerals have long been known to be one of the few indispensable necessities for healthy tree growth (and calcium is one of the key mineral nutrients).

Richard St. Barbe Baker, the late founder of Men of the Trees (one of the first environmental organizations) who has been credited with organizing the planting of some 26 million trees during his lifetime, pointed out something remarkable about the way the earth's trees have been dying off. He said that the trees that die off first are those with the greatest leaf area per tree: chestnuts, for example, with maybe 60 acres of leaf per tree, followed by elms, running about 40. Then the beeches, the oaks, and the eucalyptus. And finally the conifers, with the smallest leaf area: needles.

Lush tree species with the greatest leaf area need the most soil nutrients. If the soil becomes demineralized, these trees tend to die off first, leaving fewer trees and species with a lower rate of metabolism.

Evidence that soil demineralization is a major factor in the contemporary decline and death of the world's forests comes from a remarkable study done by Danish climatologist Svend Andersen (1966). Studying sediments found at the bottom of lakes in Denmark, he counted the types of pollen found at different depths. Knowing that sediment is laid down at a fairly constant rate over thousands of years, he could calculate about how long ago each layer was deposited, deeper layers of course representing earlier times. The different types of pollen indicated what kind of vegetation was growing at that period. And his sample spanned hundreds of thousands of years. (See Figure 8, next page.)

Focusing on changes in vegetation during the last warm interglacial period, a time comparable to our own, Andersen found that lush shade trees (such as elms, yews, and ashes), which require rich soils, began to predominate as soon as the climate warmed up after the previous ice age. They continued to thrive for thousands of years. Then, almost abruptly, they disappeared almost entirely from the scene. Why? Andersen found they were replaced by plants which thrive on more acidic soils (such as spruce and heather) and concluded that the soils became acidic primarily by the progressive leaching of minerals, which are known to buffer and minimize acidity. (He also found a simultaneous increase in the remains of ancient communities of microscopic animal life in the lake, leading him to conclude that some of the eroded minerals were washed into the lake, where they fed its inhabitants.) He found a similar pattern at four different sites, representing not only the last warm interglacial period but also the one before that.[12]

Gene Likens and his colleagues (1977) have measured the loss of minerals from the soil directly in recent studies of a temperate forest ecosystem. They found that the loss of calcium, for example,

**FIGURE 8**

## Cumulative Pollen Curves for Plants of
## Various Ecological Categories from
## the Interglacial Deposit at Hollerup, Denmark

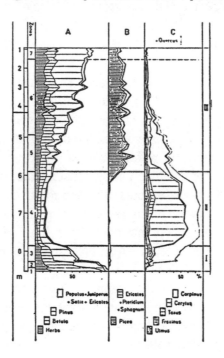

The top of the graph represents the end of the last warm interglacial period. The deeper layers were formed at earlier periods of time, and successive layers of pollen laid down on top of one another, 100,000 years ago.

Category A includes the light-requiring plants, which thrive as soon as the climate warms up, but are forced out by the spread of the larger, rich-soil plants of Category C. The rich-soil plants take over as the climate warms further, and the new postglacial soil is built up with many generations of organic matter from the earlier interglacial trees. (*Quercus* = oak, *corylus* = hazelnut)

The rich soil plants of C die out rather suddenly after a few thousand years of the interglacial, which Andersen attributes to the loss of soil minerals by erosion and leaching. This loss of minerals also results in an increasingly acid soil, and explains the simultaneous rise in the plants of Category B, which thrive mainly on acid soil. (*Picea* = spruce, *ericales* = heather, *pteridium* = ferns, *sphagnum* = moss)

Source: Svend Th. Andersen (1966), p 120.

which they determined to be a precursor to severe demineralization, averages about 12½ pounds per acre each year. Over the 10,000-year span of an interglacial period, that would amount to a loss of some 62 tons of calcium per acre, clearly an enormous depletion.

## An explanation of the ice ages

Based on scientific findings in a large number of different disciplines as well as his own observations, John Hamaker has finally discovered an explanation for the 100,000-year ice age cycle. It is his thesis that most of the soils of the earth have become severely demineralized, due to the natural processes of erosion and leaching over the centuries and millenia since the last ice age. That the resulting succession and die-back of much of the world's plant life—in the temperate regions primarily[13]—leads to a greatly increasing amount of carbon dioxide and other greenhouse gases in the atmosphere.[14] (The succession is eventually to conifers, which do better on acidic soils but have only one-quarter to one-third the annual leaf production of deciduous trees to consume $CO_2$; the lost trees and leaves that formerly consumed $CO_2$ decompose when they die, giving off additional carbon to the atmosphere, which forms carbon dioxide.) And that the continuing increase of atmospheric carbon dioxide, by widening the world's climatic temperature differentials and evaporating the tropical oceans faster, builds up the polar glaciers and eventually brings on the next ice age.[15]

And finally: As the glaciers inch their way over thousands of square miles of the earth's surface, they slowly grind up millions of rocks—rocks which are essentially made up of minerals—into a powder-fine dust which is carried away on the wind and the water. It can blow for thousands of miles and has been found deposited in some areas in layers up to 80 feet deep. Moving at only a few feet per year, the glaciers take some 900 centuries to remineralize the

*Drawing of the ice age mechanism. The greenhouse effect evaporates more water from tropical oceans, forming more clouds. These are moved by the increasing wind systems toward the poles. In the mid-latitudes they produce more rain, in the higher latitudes more snow and ice.*

earth. The earth's vegetation responds to a new presence of life-giving minerals, and another cycle begins with some 10,000 years of warmth and fertility.[16]

The major piece of this gigantic puzzle that Hamaker contributed is the differential greenhouse effect. All the other pieces—the importance of soil minerals, the demineralization of the earth's soils by erosion during interglacial periods, the role of forests in controlling $CO_2$, the role of $CO_2$ in trapping heat from the sun, the weather and climatic changes caused by an increased tropic-polar temperature differential, and even the buildup of polar ice from heating in the tropics—are well-known to science, in one or another of a number of different specialties (botany, geology, forestry, climatology, glaciology, and so forth).

Hamaker simply combined and synthesized the elements into a single theory. His position as an outsider, with no specialty and no status in any of the disciplines, paradoxically seems to have provided the crucial perspective needed to perceive such a grand design.[17]

# *Earthquakes and volcanic eruptions*

Hamaker believes the rising incidence of earthquakes in recent years can be attributed to the increasing weight of polar snow and ice cover pressing on the molten layers just beneath the earth's crust, causing shifting. Increased weight on the polar regions doesn't have to move the whole surface of the earth to cause an earthquake. It just has to trigger a slippage, a brief release of the friction binding the earth's gigantic plates against one another.

Hamaker notes that the sharp rise in major earthquakes began about ten years after the climate began to get noticeably colder around 1940[18] (Figure 9, see next page).

He also predicts a steadily increasing incidence of volcanic eruptions for a similar reason: accumulating snow and ice pressing down on the poles puts increased pressure on the vast layer of what is essentially a hydraulic fluid in one place and it tries to pop out somewhere else: a volcano, a rift in the seabed, and so on.

Hamaker suggests the increase of volcanism has already begun in the last few years—Mount St. Helens, El Chichon, Mount Etna, Mount Kiska, Mount Luzon, Mount Hekla, Chokai, Sangay, Kilauea, and Mount Mihara; the undersea activity that caused El Niño; and so on. Reid Bryson, director of the Institute for Environmental Studies at the University of Wisconsin, has presented data showing that the number of volcanic eruptions more than doubled between 1945 and 1970[19]. And that in this century there have been more volcanic eruptions when the earth's climate has been colder.

Other researchers have gone much further in connecting volcanic activity and ice buildup. Writing in *Science* (1979), Michael Rampino of NASA, Stephen Self of Dartmouth, and Rhodes Fairbridge of Columbia reported on the last 85,000 years of volcanic activity. Their conclusions:

Many major volcanic eruptions coincide with cooling trends of decadal or longer duration that began significantly before the eruptions ... variations in climate lead to stress changes in the earth's crust—for instance, by loading and unloading of ice and water masses and by axial and spin-rate changes that might augment volcanic (and seismic) potential.

Volcanic eruptions also spew a great deal of carbon dioxide and other gases into the atmosphere, which then accelerate the climatic

**FIGURE 9**

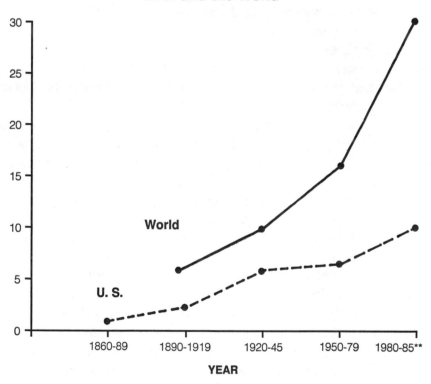

## Average Number of Earthquakes of Richter Magnitude 6 or Higher, U. S. and the World*

**Source: James M. Gere and Haresh C. Shah, *Terra Non Firma* (New York: W. H. Freeman, 1984)**

*Again, there is probably an error factor due to increased reporting, but it is most likely significantly less than the dramatic increases shown here.

**Prorated for the decade from earthquakes 1980-85.

extremes described earlier, leading to a greater buildup of snow and ice and hence more volcanic eruptions. Sulfuric and other volcanic acids also accelerate the destruction of the earth's vegetation, accelerating the transfer of their $CO_2$ to the atmosphere. The cooling cycle develops greater and greater momentum.[20]

# Ice ages seem to come on very quickly

Dr. Genevieve Woillard of the Institut de Botanique of the Université Catholique de Louvain, working with a deep, undisturbed pollen bed in northern France, also studied the succession of trees through the last glacial cycle. Counting a thousand or more grains of pollen at each millimeter of depth, she could estimate with considerable precision the time it took for the last ice age to begin.

Writing in 1979, Woillard reported that the transition, at the end of the last warm interglacial period some hundred thousand years ago, from a warm climate on much of the earth, supporting nut and apple trees, to the kind of cold climate which is now found in northern Sweden and Alaska and supports only cold-weather pine and birch forests—trees that do not produce a food crop—took only 150 years. Even more unexpected and ominous was this finding: "The main shift in vegetation apparently took place in only a few years...." She estimated it to be less than twenty.

Four months later Professor John T. Hollin of the University of Colorado reported that his studies of Greenland ice cores reveal the same cooling (he called it "catastrophic" because it happened so quickly) occurring in "something less than 100 years." He could not pin it down any closer than that from his ice core data.

In 1979, two years before her death from cancer at the age of 33 (her work routinely brought her in proximity to volatile acids strong enough to eat through glass), Woillard warned that the worldwide decline of forests now taking place suggests that we may have *already* entered the brief climatic period of less than 20 years which seems to characterize the end of a warm interglacial and the beginning of the next ice age. ("We thus cannot exclude the possibility," she understated it in the scientific manner.)[21]

Based on his reading of climate extremes of many kinds, widespread forest death, and the rising $CO_2$ curve in recent decades, John Hamaker believes that the earth may well have entered that less-than-twenty-year period around 1975.[22] That would put us, in 1988, some 13 years into it, with the rapid shift into severe cold, drought, and other conditions inhospitable to food growing conceivably concluding sometime before 1995—or within the next 7 years at the time of this writing. And since Woillard said "less than" 20 years, conceivably the transition could come even within the next 5 years. We may be on the very verge of it.

Hamaker also points out that once that extreme climatic shift occurs, accompanied as it will be by the massive death of warm climate trees with their ability to bring down $CO_2$, nothing human beings could do would be able to reverse it. The earth would then be irrevocably committed to the 90,000 years of the next ice age.

# Our own contribution to atmospheric $CO_2$

In the year 900 some 90% of the earth's land was still covered with forests. As the human population began to expand rapidly in the next few centuries, however, larger and larger areas of forested land were cleared for agriculture, settlements, and wood to build with and to burn. By 1900, only 20% of the land still had forests on it.

With the transition to fossil fuels the forests rebounded slightly, to 30% by 1950. But we have been destroying them again ever since, at an accelerating pace. Half the trees left standing in 1950 were gone by 1982. And now the world's few remaining forest lands are being cleared at a rate exceeding 75 acres a minute, almost 5,000 square miles a month.

Nowhere is the deforestation more alarming than in the earth's rainforests, located in a band along the equator in Central and South America, West Africa, Southeast Asia, and the Pacific Islands. The rainforests have often been called "the lungs of the earth" because they give off so much oxygen and take in so much carbon dioxide. The Amazon basin in Brazil, the largest of the remaining rainforests on earth, is two-thirds the size of the United States. An area of Amazon rainforest the size of France is razed every 5 years—the equivalent of a football field *every second.*

When forests are destroyed—especially large forests in tropical regions—they are often replaced by deserts. Dense rainforests hold tremendous amounts of water, which evaporates and falls back as rain. When forests are clearcut, the soil dries out and little rain falls, making it difficult if not impossible for the forest to reestablish itself. Erosion of denuded slopes exacerbates the problem. Rainforests are huge sponges that soak up rainwater and release it gradually into rivers, fostering agriculture downstream. When the forests are clearcut, rivers silt up and dry up, making whole regions inhospitable for growing food.

Deforested tropical regions also heat up substantially as the sun beats down on the now bare earth—increasing the temperature difference between the tropics and the poles still further, with all the climatic consequences that leads to.


Why are the rainforests being cleared, and at such a rapid rate? For several reasons, unfortunately.

The governments of rainforest countries are destroying their own forests in the name of "development," trying to catch up with the most highly industrialized nations. So they cut roads through the forest, encourage new settlements, clear land for agriculture, and build dams that drown billions of trees. The native peoples who lived in harmony with the land for eons are displaced, their cultures destroyed. Brazil has recently been contemplating the destruction of more than 700 square miles (2000 square kilometers) of Amazon rainforest with toxic herbicides in order to flood the land for a giant dam. No matter that the local population will be poisoned, and people who drink the water. The government is in too much of a hurry even to cut the trees into wood.

The industrialized countries have also been responsible for a large part of the destruction of the tropical rainforests in recent decades. The less developed countries are seen as prime targets for investment by multinational corporations, and pressured to develop rapidly with enormous lines of credit. Much of the Central and South American rainforest is being bulldozed by multinational conglomerates to raise cattle, for example, more than 90% of whom end up as fast-food hamburger in Americans' mouths.

The Volkswagen corporation is one of the companies which has been profiting from the destruction of our ecosystem by raising cattle on cleared rainforest land. Recently they set fire to a large forested area in Brazil, which got out of control and burned an additional vast area the size of an entire Brazilian state. Pesticides and herbicides so toxic they are banned in the U.S. are also used to defoliate these cattle ranges, coming back to people in their hamburgers.

When an area is cleared for cattle the soil gets used up within a few years, because tropical soils surprisingly are not very fertile—all the nutrients are in the rapidly growing vegetation and get recycled quickly when each generation of highly efficient plants dies. (Huge tropical trees often have above-ground buttress roots propping them up because the soil underneath them is so hardened and poor.) So every few years more land has to be cleared. Often they do this by burning, and the fires they set often get out of control, releasing enormous amounts of $CO_2$ into the atmosphere.

The lending policies of the World Bank, controlled by the American-European-Japanese corporate establishment, have locked Third World countries into "development" at any cost with little concern for the environment. The World Bank has loaned Latin American cattle ranching projects billions of dollars in the last 25 years.[23]

Slash-and-burn agriculture by native people is another way the rainforests are being destroyed. Most farmers resort to slash-and-burn only when more suitable land has been taken away from them by people with more economic or political power. In Latin America, home to much of the world's remaining rainforests, 93% of the farmland is controlled by 7% of the people. For the past three decades large landowners in Central America have been confiscating peasants' farms at a rapid rate to increase their profits from exports. Now millions of peasants have no land at all, or not enough even for subsistence farming. Giving poor people rainforest land to clear is a way of keeping unrest down temporarily, while leaving the social structure unchanged.[24] Greed and gross political and economic inequalities are much more serious causes of the destruction of the world's rainforests than increasing population.

In most parts of the world more trees are cut down for firewood than for building. Deforestation from this source alone has become a major problem.

The earth's rainforests have also been destroyed by large-scale war. Faced with the American public's revulsion at the Vietnam war and questioning of its human toll, the U.S. military began a "scorched earth" and defoliation tactic to destroy ground cover and reduce the need for troops. The motto of American defoliation squads in Vietnam was, "Only we can prevent forests."

It is important to understand that wars like this are not started over ideologies but for industrial raw materials. Shocking as this may be to many people, 500,000 young men were not sent to Vietnam to face death and 50,000 did not die to stop Communism. They were sent to try to secure Southeast Asia's oil, rubber, tin, and other minerals for American corporate interests, as French troops had been sent for similar reasons earlier. It may have been about to happen again in Central America when the Reagan administration's Iran/contra scandal became public. It may yet happen if there is not sufficient resistance by the American people, and the rainforest will be destroyed that much faster.

Even at the present rate—and primarily because of cattle raising and other development-related reasons rather than peasant agriculture—there will be no rainforests left in all of Central America by the end of this century, just a few years away. (Nicaragua may be the one exception, since the U.S. has stopped trading with them, and they seem to be less committed to development at any cost.)

The destruction of these tropical jungles is also extinguishing the world's largest aggregate of animal and plant species. As many as 30 million different species have not even been catalogued yet! The jaguar, the gorilla, the giant armadillo, and the Amazon parrot are among the endangered rainforest species. The rainforests are also the winter haven for millions of migratory birds, whose extinction would bring on unprecedented swarms of insects and devastation of crops throughout the world.


The forestry practices of many of the industrialized nations are also wasteful, destructive of the land, and ecologically disastrous. Millions of trees are cut down unnecessarily for products that could be recycled: paper of all kinds, some plastics, and so on. Clearcutting whole areas leads to erosion and flooding. Nowadays clearcutting is often combined with "whole-tree harvesting," in which even the branches, twigs, and leaves—which may contain two-thirds of the nutrients—are removed from the area, further depleting the soil. Then the stumps and stubble are burned, depleting it still further and adding to the $CO_2$ and other greenhouse gases in the air.

And they don't even replant as many trees as they cut down. The Canadian government spends so little money on reforestation that Jack Walters, professor of forestry at the University of British Columbia, says, "They are lunatics. We have gutted the forests across the nation...." George Marek, recently retired as a forester in Ontario, says "Our forest companies have to start acting like civilized people instead of pigs. In Europe they would never get away with the things they do here. People in Europe worship the land."

Apparently worshipful of the Vietnam experience, the U.S. Forest Service is now using Agent Orange, flame throwers, and bombs of napalm-like jelly to achieve what they call a "clean burn" of all the "debris" left after clearcutting, rather than recycling its precious nutrients back into the soil, and to destroy thousands of acres of national forest trees that are deemed a hindrance to the growth of "more desirable" trees—trees that can be sold for more money.

Richard St. Barbe Baker said it this way: "Man has been skinning the earth alive."

Our other major contribution to atmospheric carbon dioxide is our unparalleled burning of fossil fuels—coal, oil, and natural gas—for the past century and a half.

Each year now we send back into the atmosphere the carbon it took lush vegetation millions of years to take out. Some have even called our rapid burning of these ancient carbon deposits a reversal of evolution—undermining the atmospheric development nature seems to have evolved over hundreds of millions of years, from the time when dinosaurs roamed the earth until now.[25] Certainly this mindless burning is now threatening our own species with extinction. That less-than-20-year plunge into an ice age climate which we may be in the middle of would probably have happened hundreds, perhaps thousands of years later in the absence of our own fossil fuel burning and clearcutting.

Another side effect of our fossil fuel burning—acid rain—is also contributing to the progression of events that is bringing on the next ice age more rapidly than nature intended. For acid rain also kills the trees and other vegetation whose fate, we can now see, is most inextricably linked with ours.

The rain has been becoming more acid each year, strong enough to kill fish as well as trees. And it is killing lakes and soils all over the planet, not just downwind from heavy industry. Eight years ago a study of rainfall in the Rocky Mountains—where there is very little pollution in the direction of the prevailing wind—found that the acidity of the rain, already quite acidic, increased 500% in only three years.

The earth's soils become quite acidic naturally during the interglacial period, as the soils become demineralized by erosion. Minerals are a buffer against acidity, and as they are eroded away the soil becomes inhospitable to most forms of life, including beneficial worms and insects. This is part of the process whereby the earth's vegetation withers and dies, giving off carbon dioxide and bringing on the next glacial cycle. We are only accelerating the process this time.

**FIGURE 10**

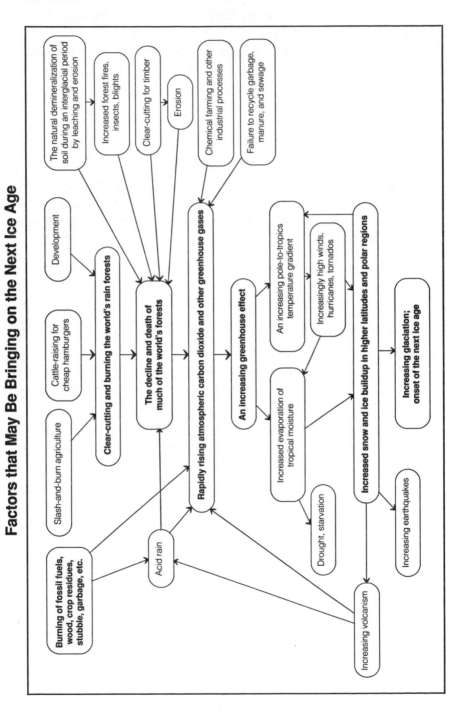

Factors that May Be Bringing on the Next Ice Age

Other greenhouse gases of human origin—methane from the un-recycled manure produced in huge cattle feedlots, from coal and gas mining, and from unrecycled garbage, burning vegetation, and the natural cycle of demineralization and forest fires, among other things; nitrous oxide from automobile exhausts and massive quantities of artificial nitrogen fertilizers (which also "burn" organic matter in the soil, producing more $CO_2$ and methane); carbon monoxide from internal combustion engines; industrial chlorofluorocarbons (such as freon from refrigeration, styrofoam, and other things, which is also destroying the ozone layer);[26] and so on *ad nauseum*—are collec-tively contributing *even more than carbon dioxide* to the greenhouse effect. Atmospheric methane, for just one example, was recently found to have *doubled* in the last few centuries, an enormous change.

You can see what a pickle we're in.

## Stopping the next ice age

Are you ready for some good news?

John Hamaker's thesis, and much scientific evidence, leads to the astounding conclusion that we can control our own climate and prevent the next ice age from ever occurring: simply by taking over the glaciers' job and remineralizing the earth's soil ourselves, planting billions of new trees; and quickly cutting back dramatically on fossil fuel burning in favor of renewable energy sources.

Remineralizing the soil would regenerate the earth's forests, which will absorb the excess $CO_2$ from the atmosphere. This will decrease the greenhouse effect, which will slow down the evapora-tion from tropical oceans and reduce the extreme temperature differentials between the tropics and the poles. That will quiet the fierce winds that have been transporting all that tropical moisture to the polar regions and dumping it as snow and ice, building up the glaciers.

Hamaker's magnificent, terrifying theory is supported by a great deal of theoretical writing and experimental research on soil demineralization and remineralization over the past few decades. Scientists at Oxford, Cambridge, Columbia, Yale, and other universities have learned that the earth's soils normally become severely demineralized during interglacial periods, and that the glaciers' function is to remineralize them.

More than half a century of research on the beneficial effects of soil remineralization on trees and forests has been compiled in a book by Marcus Bell and his colleagues (1974). They describe the work of R. Albert, who began in 1905 to experiment with many kinds of crushed stone quarry rocks as a fertilizer and reported great increases in fertility regardless of the poorness of the soil, because of the many elements supplied by the glacial rocks. He fertilized degraded soil with crushed basalt rock (117 tons per acre) and two years later planted pine seedlings. Twenty-two years later the pine trees planted on this remineralized soil were so healthy and vigorous they had a timber volume *four to five times* that of unmineralized

*John Hamaker*

PHOTO: FRITZ LEIBOLD

*Two fir-tree branches*

plots nearby. Other researchers have independently reported comparable results in similar experiments.

Werner Koch, professor of forestry at the University of Munich, shows photographs of remineralization experiments done by his friend Fritz Leibold, a scientist and government official. In the picture above, the fir branch on the left is from a tree that was remineralized with rock dust. Its needles are clearly thicker, more numerous, darker green, and stronger than those of the control tree, which was not remineralized.

Georg Abermann, an agronomist and engineer with the Sanvita rock dust company in Kitzbuhl, Austria, remineralized part of a national park forest in which most of the trees were dying, contaminated by toxic heavy metals from a nearby chemical plant. Officials had been saying that the only way to save the trees would be to replace all the soil in the park, and were preparing to do it, at enormous cost. The trees that Abermann remineralized, with a small amount of rock dust, stopped dying and grew new green needles within only six months. In the photograph at the top of page 40, he shows how little this tree had grown in its first 7 to 8 years, on contaminated soil. At right, he shows how much it grew in the first four and a half years after it was remineralized.

An article in *World Wood* describes how degenerating pine forests

*Georg Abermann indicating the dramatic increase in growth achieved by remin-
eralizing. His left hand shows the height of the tree after the first 7–8 years of
growth, before remineralizing. After its soil was remineralized, the tree grew to its
present height in only 4½ years. Its growth rate seems to have increased by more
than 300%.*

*The oak trees were dying on Jeannie Stevens' land in Australia. She remineralized
some of them and left others untouched. About 2½ years later she picked these two
leaves, the largest leaves she could find from one tree she had not treated (left), and
a similar one she had simply spread finely ground gravel dust around. The tree she
had remineralized had also put out many new seedlings. The other had not put
out any.*

*A blower-truck spraying finely ground gravel dust into the forest. Sanvita Company, Kitzbuhl, Austria.*

in New Zealand were "bombed" with "super-phosphate" rock, and that this "proved adequate for arresting deterioration and restoring vigor." A. L. Poole, Director General of Forests for the New Zealand Forest Service at the time, called it "a spectacular success in increasing growth."

Several countries have already been spraying crushed limestone on lakes and forests to counteract the effects of acid rain. Gravel dust is better at buffering acid soils, because it is milder and lasts longer than lime, besides providing the full spectrum of mineral nutrients to feed growing plants. Normal soil is filled with tiny life forms, from earthworms to millions of microorganisms in every square inch. All of them are nourished by the minerals supplied in finely ground gravel dust, and the health of all of them is essential to the healthy growth of the forests above them.

So there is a way out, if we're willing to take it. We can spray most of the forests of the world with crushed glacial rock, remineralizing their soils and restoring the trees so they can deal with our common, life-threatening climate problem. And we can plant lots of new, fast-growing trees to help bring down the $CO_2$ and store it. We can reduce our fossil fuel burning drastically, substituting renewable fuels made from some of the new trees and from non-$CO_2$-producing energy sources like solar, wind, and geothermal energy (and a lot more people power, such as walking, bicycling, and roller skating rather than driving).

The solution is simple. Monumental, but essentially very simple. Well within the capabilities of creatures who put some of their own on the moon.

If we intend to take over the glaciers' job, however, we'd better do it *very* fast; or it may soon be too late to reverse the process.[27]

# How long do we have?

How much time do we have to remineralize the earth before the progression of climate toward the next ice age becomes irreversible? And how long before the climate becomes too extreme to grow food?

It is clear that the sharply rising curve of $CO_2$ is now much steeper than the gradual upward curve of fossil fuel consumption. The difference is attributable to the destruction of the world's forests by a set of interrelated factors including clearcutting, demineralization, acid rain, summer drought, cold winters, disease, insects, and forest fires.

Hamaker says there are only four things we can and must do to bring down the level of carbon dioxide and other greenhouse gases in the earth's atmosphere quickly, and reverse the inexorable progression of climate toward the next ice age—and that we must do them all *immediately:*

- Stop the massive cutting down of the world's forests, and especially the rainforests;

- Remineralize the soils of the earth's forests, bush country, agricultural lands, and coastal waters with gravel dust, in order to rejuvenate the planet's vegetation so it will stop dying and soon begin to consume the excess $CO_2$ in the atmosphere;

- Plant huge plantations of fast-growing trees to consume $CO_2$, and soon to provide renewable wood-based fuels (methanol, methane, and so on) as one alternative to fossil fuels;

- Cut back drastically on our use of fossil fuels of every kind, beginning immediately with coal and oil (90% of the world's energy currently comes from burning fossil fuels; almost one-third of them are burned in the United States).

If we do none of these things, Hamaker thinks that our rapidly deteriorating climate may well lead to massive *worldwide* starvation by 1995 if not before, with the possibility of nuclear war over dwindling resources. If we do only some of them, or do not act quickly enough, the ice age progression may be slowed down but may become irreversible anyway before very long, partly because too many trees may be gone, partly because increasing volcanic activity may create an unstoppable feedback loop, spewing out $CO_2$ and other greenhouse gases that lead to more ice buildup and thus more volcanic eruptions.[28]

Even if we begin tomorrow, the severe climatic changes already set in motion may lead to the death by starvation of unprecedented numbers of people in the next few years before we can bring things under control—perhaps as many as half the people on earth, because we are so unprepared for this emergency with huge stockpiles of food. There is now reportedly less than three weeks' worth of food stored on the planet.

Because of the size of the job we have to do and our inexperience in organizing this type of global-scale project, because we are starting so late and so few people recognize the scope of the problem and the gravity of the situation, Hamaker thinks we now (1988) have less than a 50% chance of surviving. If we wait another year or two even to begin, he feels our chances may drop precipitously toward zero.

## NOTES TO CHAPTER ONE

1. The first evidence of recurrent ice age cycles lasting tens of thousands of years was reported by Emiliani (1955), who studied the chemical isotopes in the shells of microscopic sea life found in cores taken from the bottom of the ocean. Since sediments settle out of the ocean at a fairly regular rate and deeper deposits were laid down earlier, a rough calibration can be made of depth equals time. Broecker and van Donk (1970) used similar cores to determine a recurrent 100,000-year cycle, while Kukla (1970) independently confirmed its existence based on alternate layers of soil and glacial silt at an abandoned brickyard in Czechoslovakia. Fink and Kukla (1977) later reported evidence for the existence of at least 17 such cycles during the past 1.7 million years, and further research on sea and ice cores by a number of other scientists eventually found evidence of at least 25 such cycles over the past 2.5 million years. The best popular account of contemporary research on climate is presented in Schneider and Londer (1984).

2. I analyzed the data provided in *State, Regional, and National Monthly and Annual Temperature, Weighted by area for the contiguous United States, January 1931–December 1985* (Asheville, N.C.: National Climatic Data Center, May 1986). Here are the results. The figures in the last column are a measure of the likelihood that a difference as large as that found in each comparison might have occurred by chance (Table 1, page 45).

**FIGURE 11**

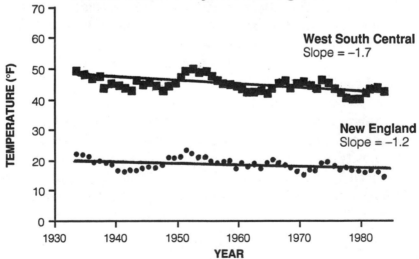

## Average January Temperature
## 1933-1983, New England and West South
## Central States*:  5-year Running Means

Source: NOAA, State, regional and national monthly temperature, Historical Climatology Series 4-1, May 1986     *West South Central states include Arkansas, Louisiana, Oklahoma, and Texas.

**TABLE 1**

## Average January and February Temperature in Seven Regions of the United States, 1931–1955, 1956–1975, and 1976–1985.

| REGION | MO. | YEARS | MEAN TEMP. (F) | T-VALUE | α |
|---|---|---|---|---|---|
| New England (ME, VT, NH, MA, RI, CT) | Jan. | 1931–55 | 19.6 | | |
| | | 1956–75 | 18.0 | 1.205 | |
| | | 1976–85 | 15.0 | 1.863 | .05 |
| | Feb. | 1931–55 | 20.7 | | |
| | | 1956–75 | 19.1 | 1.459 | .10 |
| | | 1976–85 | 21.0 | −1.184 | |
| East North Central (IL, IN, MI, OH, WI) | Jan. | 1931–55 | 25.3 | | |
| | | 1956–75 | 21.1 | 2.961 | .005 |
| | | 1976–85 | 17.5 | 1.925 | .05 |
| | Feb. | 1931–55 | 26.5 | | |
| | | 1956–75 | 24.5 | 1.655 | .10 |
| | | 1976–85 | 24.5 | 0.257 | |
| West North Central (IA, KS, MN, MO, NE, ND, SD) | Jan. | 1931–55 | 20.6 | | |
| | | 1956–75 | 18.2 | 1.534 | .10 |
| | | 1976–85 | 16.0 | 1.925 | .05 |
| | Feb. | 1931–55 | 24.4 | | |
| | | 1956–75 | 23.3 | 1.655 | .10 |
| | | 1976–85 | 24.3 | 0.257 | |
| West South Central (AR, LA, OK, TX) | Jan. | 1931–55 | 45.9 | | |
| | | 1956–75 | 43.8 | 2.070 | .025 |
| | | 1976–85 | 40.5 | 2.531 | .01 |
| | Feb. | 1931–55 | 49.3 | | |
| | | 1956–75 | 47.5 | 1.890 | .05 |
| | | 1976–85 | 46.5 | 0.685 | |
| East South Central (AL, KY, MS, TN) | Jan. | 1931–55 | 44.4 | | |
| | | 1956–75 | 40.4 | 2.846 | .005 |
| | | 1976–85 | 35.4 | 3.289 | .001 |
| | Feb. | 1931–55 | 46.1 | | |
| | | 1956–75 | 43.2 | 2.215 | .025 |
| | | 1976–85 | 41.8 | 0.779 | |
| Middle Atlantic (NY, NJ, PA) | Jan. | 1931–55 | 26.6 | | |
| | | 1956–75 | 23.7 | 2.041 | .05 |
| | | 1976–85 | 19.9 | 2.569 | .01 |
| | Feb. | 1931–55 | 26.6 | | |
| | | 1956–75 | 24.8 | 1.548 | .10 |
| | | 1976–85 | 25.4 | −0.385 | |
| South Atlantic (DE, MD, NC, SC, VA, WV, GA, FL) | Jan. | 1931–55 | 47.0 | | |
| | | 1956–75 | 44.0 | 2.206 | .025 |
| | | 1976–85 | 39.7 | 3.002 | .005 |
| | Feb. | 1931–55 | 47.3 | | |
| | | 1956–75 | 45.8 | 1.283 | |
| | | 1976–85 | 45.0 | 0.469 | |

**FIGURE 12**

## February Central England Temperatures, 1860 to 1960, 25-year Running Means (Centered on Year Given)

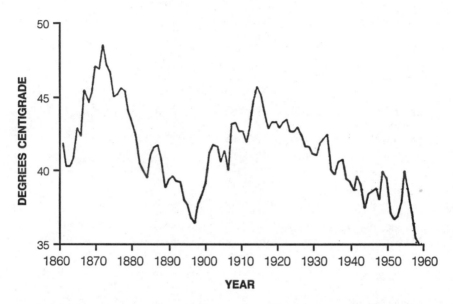

YEAR

3. Figure 12 is the graph referred to. The source is N.E. Davis, *Quarterly Journal of the Royal Meteorological Society* 98 (1972): 763, 767.

4. Notice that the increase in tornados reported per year has been more than 300% since 1950. Since tornados are pretty recognizable, usually do indisputable damage, and are widely written about, probably only a portion of this difference is attributable to better reporting or increased population.

5. Richard Anthes, director of the National Center for Atmospheric Research, has been quoted as saying that the link between sea surface temperature and greater intensity of hurricanes is well known and supported by many studies and that oceanic and atmospheric warming could also lead to more frequent hurricanes. *Austin-American Statesman,* April 5, 1987. See also Schneider and Londer (1984, p. 248n); and Adam (1975).

6. Africa has been particularly hard hit by tropical heat and drought because it straddles the equator more than any other continent. The northern summer hits the northern half, the southern summer the southern half. In the Sahel

region of Africa, for example (a band across the northern part of the continent just below the Sahara desert), a drought began in the late 1960s (as Northern Hemisphere winters were cooling and snow cover began increasing) and continued uninterrupted to at least 1985. The possibility that this extended drought was a random fluctuation of dry years was calculated at about 1 in 130,000 (Weisburd and Raloff, 1985).

7. In his recent summary of a great deal of research on climatic change, Stephen Schneider states, "... no verified mechanism has yet been found to translate this very weak forcing into more than a small climatic signal" (Schneider and Londer 1984, p. 265). A similar point is presented by Pisias and Shackleton (1984).

8. A number of theories have tried to explain why a very regular 100,000-year orbital cycle, presuming it were large enough, should result in ice ages that are 90,000 years cold and only 10,000 warm. Generally they presume some "resonance" of processes on earth, such as a lag in the rebound of the earth's crust after glaciation; but as Imbrie and Imbrie point out (1980, p. 951), "Unfortunately, the physical basis for such response characteristics seems to be lacking." See also Mitchell (1976).

The Milankovitch theory has also been unable to explain why the ice ages seem to begin and end about the same time in both hemispheres, since these orbital variations do not change the total amount of solar energy received by the earth, only the relative amount received at different latitudes, (Berger *et al.* 1984, pp. 687–688; Ruddiman in the same volume, p. 867).

Each of these problems makes an astronomical explanation for the 100,000-year ice age cycle seem fairly unlikely. Together they seem to make one very unlikely.

Yet die-hard Milankovitch theorists continue to insist that these minute changes will eventually be shown to explain the 100,000-year ice age cycle, and continue to look for "resonances" which are not forthcoming. A few other climatologists believe that the 100,000-year cycle of ice ages is a natural oscillation of the earth's own processes (heat exchange between ocean and atmosphere, etc.). But Schneider calls these "highly simplified models compared to reality, and each is laced with speculative assumptions" (Schneider and Londer 1984, p. 267). None of them has been willing to consider Hamaker's ideas seriously.

9. Imbrie's own words had best be reprinted here, lest confirmed Milankovitch theorists assert that I made these things up. (They sometimes neglect to cite this paper of his, in favor of his earlier papers which are more favorable.) "At least over the past 600,000 years, almost all climatic records are dominated by variance components in a narrow frequency band centered near a 100,000-year cycle.... Yet a climatic response at these frequencies is not predicted by the Milankovitch version of the astronomical theory—or

any other version that involves a linear response.... All of these failures are related to a fundamental shortcoming in the generation of 100K power" (Imbrie and Imbrie, 1980).

10. Bradley and his colleages conclude that "these large-scale trends are consistent with general circulation model projections of precipitation changes associated with doubled concentrations of atmospheric carbon dioxide ..." (though they are unwilling to make the connection). But $CO_2$ *hasn't* doubled—it has increased by a little over ⅓. That these large-scale trends are already occurring seems to cast doubt on the assumptions usually built into the general circulation models of the atmosphere—at least those models in which increasing cloud cover is not a major variable.

There has been considerable debate in recent years about whether the earth's climate is warming, cooling, or staying essentially the same, perhaps with more variation. P. D. Jones, T. M. L. Wigley, and P. M. Kelly (1982, 1986) at the University of East Anglia in Norwich, England, tell us there was little trend in the 19th century but warming most of the time ever since, which they believe represents the effects of $CO_2$. They note that the three warmest years have all occurred in the 1980s. Kukla and Gavin (1981) reported that antarctic sea ice decreased substantially from 1973 to 1980. Sue Ann Bowling at the University of Alaska writes me in March 1986: "Here in Fairbanks this has been the warmest string of 10 winters on record. We haven't had the normal 40 below weather since 1975." Lachenbruch and Marshall (1986) present evidence suggesting that much of the Alaskan permafrost has warmed over the past few decades or more. And every month there seems to be another story in the mass media quoting some scientist saying the climate is getting warmer and attributing it to the greenhouse effect.

On the other hand, Bentley reported to a 1986 meeting of the American Association for the Advancement of Science that the Antarctic ice sheet has been getting *bigger* for the last ten years (overlapping with Kukla by four years). Reporting on his studies of glaciers in West Greenland, John E. Gordon (1981) speaks of "a marked climatic deterioration during the 1960s and early 1970s." Dewey and Heim (1982) reported that the Northern Hemisphere snow cover increased by an enormous million square miles from 1972 to 1980. This is attributed to "unprecedented cold winters in the contiguous United States" from 1977–79, according to Diaz and Quayle (1980), Matson and Weisnet, (1981), and Matson, Berg, and McClain (1979).

What are we to make of these apparent inconsistencies? Kenneth Watt and others have presented evidence that much of the so-called global warming from 1880 to 1940 may be an artifact of biased data: Most of the thermometers used to calculate global temperatures have been located in cities, whose temperature is not only significantly higher than the surrounding countryside (as much as 18°F), but rises over time with increasing population density. Griffiths and Vining (1984) reported quite recently that of the 11,600 cooperative climate stations used by the U.S. National Weather

Service Network, "a maximum of only 270 can be considered as base reference stations for the 1900–1979 period (i.e., unbiased). " Working with 28 unbiased stations from the Reference Climatological Network, Watt found a cooling trend in the U.S. from 1941–83, with the exception of a few areas. He states, "Florida is very far south to find an increase in the frequency of freezing winters if indeed the world is warming."

Some mountain glaciers have been reported to be receding, but they are primarily those at low altitudes. Barry (1985) has reported that the percentage of advancing glaciers in the high Swiss and Austrian Alps has been increasing for the last two or three decades, to the point where more than half of them were advancing by 1985.

Bowling points to "a tendency for the warm parts of the globe (those where tropical air is travelling northward) to be over the oceans, while the arctic air is moving southward over the continental areas where the low temperatures it produces can be recorded." Thus sea ice might melt at the same time land ice is building up. Most of the temperature probes are of course on land rather than at sea. And even sea temperature data has recently been thought to be biased, because of a significant change in the way the temperature of the seawater is measured.

The apparent warming of Alaska in recent years may be due to the fact that it has recently been the recipient of more warm tropical air currents moving northward, an unusual situation but consistent with H. H. Lamb's contention that the normally gentle s-shaped path of the jet-stream around the north pole has become more extreme in recent years. It is also consistent with the increase of freezing temperatures and snowfall in the Northern Hemisphere as a whole, and with recent record cold spells throughout Europe and Scandinavia (see Associated Press, 1984). The fact that the Southern Hemisphere does not show any cooling yet is attributable to the fact that there is more ocean there, and less land mass for glaciers to build up on. But South American and Asian glaciers will build up there too, tipping the Southern Hemisphere into ice age conditions as well.

Certainly it becomes clear that looking primarily at *global* temperature changes is not particularly useful when summers and the tropics are getting hotter while winters and the northern latitudes are getting colder: enormous changes are completely overlooked by studying only yearly and geographic averages.

A good overview of many articles in this area can be found in a paper by Fred B. Wood (1986), who works out of the U.S. Congress' Office of Technology Assessment.

11. Though he didn't get the source of energy right, Simpson well understood how an increased energy input would lead to glaciation under some conditions—he even did ingenious laboratory experiments to validate his ideas. His explanation of the consequences of a theorized increase in solar radiation can be directly applied to the energy increase provided by a greenhouse effect trapping additional heat from the sun: "increasing the solar radiation

... the equator would be warmed up more than the poles. Hence the difference in temperature between the equator and the poles would be increased, and this would lead to an increase in the general circulation of the atmosphere. The increased temperature and the increased wind cause an increase in the amount of water evaporated from the oceans. This increased water in the atmosphere leads to greater formation of cloud and ... to an increase in precipitation ..." (Simpson 1938, p. 595).

Today's general circulation models (GCMs) theorize that a greenhouse warming would be most pronounced at the poles, the opposite of Simpson's conclusions. Since the tropics get much more sunlight than the poles, this appears counterintuitive, regardless of air circulation patterns. The GCMs also assume that a greenhouse warming would melt polar ice, and the resultant lowering of reflectivity (albedo) would contribute to a polar warming. But the poles contain an abundance of cold, and would require more than a degree or two of warming to change the albedo much. Before that happens, the increased cloud production and precipitation produced by the greenhouse effect seems likely to increase snow cover and more than offset any melting.

Schneider points out that the GCMs usually compute some future equilibrium conditions (typically, for a *doubling* of current levels of $CO_2$), which may be quite different from the time-evolving or transient response: "Thus, although albedo/temperature feedback processes in high latitudes eventually (that is, in equilibrium) may cause those regions to be warmed more than the lower latitudes for a given $CO_2$ increase, midlatitudes or even high-latitude regions would not necessarily warm up as fast as lower latitudes during the transition period toward a new equilibrium. In the transition, the larger thermal inertia of the deep high-latitude mixed layer could actually slow the temperature rise relative to tropical waters.... If $CO_2$ increases rapidly ... neglecting the transient would be a more serious error" (Schneider and Londer 1984, pp 332–333).

12. It is sometimes argued that some well-established tree species all but died out in America, for example, because waves of immigration inadvertently brought new parasites and microbes to which American trees had no immunity. There may be some truth to this. However, the findings of Andersen, St. Barbe Baker, and others relating tree species succession to a predictable, progressive loss of soil nutrients seems a more general and useful explanation. The species that have died off are those having the greatest leaf area per tree and therefore the greatest nutritional requirements, which suggests that the underlying cause is loss of soil nutrients. See also Iverson (1973) and Davis (1976).

13. Temperate region forests are most likely the ones that participate in this cycle. The tropical rainforests are probably remineralized primarily by volcanic eruptions, perhaps along with some minerals caught up in sea spray and distributed in coastal regions by winds. The rainforests seem to conserve

and recycle their nutrients, including minerals, very effectively: When plants die, their constituents are quickly broken down and used by others. The tropical soils on which the giant trees of the rainforest grow are notoriously poor, which implies that tropical forests do not need a large supply of minerals to survive. And the hardpan of congealed minerals typically found a few inches under the surface of tropical soils also helps prevent nutrients from leaching into the subsoil.

14. The weakening of trees by loss of minerals plus drought leads to a major increase in forest fires toward the end of the interglacial period. Burning trees give off not only $CO_2$, but also other greenhouse gases, including carbon monoxide and methane. The water vapor that is evaporated from warming oceans is also a greenhouse gas, though a relatively inefficient one.

15. W. L. Gates (1976) showed that glacial periods have increased pole-to-equator temperature gradients and, consequently, stronger winds. T. R. Janacek and D. K. Rea found a similar scenario when examining the size of wind-blown grains of sand as a measure of wind strength (Berger *et al.* 1984, p. 343). And CLIMAP scientists estimated tropical sea surface temperatures to be significantly *warmer* 18,000 years ago than today—up to 4°C—while the ice sheets were at their maximum (Schneider and Londer 1984, p. 66ff).

16. The wind-borne portion of this glacial dust, usually called loess, is found today primarily in certain regions near ancient glacial rivers, sometimes in drifts up to 60m (200ft) deep. Hamaker points out that a more finely ground gravel dust, which can be found today in large deposits in formerly glacial regions and which is lighter than loess, can be presumed to have blown over and remineralized a much wider area, and to have been mostly used up or leached and eroded away by now.

17. Hamaker's theory also seems to be supported by ocean core data analyzed by Nicholas Shackleton and his colleagues at the Cambridge University, which approximates atmospheric $CO_2$ and global ice over the past 150,000 years (Shackleton *et al.* 1983). In the graph on page 52, the dip in ice volume from about 130,000 to 120,000 years ago represents the last warm inter-glacial period. Our present interglacial period started about 10,000 to 11,000 years ago. The general curve of the two graphs—almost a mirror image of one another—might seem at first glance to support the generally accepted view that increased $CO_2$ leads to warming and decreased $CO_2$ to cooling and ice formation.

    An interesting exception to the general shape of the two curves, how-ever, is seen in the period between the two dashed lines—approximately the last 5000 years of the last interglacial period, which corresponds to our own time. During that period $CO_2$ was distinctly *rising*, while the beginning of the largest ice buildup on the graph was taking place. The only plausible explanation for this is the cycle that has been described here, with tropical oceans overheated by a differential greenhouse effect, increased winds resulting from the increased air pressure differentials, and the movement of tropical clouds toward the higher latitudes and the poles where they precipitate as snow and ice. It is especially significant that this rise in $CO_2$ corresponds exactly with the later phases of the interglacial period as shown in Andersen's studies—when gradually increasing soil demineralization is known to result in the succession, loss of vitality, and finally massive death

## SHACKLETON GRAPH

### Estimated Atmospheric $CO_2$ and Global Ice During the Past 150,000 Years

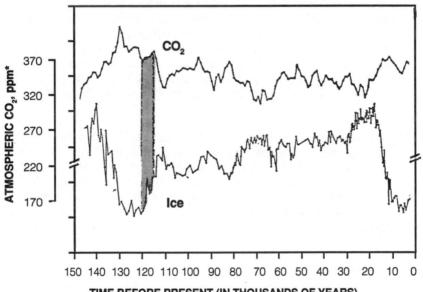

The global ice proxy is the oxygen isotope record from the deep water organism *Uvigerina senticosa*; the $CO_2$ proxy is the carbon isotope difference between ocean surface (from *Neogloboquadrina duterei*) and sea floor (*U. senticosa*); both from core V19-30. The $CO_2$ scale is placed off the graph because it is not certain what atmospheric values of $CO_2$ the ocean core data correspond to. I have changed the labeling on this scale slightly to represent more recent evidence for the preindustrial $CO_2$ baseline; and have added the vertical lines and letters.

**Source: Shackleton et al. (1983). The graphs were rotated and combined from two different graphs.**

**BARNOLA GRAPH**

## Estimated Atmospheric CO₂ and Temperature
## During the Past 160,000 Years

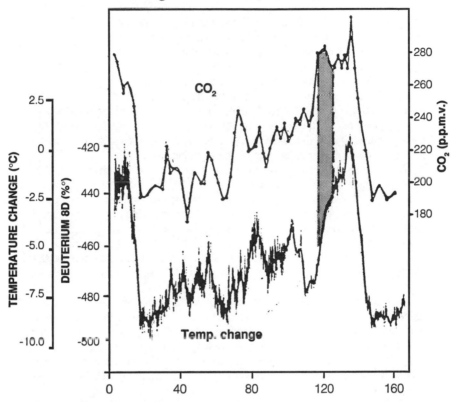

Source: J. M. Barnola et al. (1987).
Notice that in this graph, the present time is at the left.

of the earth's $CO_2$-consuming vegetation, which finally releases $CO_2$ into the atmosphere in great quantities.

Another, very recent study of $CO_2$ and temperature over the last 160,000 years was carried out by Barnola and others (1987) from the Vostok ice core in Antarctica. Although there were some differences in detail from the Shackleton data, the general shape of the curves was found to be quite similar. (In the Barnola graph, the lower curve represents temperature rather than ice volume, so higher values on it represent warmer periods of time.) A similar, several-thousand-year period of rising $CO_2$ can be seen between the two dashed lines, at the end of the last warm interglacial period and the initial rapid cooling (ice buildup) that ushered in the last ice age. In spite of admitted differences between the Barnola and Shackleton graphs (the Vostok researchers interpret their data as indicating an interglacial of some 22,000 years), the time period of rising $CO_2$ corresponding with the end of the interglacial is almost exactly the same in both studies.

The long downward trend of $CO_2$ during the last ice age is probably attributable primarily to the fact that $CO_2$ continues to be absorbed by increasingly cooling ocean waters. Carbon dioxide is that gas that makes carbonated drinks fizz. When your bubbly drink gets warm, it goes flat—the gas escapes into the air. The same thing happens in the ocean—warm oceans release $CO_2$ into the atmosphere. When the ocean gets colder, it absorbs more $CO_2$ from the air. Thompson and Schneider (Schneider and Londer 1984, p. 337) have pointed out that the minimum level of $CO_2$ at the end of the last ice age, and the possible maximum some 8,000 to 10,000 years ago, both occurred several years *after* the largest climatic changes had already taken place. In other words, the widely held idea that increased $CO_2$ causes warming and decreased $CO_2$ causes cooling does not seem to be borne out by at least this portion of the geological record.

A few years ago Shackleton and Pisias reported that the changes in $CO_2$ led to changes in ice volume over the last 350,000 years of the geologic record. But Alan Mix, an associate of Pisias at Oregon State University, recently told me (April 29, 1987, when Pisias was unavailable) that five partial replications led to the tentative conclusion that the two might actually be in phase, changing simultaneously. Moreover, he said that the variable on which $CO_2$ is based in the Shackleton studies, carbon-13, may not be the whole story since there are other components that are not included in these curves.

The differential greenhouse effect central to Hamaker's theory is magnified by the fact that warm tropical oceans give up $CO_2$ to the atmosphere while cold, high-latitude oceans absorb it. The net difference—on the order of 100 parts per million of $CO_2$—is quite large relative to recent changes in $CO_2$. The greenhouse effect in the tropics, which leads to increased evaporation as well as high winds, is thus substantially increased by this factor. (see Brewer, 1978)

If rising $CO_2$ leads to glaciation during that geologically rather short period of time between the two dashed lines (the last half of the last warm interglacial period), why shouldn't it always do so—especially during the much longer and steeper rises of $CO_2$ seen on the graph? The answer, I suggest, is that only that rise of $CO_2$ occurred well into a major interglacial period, when global ice was at a minimum. The largest rises of $CO_2$ during this whole period—as the last and present interglacials were beginning— occurred at times when the oceans had been cooling for tens of thousands of years, and cold glacial meltwater was cooling them still further. The evaporation and cloud production from a greenhouse effect, which are proposed here as the major source of glaciation, occur primarily in the presence of warm oceans, such as would be found after several thousand years of a warm interglacial period.

Carbon dioxide may have declined during the last ice age for another reason in addition to cooling oceans. Billions of microscopic sea animals build their shells (made of calcium carbonate—limestone) with the ocean's carbon and other minerals; when they die they form layer upon layer of the ocean floor. (The ocean research cores are going after their shells; ice cores go after tiny bubbles of trapped air, the elements which can be analyzed.) As sea life extracts $CO_2$ from the ocean, the ocean can absorb that much more from the air.

And then there's the role of the nutrients, which reach the ocean in greater quantities during ice ages. Minerals in the glacially ground rock sediments flow in streams to the sea. As ice builds up and sea level drops, nitrogen that was trapped in coastal sediments also gets exposed and then carried by glacial rivers toward the deep ocean, where it nourishes plants and sea life that extract $CO_2$ from the atmosphere (McElroy 1983).

The orbital cycles described by Milankovitch and others probably do have some influence on the shape of the ice volume curve. Combined Milankovitch maxima (maximum Northern Hemisphere solar radiation, primarily from the 41,000- and 22,000-year cycles) at about 103,000, 85,000 and 52,000 years before the present may account for the dips in ice volume during those periods, while minima at 70,000 and 25,000 years ago may explain the additional rises around those times. The smaller zigs and zags in the $CO_2$ curve may be partly attributable to the generational cycles of the shelled sea life, which may alternately multiply to the limit of the carbon supply and die back along with the whole ocean food chain as available supplies of carbon are used up.

There may be some evidence that sea level has risen about 7 centimeters in the last hundred years of so, which is taken as a sign by some warming theorists that polar ice has been melting because of $CO_2$. There is no certainty that sea level has in fact risen at all, however, because of the way measurements are taken, and in some areas measurements show it to have declined in recent decades. Barnett examined the evidence recently and concluded that the existence of a global rise in sea level "has not been proven" (Barnett 1985).

Even if sea level has risen a few centimeters in the last century, events consistent with cooling could have caused such a rise: half a century of worldwide deforestation, leading to much runoff into the sea of waters previously obsorbed by and held in soils; mineral depletion of the world's soils, with similar effects; a slight expansion of tropical oceans due to the warming in that large area; the wholesale drainage and filling of wetlands (now at a rate of about 450,000 acres a year); and the widespread use of groundwater for irrigation during the last quarter century or more, much of which runs off to the sea.

A very recent report by John Maddox (1986) describes the difficulties and uncertainties of measuring sea level rise. He refers to the work of Peltier, Drummond, and Tushingham (1986), which showed that sea level, and the "rebound" of the earth's surface after glaciation, "can be accounted for only by supposing that the present rate is controlled by viscous processes deep in the mantle of the Earth." This approach is consistent with Hamaker's. Hamaker has written extensively on the earth's tectonic system, work that should be published to further our understanding of various geological phenomena, including earthquakes and tectonic plate movement.

If the earth's vegetation and sea life needs periodic infusions of minerals, where did it get them during the billions of years before the Pleistocene ice ages began only a few million years ago? Presumably from volcanic eruptions, which are believed to have been considerably more extensive than present throughout much of Earth's history; from the erosion of uplifted rocks, erosion that was probably much greater than today's when the climate was much warmer and more humid millions of years ago; and from long, early periods of glaciation, perhaps much more extensive and prolonged than any ice ages in more recent times.

For a reconstruction of possible levels of volcanic activity over the past 600 million years, see Schneider and Londer (1984, p. 242). Schneider also cites evidence which might suggest that there were ice age cycles during the Tertiary (p. 20) and that there may have been extensive ice sheets in some earlier periods as well (p. 15).

Many climatologists have recently gone on record to say that climate change can be understood only from an interdisciplinary perspective, including soil science, forestry, biology, and paleobotany. See, for example, Marland and Rotty, (1979); Hare (1982), and others cited in Wood (1986).

18. In view of the data presented in the graphs, it is puzzling that every seismologist I talked to (about four) said there was no evidence that the number of major earthquakes has been increasing in recent decades. Published research, with the exception of the book cited for the data used in the graphs, also seems to say there is no trend.

19. There is considerable controversy about whether volcanism has in fact increased during this century. Bryson's work correlating volcanism and cooling is presented in Bryson and Goodman (1980). Others have reported increased volcanic activity over the last century or more. Simkin, Siebert, McClelland, Bridge, Newhall, and Latter (1981) report that the number of active volcanoes has more than doubled from 1860 to 1980, from 25 to 55. The number of *major* volcanic eruptions has also been found to be increasing over the last three decades (Simkin et al., cited in Bradley and Jones 1985).

The fact that the dust veil index, a measure of the amount of fine particles in the stratosphere, does not show a significant trend in this century is often presented as evidence that volcanic activity has not increased. Bryson argues, however, that the dust veil index primarily reflects larger eruptions whose products reach the stratosphere and is not an adequate measure of overall volcanic activity, most of which is smaller.

20. Here is a summary of the major points of the Hamaker theory, in the form of a proposed explanation of what appear to be the long-term components of the $CO_2$ and ice curves in Shackleton's 130,000-year graph of ice and $CO_2$. During the last interglacial period from about 130,000 to 122,000 years ago, a temperate climate and an abundance of minerals spread by the previous

glaciation fostered the spread of land vegetation, which brought down the $CO_2$. As some of the minerals eroded into the sea, sea life expanded and consumed more $CO_2$, storing much of it in their shells on the ocean floor.

As much of the minerals on land and in the ocean were eroded away or used up around 122,000 years ago, land vegetation and sea life began dying off, giving their carbon back to the atmosphere. Rising $CO_2$ created a greenhouse effect, evaporating more moisture from tropical and eventually mid-latitude and even some high-latitude oceans, some of which fell as snow and ice, building up the world's ice cover. This raised the polar regions' albedo (reflectivity), increasing the temperature gradient between the poles and the tropics still further and accelerating the process.

As the glaciers began building, they cooled higher latitude oceans, which began absorbing more $CO_2$. The ice continued to build for a few thousand years after the temperate forests had given up most of their $CO_2$ because of a combined Milankovitch minimum at 115,000 years ago (primarily the higher-frequency cycles). Then volcanism increased greatly from the enormous new weight of ice at the poles, raising the $CO_2$ curve again. By this time the mid- and higher-latitude oceans were considerably cooler, however, so that from this time on new glacial buildup was slower than at the end of the interglacial.

The long upward slope of ice during the glacial period is the result of the more-or-less continuous transfer of new moisture to the higher latitudes from tropical oceans, which remain warmer throughout the period because of the continuing greenhouse effect. The widening temperature difference caused by warm tropical oceans and an increasing high-latitude albedo as the ice builds up means that less and less $CO_2$ is needed to accomplish the process: The resulting increasingly high winds throughout the period continue to move abundant quantities of evaporated tropical moisture to the growing glaciers—some of it evaporated by the heat of the tropics, some by the high winds themselves.

The long downward slope of $CO_2$ during the glacial period results from two processes. Cooling high-latitude oceans absorb some $CO_2$. And some of the glacially ground rock dust is carried by water and wind to the oceans where it nourishes foraminifera and other shelled sea life, which are then able to expand greatly, consume large quantities of carbon, and deposit it on the ocean floor.

Combined Milankovitch effects from about 103,000 to 52,000 years ago help shape the major dips and peaks of the ice curve, with the $CO_2$ curve closely following suit as colder high-latitude oceans gradually absorb more and more $CO_2$. Periods of increased volcanism temporarily send more $CO_2$ into the atmosphere. And even in the shorter fluctuations, increasing glaciation feeds more sea life, which brings the $CO_2$ curve down.

As the ice sheets finally reach more temperate regions, they begin to melt as fast as they are growing, and ice buildup stops. With the temperate-region climate temporarily stabilized, some coniferous forests begin expanding, fed by a great deal of mineral-rich glacial runoff in the middle latitudes. The albedo is lowered somewhat by the spread of dark forests, and the temperate regions begin to warm up. The glaciers start melting back, the climate begins warming, and the forests expand further. As cold glacial meltwaters cool down the overheated tropical oceans, $CO_2$ production decreases, the greenhouse effect subsides, glacial melting greatly exceeds buildup, and the next interglacial is underway.

George H. Denton and Terence J. Hughes (1981, Chapter 8) believe that the late Pleistocene glaciers finally slid into the sea in a series of glacial surges rather than slowly melting in place, before the climate had warmed up substantially. Their view is not inconsistent with that presented here. See also Ruddiman and McIntyre (1981).

As the climate warms, the oceans begin giving off $CO_2$ and the $CO_2$ curve rises—perhaps abetted by a dieback of sea life resulting from the reduction of the stream of new minerals that had been supplied by glacially ground rock dust for so long. Mid- and higher-latitude oceans are still cold from 90,000 years of ice and now from melting glaciers, and tropical oceans are cooling; so the high $CO_2$ level during this period does not lead to renewed evaporation and glaciation.

As the climate warms up, spreading forests, fed by newly remineralized soils and an abundance of $CO_2$, begin consuming the atmospheric carbon. As the soil becomes enriched with the organic remaining generation of trees, and the rock dust broken down, larger trees with greater nutrient needs begin to spread. They begin to consume carbon in great quantities, lowering the $CO_2$ curve and beginning to cool the climate from the high temperature of the climatic maximum some 8,000 years ago. The temperate and higher-latitude oceans warm up during the next few thousand years, the soil minerals are finally used up or leached and eroded away, land and sea life dies back once again, carbon is given up to the atmosphere, and the cycle begins again.

21. Genevieve Woillard (1979) presented this paper in the scientific journal *Nature*. Her last paragraph reads: "My pollen work shows that, in Grande Pile, the change from a temperate to a boreal vegetation occurred over 150 yr ±50%. The accompanying gradual decline in temperate elements would probably now be hardly perceptible to man, because of the artificial management of many European forests. We thus cannot exclude the possibility that we already live at the beginning of the present equivalent of the terminal interglacial pollen zone, and that we are heading towards a relatively fast, perhaps dramatic, 'borealization' of West European forests which, some 115,000 yr ago, took less than 20 yr." She suggests that the final perhaps-less-than-20 years of our warm interglacial may have begun around 1979.

22. The unusually high precipitation to which the Great Lakes flooding has been attributed is reported to have begun around 1970 to 1972—precisely when Northern Hemisphere winters began getting substantially colder, snow cover began increasing dramatically, summers began getting hotter, and the

tropics began experiencing record heat and drought, in accord with the theory presented here. The date of onset of high precipitation in the Great Lakes region is attributed to Frank Quinn, chief hydrologist with the Great Lakes Environmental Research Laboratory (*Washington Post,* Feb. 18, 1987, p. A8).

23. Many tropical trees produce food (for humans or animals) extremely efficiently. Many of these trees are able to produce *ten times* the food per acre produced from the cattle that replace them when they are cut down for grazing land, which then typically becomes barren within five or six years.

24. Here is the rate at which each of a number of Central American countries are destroying their rainforest by cattle ranching and logging:

| Country | Square Kilometers per Year |
|---|---|
| Guatemala | 900 |
| Honduras | 800 |
| Costa Rica | 600 |
| Panama | 500 |
| Nicaragua | 500 |

Source: The Environmental Project on Central America, Green Paper Number Two (c/o Earth Island Institute).

I think you would find a high correlation between rainforest destruction and political repression, as measured, say, by the number of political murders and disappearances in each country, though accurate figures on repression are not available. Under the Somoza dictatorship, before its revolution, Nicaragua was destroying 1,000 square kilometers of rainforest a year. The point is that land reform—equitable distribution of decent farmland to the people—may be essential if we are to save enough of the world's rainforests to make it through this crisis.

25. The idea that our massive burning of ancient plant fossils as fuel might be a reversal of evolution is developed as follows. Tens of millions of years ago the earth's atmosphere contained several times the $CO_2$ it does now, and the climate was consequently much hotter. Huge tropical vegetation flourished over most of the globe; there were no ice caps on the poles; and huge animal life including dinosaurs lived off the lush vegetation. When succeeding generations of this vegetation died, much of it was buried under successive layers of earth and rock where its carbon could not be recycled back to the atmosphere. Gradually, most of the carbon in the atmosphere was withdrawn into these plants and buried in the earth. As they decomposed under great pressure, they formed deposits of coal, oil, and natural gas.

As the atmosphere's $CO_2$ was diminished in this way, the climate got cooler and cooler, which eventually brought on the 100,000-year cycles of ice ages about three million years ago. (Since the extinction of the dinosaurs took millions of years, they probably died out because the climate got colder and their abundance of food diminished—not some sudden catastrophe like an asteroid hitting the earth and putting up a dust cloud for a few years.)

If much higher levels of $CO_2$ made the earth much warmer in the age of the dinosaurs, how could today's rising levels of $CO_2$ bring on the next ice age? Because at much lower levels of $CO_2$ when the whole climate is much cooler, relatively small increases in $CO_2$ can move the planet's moisture around and build up the glaciers. At much higher levels, however, the heat trapped by massive quantities of $CO_2$ in the atmosphere overrides any possible buildup of ice and creates a much warmer climate where no ice could remain.

How could our burning of massive amounts of fossil fuels—now a million years' worth every year—be a reversal of evolution? Well, perhaps it is no accident that the human species evolved only in the last, cool million years or so of the earth's four billion year history, most of which was much hotter. Can you imagine living year-round in a climate much hotter and more humid than the hottest, most humid tropics? You certainly wouldn't be comfortable, and you almost certainly wouldn't get any work done. Most of humanity's technical progress has been achieved by people working in the temperate zones. And would you want to be competing every day with dinosaurs and huge winged monsters that are more adapted to the climate and vegetation than you are?

The "hole" in the earth's ozone layer over Antarctica during winter, which was first noticed in 1985 and which has been growing larger every winter since, may also be related to the climatic changes described here. Most scientists now believe that the earth's ozone layer is being destroyed by industrial chlorofluorocarbons (CFCs). These chemicals tend to become more concentrated over Antarctica because of the polar vortex, which tends to trap them there, where they destroy the ozone layer and create a "hole." Since ozone is one of the substances in the atmosphere which normally absorbs heat from the sun, its absence contributes to the increasingly cold temperatures over Antarctica. Colder temperatures increase the polar vortex, which traps more chlorine molecules and accelerates both the cooling and the destruction of the ozone layer.

In 1987 the ozone "hole" lasted until late in the Antarctic spring, at least two weeks later than ever monitored before. The loss of ozone permits more destructive ultraviolet radiation to penetrate the atmosphere, which has harmful effects on many forms of life. In the Antarctic winter, the low angle of the sun's rays produces relatively little ultraviolet radiation; in spring and now late spring, however, more and more ultraviolet radiation is penetrating through the ozone "hole," and many forms of life in Antarctica may be at risk. The ozone "hole" was even recently found to have covered all of Australia for a time.

26. Destruction of the ozone layer lets in a little more ultraviolet light and enhances the greenhouse effect slightly, but this is a very minor factor. And up until now, most of the ozone loss has been over Antarctica and primarily during the winter and early spring, when there is little sunlight to be let in.

27. We've been talking primarily about how an ice age begins. Since we're primarily concerned with stopping the next one, it may help to reiterate why ice ages eventually stop. When does the ice age come to an end?

    When sufficient minerals from glacially ground rocks have been spread by streams and high winds and have provided the nutrition for the world's plant and sea life to expand greatly, consuming and bringing down the excess $CO_2$. When sea level has lowered enough (from water transferred to glaciers) that huge areas of the continental shelves have been exposed to the air, so that the nitrogen held in them is carried by rivers to deeper areas of the ocean, where it also nourishes sea life and allows it to expand still further. When the glaciers have moved far enough from the poles that their melting equals or exceeds new buildup: cold glacial meltwater flows into the oceans, lowering their temperature and stopping excess evaporation and cloud production. As the glaciers stop expanding, the volcanic activity that was caused by the increasing weight of ice eventually diminishes, and with it this source of additional $CO_2$ to the atmosphere. As plant life fed by mineral-rich glacial runoff flourishes, and consumes more $CO_2$ and the level of atmospheric $CO_2$ comes down, the differential greenhouse effect dies out, the transfer of new moisture to the glaciers diminishes greatly and glacial melt exceeds buildup.

    One of the most important factors in bringing on and ending the ice ages, one which was not sufficiently emphasized in the text, is the earth's albedo, the extent to which it reflects the sun's heat back into space rather than absorbing it. Ice of course has a very high albedo (80 to 90%), deep forests very low (10 to 20%), deserts somewhere in between. As the earth's vegetation gradually dies off from a lack of nutritive minerals, it gives way to treeless plains and deserts which reflect back more of the sun's warmth. And as snow and ice begins to build up, its high reflectivity helps keep the region cold from year to year; as ice takes over other areas their reflectivity increases and cooling spreads. As the earth's plant life finally rebounds from a new infusion of minerals in the latter part of an ice age, it captures more of the sun's warmth than the barren lands it replaces, and this helps the earth warm up again and melt much of the remaining glaciers.

28. The glaciers are not going to cover the land in a few years, creating mile-high ice sheets over New York City—that will take tens of thousands of years, like it did last time. What seems likely to happen within the next few years if we don't act fast is that all the climatic extremes which are already occurring—record cold winters, summer freezes, flooding, droughts, high winds, hail—will continue to become more and more extreme, each de-

stroying more food crops as it does so. The combined result may well be worldwide starvation in the very near future.

A lasting ice sheet the size (not yet the depth) of the last ice age might well occur in the same time frame, however, if a series of six or seven severe winters in the higher latitudes leaves more and more snow on the ground throughout the year. Large snow fields create a colder regional climate, which makes it increasingly likely that larger areas of snow and ice will remain throughout the following summer. For the next ice age to begin, however, it will be sufficient for an unstoppable momentum of the climatic changes associated with glaciation to occur. Those changes in themselves will be devastating for human life, regardless of whether the ice fields have expanded greatly yet.

*Chapter Two*

# A REVOLUTION
# IN AGRICULTURE

Remineralizing the soils we grow our food on will produce the most dramatic results imaginable:

- *Greatly increased* yields
- *Lower costs* of agriculture and of food
- Hardier, insect- and disease-resistant crops, *without the use of any toxic pesticides or other chemicals*
- A great improvement in the *nutritional quality* and the *taste* of our food

And as you will see, all of these things go together.

One of John Hamaker's earliest insights about the nutritional value of the minerals bound up in rocks came when he was looking at maps in the 1969 *Encyclopedia Brittanica Atlas:*[1]

A few weeks ago a CBS Special, "The Frozen World of Seals and Walruses," emphasized that the waters of the Bering Sea around St. Lawrence Island are teeming with life.... The water is 28 degrees Fahrenheit. Most of the rest of the ocean has warm water and almost no life. Why?
    The answer is that the East Siberian Coastal Current picks up the flow from at least a half-dozen glacial rivers and sends it

through the Bering Straits. By superimposing the fish catches . . .
on the ocean currents . . . one can see that the fish are where the
crust of the earth is being ground.

In 1973 Hamaker built a very small gravel grinder. On August 4
he put in a small (10 by 12 feet) test plot for fall vegetables on his
farm in Lansing, Michigan (close to the Canadian border), and
remineralized one end of it with about 4 tons per acre finely ground
gravel dust.

He says,

> Anyone who plants a fall garden on the fourth of August in this
> area should not expect to get anything to eat. The 7-foot-long
> rows of the control plot produced nothing edible except for a few
> leaves of half grown pale lettuce and Swiss chard. The gravel
> dusted strip produced good lettuce, Swiss chard, and turnips.
> Carrots, beets, and parsnips did not have time to mature but some
> were usable.

In 1974 he put 3 tons of dust per acre on his whole garden, but
heavy rains eroded some of it away and damaged the crops. His
farmed-out soil was still too compacted to absorb rainwater fast
enough to prevent erosion. (He had started working it only in 1971.)

In 1975 spring planting couldn't be done until June, then drought
followed by more heavy rains took their toll, as did a neighbor's
cows. There were only 65 to 70 days for crops to grow. Yet Hamaker
and his wife got "the best quality and the most produce put away for
winter that we have ever had off that garden." He wrote, "that
garden patch is probably the richest piece of land in Michigan."

In 1976 Hamaker spread 46 tons per acre of gravel crusher
screenings (crushed gravel which had been passed through a screen,
containing a mixture of small particles ranging from dust to about ⅛
inch) on several acres of his 10-acre farm.

The following year, while other farmers in the area were getting
25 bushels to the acre using chemicals, in an area of sparse rainfall
and dry summers Hamaker's corn produced 65 bushels per acre—
with no irrigation. The next year, after the minerals had had more
time to work into the soil, he got 75.

Moreover, when the Detroit Testing Laboratory in Oak Park was
asked to do an analysis, Hamaker's corn was found to contain 46%
more calcium, 57% more phosphorus, 60% more magnesium, and

87% more potassium than the same type of corn grown nearby with chemical fertilizers.[2]

In 1978, in spite of a severe drought as the summer went on, Hamaker grew a soybean crop of 25 bushels per acre. "Local crops just dried up and quit in late August of that year, leaving most of the beans in an immature state."

Planting wheat on this same parcel a couple of years later, Hamaker again got an exceptionally high yield, even though the soil cracked open twice from drought during the growing season. The agricultural extension agent estimated the county average to be around 45 to 50 bushels of wheat per acre. Hamaker got more than 60.

Don Weaver, who eventually wrote a book with Hamaker, grew 20-foot pole beans (most farmers get 5- to 8-foot plants) on remineralized soil, and got two to four times the normal yield of organically grown farms. Alan LePage grew a crop of carrots on remineralized soil which averaged one-and-a-half feet long (your elbow to your fingertips).

And there was *no insect damage* to any of these crops.

Mark Williams, who is now building gravel grinders, planted corn in 11-inch pots and did a little home experiment. One set of pots was left unfertilized; one was fertilized with Miracle-Gro, a widely used commercial chemical fertilizer; and one was fertilized only with his silt-fine rock dust, at a rate equivalent to about 5 tons per acre. The results can be clearly seen in the picture of the three small corn plants. He estimated that the remineralized plants already averaged about 30% larger than the chemically treated plants after only about six weeks from the time of planting.

Dan Hemenway, a science writer by trade, heard about a lot of granite dust left over from water drilling in his Massachusetts neighborhood. He got himself a pickup truck full ("the small-diameter stuff that had washed further from the pile") and put it on part of his vegetable garden while he was planting it—the part with the poorer, less-fertile soil—just to see what would happen. When his carrots came in he picked ten from the remineralized bed and ten from his

*Dan Hemenway's carrots.*

*Don Weaver with one of the huge heads of lettuce from his remineralized garden.*

*Mark Williams' corn. Plant on left was grown with Miracle Gro. Center plant was grown in soil with stone flour added. Plant on right is a control.*

normal soil, and took a picture of them all in a flat. The remineralized carrots are several times as big.[3]

Other people have reported growing 12-foot clover, 6- to 7-foot buckwheat, 2-pound beets, 3-pound potatoes, and so forth on remineralized soil.

## Some studies

In Germany, Helmut Snoek has been scientifically studying the fertilizing effects of rock dust for 28 years. A book on his discoveries was published in 1983, another is in preparation. Using small pots about 4 inches on a side (10 centimeters), he added tiny amounts of rock dust, starting at only one gram—the equivalent of less than 1 ton of dust per acre. Seeds were planted and the pots photographed every ten days with a ruler behind each of them. He says,

> With rock dust, the plants were growing at least twice as high as the controls, with incredibly green leaves and a growth of roots you cannot imagine! The pot nearly exploded![4]

Werner Koch, the University of Munich forestry professor mentioned earlier, has photographs of Fritz Leibold's remineralization experiments that show this dramatic improvement in root growth quite graphically in two tomato plants from the same location. The obviously much healthier plant was taken from a plot fertilized only with finely ground rock dust. There was no other difference in the treatment the two plants received.

Koch also shows pictures of apples grown on remineralized soil. He says,

> This is a very sensitive type of apple, known as the Cox Orange, and these soils have never seen a chemical. These trees have been fertilized exclusively with rock dust.... It is almost incredible that one can achieve such a result without chemical fertilizers. There are more apples in the tree than leaves! ... In the close-up photograph, one can see that these apples have no defects, they are without blemishes.

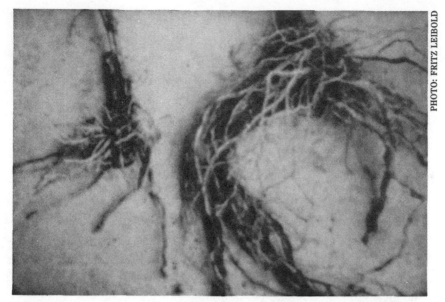

*The roots of two tomato plants. The plant on the right was fertilized with rock dust.*

*Unblemished apples fertilized only with rock dust. No pesticides or other chemicals were used.*

Perry Spiller is an officer of The Soil Association of New Zealand. He became enthusiastic about John Hamaker's discoveries and suggested to his daughter Jean Marie that she might want to do something on remineralization for her high school science project. She did. Growing clover in pots, she showed that the plants fertilized with rock dust were *400 to 500% bigger* than the controls.

In a less-controlled experiment, I planted collard greens in three boxes filled with potting soil, remineralizing two of them with a liberal quantity of finely ground gravel dust. The difference was clearly visible after only a few weeks.

*My collard greens.*

John Hamaker estimates that on fully remineralized soil, American agriculture, for example, could grow *four times* as much food as it is capable of now—or the same amount of food at one-fourth the cost—with *no* chemical fertilizers or toxic insecticides. And yields might increase to five or more times present yields if the stalks and other leftover organic matter were put back into the soil.

Based on the results obtained by many people in several countries, Hamaker estimates that if the fields of America's corn belt, for example, were remineralized, most of it would produce super yields of over 200 bushels per acre of the highest quality, most nutritious and delicious corn. Comparable results could be expected in every agricultural region on earth.

To the extent that world hunger is an agricultural rather than political problem, it appears that we can end it by remineralizing croplands.[5]

# Chemical agriculture

The same processes of erosion that have gradually depleted all the earth's soils since the last ice age ended have of course made agricultural soils much less fertile as well. Great quantities of essential mineral nutrients have been washed away over the centuries. This may be part of the reason chemical agriculture has become so widespread in the last few decades.

Chemical agriculture began over a century ago when Justus von Leibig, a German chemistry professor, burned plants to analyze their ash residue. He found that it consisted primarily of three elements: nitrogen (N), phosphorous (P), and potassium (K). The chemical companies soon picked up on this discovery and started selling "NPK fertilizer" made from compounds of these elements, a practice that has continued almost unchanged to this day.

What von Liebig didn't know, however, was that plant ash contains *dozens* of different minerals essential for healthy crops, though some are present only in minute quantities, the so-called "trace minerals." Had he had access to today's spectrographic equipment he would have seen that plants contain more than *90* different elements.

If he had known this, von Liebig would not have given his blessing to a simplistic chemical agriculture. For he already knew that the deficiency of even *one* necessary element undermines the health and productivity of the entire plant. (We now know that even a significant *excess* of any mineral leads to deficiencies in others.)

Shortly before his death in 1873 von Liebig realized that the "fertilizer" industry he had spawned was a tragic mistake, and he wrote remorsefully, "I had sinned against the wisdom of the Creator, and in my blindness believed that, in the marvelous chain of laws binding life on earth's surface and keeping it always new, a link had been forgotten which I, weak and powerless worm, must supply."[6]

Since nitrogen is one of the most important nutrients for plant growth, chemical agriculture got increased yields by pumping increasing quantities of it into the soil. But this simplistic approach produced crops that were increasingly frail, increasingly vulnerable to insects and disease.

The plants fertilized with chemicals developed a drug habit. Within a decade farmers had to use five times as much NPK to produce the same amount of food, a need that kept growing.

The increasingly fragile plants also needed ever-increasing quantities of toxic insecticides, herbicides, and fungicides to ward off insects, weeds, and disease. Of course the strongest insects are the ones that survive, and each generation has more resistance than the last. So since large-scale spraying of pesticides began, the amount of poison being sprayed on your food every year is *ten times* what it used to be and rising every year. Yet with all this expense and ingenuity, crop damage from insects is now *double* what it was before pesticides were ever invented.

Perhaps this is one reason Jim Hightower, Texas Commissioner of Agriculture, does not have very good feelings about the people who run the U.S. Department of Agriculture: "If ignorance is bliss," he says, "these guys must be ecstatic."[7]

# Destroying the earth

Chemical agriculture is destroying our very lifeline, the soil.

The United States is such a vast country that farmers often abused their land and then simply moved on when it wore out. These kinds of practices caught up with us dramatically during the 1930s in the Dust Bowl. The prairies had become so overcultivated, so dried out and denuded of wind-breaking trees and hedgerows, that fierce dust storms rose up over much of the Midwest, carrying away the precious topsoil from plowed fields. Thousands of poverty-stricken farmers migrated yet again, this time to the still-fertile fields of California and the Northwest. John Steinbeck memorialized their plight in *The Grapes of Wrath*.

This was precisely the time when the giant hydroelectric dams were built, and one of the first things their electricity was used for was to manufacture chemical nitrogen. Some farmers began to use it as a cheap substitute for growing crops that fix nitrogen in the soil (usually beans or clover).

Much of the nitrogen was used to make explosives during World War II. When the war was over, the chemical companies found themselves with a large surplus of it, and began promoting it heavily to farmers as the answer to their problems. Large quantities of war-surplus DDT were also promoted to agriculture. (Now the nuclear power industry is trying to sell us its undisposable wastes to "preserve" our food with radiation.) Other pesticides were developed out of World War II nerve gases, substances so toxic they were banned even from warfare by the Geneva Convention.

Now tens of thousands of farmers began to use chemical fertilizers. It became the new status symbol for "progressive" farmers, to replace "old-fashioned" organic matter such as manure and compost. But these acidified chemical compounds killed the beneficial life forms in the soil—earthworms, insects, microorganisms—which keep it loose and aerated and break down last year's organic matter into nourishment for this year's crops. Paul Erlich cites a Danish study of fertile soil that counted the living beings beneath one square yard of rich dark humus: 10 million tiny roundworms, 45,000 small earthworm-type creatures, and 48,000 tiny insects and mites. (The castings earthworms leave behind are about five times more fertile than the soil from which they are made.) One-thirtieth of an ounce of soil from a fertile farm was calculated to contain 30,000 protozoa, 50,000 algae, 400,000 fungi, and more than 2.5 billion bacteria. When these essential life forms are killed by harsh chemical compounds, the soil is rendered all but lifeless. Crops squeezed out of it with more and more chemicals can only be a pale substitute for real food.

The outcome of the new chemical agriculture was devastating. As the fields lost their natural fertility and porousness, they became unable to hold rainwater, which ran off, taking more of the topsoil with it. As the soil became harder and more compacted every year, bigger and bigger tractors were needed to work it, and the weight of the tractors compacted it even further.

America's commercial farmers have now reached the point where it "costs" two bushels of topsoil for every bushel of corn. The topsoil is disappearing. Soil in Iowa, a typical state in the heart of America's food-growing region, is disappearing at the rate of an inch every 12 years. Many parts of the state have less than a foot of topsoil left.

Where farmlands have been heavily irrigated, salt builds up in the soil, eventually destroying its fertility. Hamaker says that heavily remineralizing such soils, however, can eventually restore them.

Its boosters like to argue that whatever else you might say about it, chemical agriculture is efficient: "Look how few people are needed to produce all the food we eat." Efficient? A peasant farmer usually produces 10 calories of food energy for every calorie of energy put in. America's chemical farmers can produce only 1 calorie of food for every 10 calories of energy they put in (oil, chemicals, and so on). Simple peasant agriculture, then, which fed the world for thousands of years before 1935, is *a hundred times* more efficient than high technology's modern chemical marvels. And that gross inefficiency is using up the earth's resources, destroying the topsoil, putting huge amounts of carbon dioxide and nitrous oxide into the atmosphere, and bringing us all closer to starvation.

Boosters don't seem to care much about topsoil, however. Roger Revelle, a frequently quoted American scientist and one of the major proponents of the idea that $CO_2$ is bound to cause warming, recently reassured his colleagues at a meeting of the American Association for the Advancement of Science: "topsoil probably is not very important in modern agriculture ... we can change the fertility simply by adding fertilizers."

And now the scientists have begun to use the new techniques of genetic manipulation to try to remake agriculture once again: gene transplants, recombinant DNA, cloning, etc. Again they are holding out the promise of bigger plants and animals and greater resistance to disease, some of the same promises that chemical agriculture once made.

Genetic engineering techniques are so powerful that no one can tell where they might lead, what environmental devastation might result from accidental or even planned releases of new bacteria and other organisms. The U.S. Environmental Protection Agency has been limiting and delaying most field tests of bacterial pesticides so far, but industry pressures will probably lead to large-scale releases in the next few years.

The devastating experience of chemical agriculture—for our farmland, the economic and personal well-being of farmers, and our health as consumers—is a warning we can't afford to miss. Until recently it would have been very difficult to stop the momentum of genetic engineering in agriculture, because the biotechnologists hold out to us the possibility of replacing toxic chemical pesticides with biological, bacterial substitutes.

But now we have a better alternative at hand, one that requires no dangerous new research, creates no billions of unknown new microbes, and is available immediately. Remineralizing our agricultural soils will provide most of the hoped-for benefits of genetic engineering—greatly increased yields, optimum resistance to insects and disease, and freedom from toxic chemicals—with none of the risks. And unlike some hypothetical future prospects of genetic engineering, remineralizing our farmlands will also help bring down the atmospheric carbon dioxide *now,* and store it in newly expanded crops.

# *Bread from stones*

The terrible consequences of Justus von Liebig's "blindness" might have been averted if the work of a countryman of his had been taken more seriously. In 1893, Julius Hensel published a small book called *Bread From Stones,* in which he described his discovery that remineralizing the soil with a varied mixture of crushed rocks produced superabundant yields of top-quality food crops.

A popular movement developed to promote what Hensel called "stone meal" as the ideal agricultural fertilizer. But a grinder capable of high production was not available, and the petrochemical companies, just beginning to wield their power, apparently recognized Hensel's work as the threat to them it was and suppressed it. Most library copies were quickly stolen.

Forestry professor Werner Koch says,

> You might ask me why fertilizing with rock dust, despite all its successes, which can be proved, has progressed so slowly, and is not recommended officially by our agricultural institutions and by science.... The big chemical fertilizer producers do not like competition. They want business just for themselves. They don't want to be pushed aside. That is probably the main reason.... And the other reason is that our science, agricultural science, is still going down paths that are obsolete.

West German author Helmut Snoek puts it this way:

> Rock dust was popular around the turn of the century. Then the chemical industry tried to supress the application of stone meal in favor of chemical fertilizers, which were produced artificially. But for the last 20 years now, rock dust has again gained in importance. Today the organic agriculture associations are publicizing rock

dust widely, and a number of big and well-known companies have started to produce it—grinding and selling it under special brand names and with big advertising campaigns.

The U.S. Department of Agriculture has narrowly missed recognizing the value of remineralizing the soil on a number of occasions. For example, 20 years ago it published articles describing how cement kiln dust (a by-product of cement making, ground from local gravels) supplied on the average 3 times the magnesium, 9 times the potassium, and 16 times the calcium typically removed from the soil in a five-year rotation of crops. No recommendations were made, however, and the matter was apparently dropped.

The rich supply of minerals in rocks are food not only for plants but also for the microorganisms that help nourish them. John Hamaker writes,

> Examine a stone, other than limestone, in the soil. Crack it open. Under a very drab demineralized exterior "skin," you will see the minerals. That skin represents the depth to which the microorganisms have been able to penetrate the crystal structure of the stone.

Hamaker argues that weathering alone cannot explain this process. If gravel decomposed only from freezing, thawing, moisture, and so forth, none of it would ever reach the topsoil where plants can utilize its minerals. All the gravel distributed by the glaciers during an ice age would be reduced to fine particles in the subsoil instead of being pushed up to the surface like larger rocks tend to be. It would not come up to the surface in a steady stream over thousands of years like it does. The microorganisms, however, gradually make it available as it reaches the topsoil, where it is used by countless generations of plants.

During the 10,000 years of the interglacial period, Hamaker says,

> 8 or 10 feet of glacial deposit has been cycled to the topsoil, demineralized by the soil life, and descended back into the subsoil to form a dense clay. There are only 2½ inches of the original deposit left in the topsoil, and there is no more on the way up.

From now on we must provide the minerals to the soil, or the glaciers will do it—and soon.

How can we remineralize the soils of the earth quickly when the microorganisms do it so slowly, over thousands of years? By grinding glacial rocks ourselves to a very fine dust, the fineness of talcum powder—to particles so small they will pass through a screen with a mesh of 200 holes to the square inch:

> For instance, a 1-pound stone might have a surface area of 12 square inches. Ground to about 200 mesh, it would have a surface area of about 8 acres. One ton therefore would have a surface area of 16,000 acres. The significant thing about that 16,000 acres is that it is all freshly-broken stones with the useful elements exposed right on the surface. These elements are readily available for extraction by microorganisms.

How readily? Mix ¼ inch of peat and fine gravel dust on a small plate. (Peat is nonliving organic matter. The dust can be obtained by hammering some gravel in a bag; collect the dust in half a pint of water, shake and let settle for 5 minutes; pour off the liquid into a second container and let that settle for half an hour or more; what settles will be "about as fine as rouge.") Add a pinch of dirt to the peat/dust mixture, moisten and mix. On another plate mix up the same peat and a pinch of dirt without the gravel dust. Wait six hours, then carefully crosshatch each mixture with a different toothpick or matchstick, and look at each under a simple magnifying glass. The rounded ends of the peat fibers in the plate with the dust are the work of the mineral-fed microorganisms: "... observe the points on the peat. You will see them gradually become nodulated as the colonies of organisms grow. Within six hours the material will be much changed in appearance and become granulated as all good soil is. You have produced a population explosion of soil organisms." Within six hours!

How readily? Do a simple pot test. Take two 6-inch-diameter clay pots and fill them with a 50/50 mixture of earth and peat. Add 3 heaping tablespoons of gravel dust to one, and mix each well. Plant in each a radish seed that has first been soaked in water overnight (radishes grow fast). In less than two weeks you will see a significant difference in the size and strength of the two seedlings. Topsoil is irrelevant? If the soil is left out of any of these experiments, nothing will grow. The radish will sprout but not grow. The soil contains the microorganisms that are essential for life.[8]

Hamaker puts it this way: "The foods of microorganisms are the cheapest raw materials on earth." He says we can build enormous fertility into the soil in a very short time, so much fertility "that sun energy reaching the planet becomes the limit of growth."

# Our health and the quality of our food

*"My mother puts this plastic fruit out on the table. I guess she thinks some mannequins are coming over."*

—MARVIN HAMLISCH, ON THE
JOHNNY CARSON SHOW

As early as 1948, Rutgers University professor Firman E. Bear did a study of the mineral content of vegetables, and found a tremendous range from one sample to another. Tomatoes ranged from 1 to 1,938 parts per million of iron, for example. Clearly the people eating tomatoes with much more iron are getting a great deal more nourishment.

In 1963 the U.S. Department of Agriculture published its *Composition of Foods Handbook*. Though the only trace mineral listed in it was iron, we can get a rough estimate of what has happened to the quality of American food by comparing the average of Bear's highest and lowest samples with the USDA's average (Figure 13).

The average drop in iron in these five vegetables from 1948 to 1963, a matter of only fifteen years, seems to have been more than 90%! *This is the period during which chemical agriculture replaced organic methods in America*—organic agriculture which had fed every generation of human beings since agriculture was invented some 10,000 years ago.

**FIGURE 13**

## Decline of Iron in American Food, 1948–1963
## (Before and After Chemical Fertilizers and Pesticides
## Began to Be Used on a Large Scale)

Iron content of foods (parts per million)

|  | 1948 | 1963 |
|---|---|---|
| Spinach | 801 | 31 |
| Snap beans | 118 | 8 |
| Cabbage | 57 | 4 |
| Lettuce | 262 | 14 |
| Tomatoes | 969 | 5 |

Since the other elements in Bear's study showed similar variability, it seems reasonable to assume a roughly comparable loss of the other essential mineral nutrients during this time—calcium, potassium, and so on. Hamaker says "Fields of carrots with no carotene, and alfalfa with no vitamin A have been reported."

A recent USDA study found that the *majority* of Americans—supposedly the best fed people in the world—are getting less than 70% of the recommended daily allowances of calcium, iron, and magnesium. And if a deficiency in any one nutrient is a sign of inadequate nutrition, *more than 80% of Americans are suffering from malnutrition.*[9]

Agricultural scientist William Albrecht noted that the protein content of Kansas wheat dropped from about 15% in 1940 to about 12% in 1949. Today it has dropped to about 10%. Hamaker says it was already very low in 1940, before chemical agriculture ever took over, from 10,000 years of demineralization by the weather. (Soil minerals are a key ingredient in making protein, and we need a sufficient intake of minerals to use effectively the protein we consume.) He says that if we remineralize our farmlands and grow food organically, "Protein content of grains, the indicator of health-giving potential, will run two to three times the present protein figures."

When we eat food grown on depleted soil and fertilized inadequately, we, like the plants, lose our natural resistance to disease. Suffering from more frequent colds, flues, allergies, and other infectious illnesses, we may become dependent on the human equivalent of pesticides—antibiotics and other drugs—which likewise allow microbes to build up an immunity over time. People are now dying of "superinfections" that never existed before, and all the antibiotics and drugs in the world cannot save them, because they used antibiotics too frequently (usually unnecessarily) in the past.

The chemical nitrogen used in commercial agriculture leaves residues in and on supermarket food, which end up in your stomach and are converted to carcinogenic nitrosamines. The Delaney Amendment to the U.S. Food and Drug Act outlaws any carcinogenic substance from American food. Californians also recently passed a statewide initiative banning the introduction of carcinogens into the environment. Perhaps some lawsuits under these statutes, along with education about the enormous advantages of using gravel dust instead of chemicals, can help put a stop to chemical agriculture. (One selling point is that chemical farmers have one of the highest rates of cancer in the world.) Samuel Epstein, M.D., a prominent authority on environmental sources of cancer, says, "Thousands of cancer deaths are costing billions of dollars. This is not peanuts. But industry finds it far cheaper to kill people than to institute preventive measures." Far more profitable, actually—keeping agriculture dependent on chemicals, for example, keeps lots of farmers' money flowing into a few big oil and chemical companies; organic farming is very decentralized and independent.

There is a myth that organic agriculture is obsolete now, that it can't feed the world anymore. The fact is that there are some 50,000 or more well-established organic farmers in America alone, and many of them sell their food through commercial supermarkets, where it is mixed in with chemically grown food and sold *at the same price*. Some organic farmers can grow food at a fraction of the cost of chemical agriculture, because of the high cost and ever-rising input of chemical fertilizers and pesticides. And many of them are getting a premium price for their crops, because pesticide-free food is still a specialty item that consumers are willing to pay extra for.

Monoculture agriculture, where farmers plant the same crop year after year on thousands of acres, almost invites insects and blights. The soil becomes more and more depleted, and infestations have the opportunity to spread widely. Organic farmers control insects and weeds and build soil fertility by rotating crops, cultivating, and recycling organic wastes, the way farmers have done since time immemorial. These days organic farming is sometimes called "sustainable," "low-input" or "regenerative" agriculture.

Depleted soils and increasingly empty food may be partly responsible for the increases in all the major degenerative diseases in our time: arthritis, diabetes, Parkinson's and Alzheimer's diseases, heart disease, and cancer. In a recent review of the literature relating to cancer, the National Academy of Sciences found that deficiencies of one or another of various trace minerals—iron, copper, selenium, iodine, and so on (not to mention deficiencies in several)—are directly associated in laboratory studies with an increased likelihood of cancer. Mineral depletion of soils has been found to be correlated with death rates (by region), as is "soft" water, water that is low in minerals.

In 1938 only ½ of 1% of American men were sterile. By 1980 the figure had leaped to 16%. At that rate, in another 25 years (if we make it that far) half of all American men will be sterile. Is inadequate nourishment caused by empty foods a factor? (And what about chemical residues in supermarket food? Twenty toxic chlorinated chemicals alone have been found in sperm.)

There is another pathway from depleted soils and food to degenerative illnesses of all kinds. Increasingly empty food may be one reason why Americans and other people in the overdeveloped countries eat too much: trying to get enough real nutrients. This alone may be partly responsible for our common tendency to be overweight. And unfortunately, many of the foods people turn to in their cravings are very unhealthy: too much meat (little is better, none is best), dairy products (usually high in fat), and salty foods (high blood pressure and kidney disease). Organically grown food contains significantly higher quantities of vitamins, minerals, and protein than chemically grown food, so people who eat organic food are getting more adequate nourishment and are less likely to develop the cravings that lead to overweight and death.

Heart disease actually began to taper off in the 1980s as many people got the message about a healthy diet and exercise. But cancer is still advancing on us like a glacier: One in seven of us died of cancer in 1950, one in six in 1971, one in five by 1978, one in three in 1986, probably one in two by the turn of the century, just a few years away. The many pathways to cancer—mineral deficiencies, overeating, toxic exposure, stress, and so forth—may take much individual and political motivation to avoid.

Please don't think you can make up for the deficiencies in your food by taking vitamins and minerals. The substances in pills are not absorbed in the body the way natural nutrients are. And so far only nature has figured out the right proportions between the dozens of nutritional elements, some of them not even known yet, that are necessary for health. Deficiencies or excesses of any of them may diminish or even inactivate others.

Organically grown food is the place to get vitamins and minerals, and especially organic food grown on remineralized soil. Natural food stores usually contain a wide variety of organic food. (A lot of so-called "health food" stores, unfortunately, seem to sell primarily pills these days.) If you have a garden you can start adding gravel dust and stop using any chemicals on it. Or you could get involved in the community gardening movement, where many cities provide free land and water and neighbors get together to grow food together.

The success of the Gerson therapy (an intensive nutritional therapy focusing on gallons of freshly pressed, organically grown fruit and vegetable juices) in healing degenerative illnesses including cancer further corroborates these ideas. I believe it will heal most AIDS as well. (See the Appendix: *Access*.)

You can get some of the minerals you're missing, temporarily, by adding a little seaweed to your diet. A wide variety of "sea vegetables" are now available and beginning to find their way to the tables of many gourmets. The most popular is probably the black *nori* which comes wrapped around Japanese *sushi* (sushi bars are becoming popular in many cities outside Japan). Nori comes in paper-thin sheets that can simply be toasted and crumbled into almost any soup, salad, or main dish. Some *wakame* (*wok´*-a-may) can be soaked, rinsed, and added to dishes or eaten straight with a little vinegar or lemon juice. You can find out more at your local natural food store or a good bookstore.

John Hamaker and others have said that old barren fruit trees can go into "a second childhood" and start producing fruit again. Maybe mineral-rich streams are the fabled fountain of youth we have sought for so long.

Meanwhile, though, Hamaker thinks animals may be smarter than people. As mentioned earlier, he noticed cattle avoiding agricultural chemicals. He was told of a herd of dairy cows that stuck their heads through a hole in the barn and ate more than a ton of gravel dust one summer. His cats lick gravel dust he leaves out for them. They all seem to know what they need.

# *Longevity*

The peoples of the earth who are thought to live the longest and be almost entirely free of sickness all their lives live predominantly in mountainous regions where the soil is irrigated by glacially fed rivers and streams—waters that naturally contain the mineral-rich residues of crushed glacial gravel. They include the Hunzas in the Himalayas, the Vilcabambas in Ecuador, and the Georgians in the Caucasus Mountains of the USSR. The 30,000 Hunzas and perhaps the other groups are the only known people on the face of the earth who are entirely free of cancer.

Some scientists have recently decided that Eskimos are relatively free of heart disease, in spite of the fact that they eat a lot of animal fats, because of the fish oils they consume. So now many people are taking fish oil capsules, presumably so they can keep eating a high-fat diet without dying from a heart attack. John Hamaker's research, however, suggests that the food Eskimos eat comes from highly mineralized waters fed by many glacial rivers, and that it is the minerals that are the key to their good health.

The Hunzas were "discovered" in the late 1940s by two well-known agriculturalists, Sir Albert Howard and J.I. Rodale. Each of them wrote a book about the Hunzas' health and longevity, attributing it to the richness of their soil fed by glacial silt. Both talked about the necessity of remineralizing agricultural soils with crushed rocks. Few people listened.

## *How to remineralize agricultural soils*

There are at least four potential sources of mineral-rich rocks:

- Natural deposits of glacial gravel dust
- Finely ground glacial, river, ocean, or other mixed gravel
- Crushed and screened glacial or mixed gravel
- Cement kiln dust, the residue of crushed gravel

All these are good sources. The first two are probably the best, as they will have the smallest particles and thus their nutrients will be available the most quickly. For this reason they are also the cheapest to transport: you need less of them to get the job done. Gravel companies will deliver.

Crushed gravel (also called "fines") should be checked with a 200-mesh screen if possible, about talcum powder fineness. (For fine screens try looking in the Yellow Pages under "Wire cloth.") The crushings should be close to one-sixth dust at a minimum (the gravel company can tell you), and for small batches can be screened further after delivery (use window screens if nothing else is available). Look under "Sand and Gravel" in the Yellow Pages. Some 33,000 tons of cement kiln dust, a waste material, is available each day in the U.S. alone, and probably at a good price in quantity. In some European countries, some quarries that grind gravel dust for agriculture guarantee that 80% of the particles measure less than 30 microns (25 microns = one-thousandth of an inch).

Since transportation may cost more than the gravel itself, it will be cheapest and best in most areas to get mixed gravel from local sources—creeks, rivers, gravel deposits, the ocean—and have it finely ground nearby. Gravel companies may be persuaded to do the job, though their equipment may not grind fine enough. (They tend to rely on crushers rather than grinders, so that you then need to screen the product or add more.) Perhaps they can be talked into getting a good grinder as the demand increases, or any local entrepreneur may find this a lucrative field now.

It isn't necessary to do any laboratory analyses of the mineral content of the rocks you use. Hamaker says,

> I have seen the following figures on the required elements for life, 16, 25, 52, and 70+. It keeps going up. It's now beyond the ability of the usual testing equipment. I think it's much safer to rely on a grand mixture to furnish 92 elements in normal balance.... I do not know as much as nature know, so I would use only her natural mixtures.

*Bags of finely ground rock dust for agriculture at the Zimmerli plant, Zurich, Switzerland.*

*Hamaker grinder.*

Most gravel contains a good mixture of types of rock.[10]

John Hamaker, an engineer by profession, has invented unique rock grinders which grind rock against rock so they wear out very slowly. A 6-inch diameter prototype of his rotary grinder has been built and works well. A 7-foot diameter model would probably turn out more than a ton of dust per hour, and might serve all the needs of a local area. They might be built as large as 20 feet in diameter, which would crank out a lot of dust. A simpler, "rocker-box" design could easily be built in tens of thousands of machine shops all over the world. (See Appendix: *Access* for contacts.)

And Mark Williams has recently designed a combination grinder/spreader based on Hamaker's design, which could travel across fields under its own power spreading finely ground gravel dust. The cost of grinding and blowing the mineral-rich dust over a farmer's fields would be only $3 a ton plus the cost of the gravel. He is also designing a solar-powered grinder, to work without any fossil fuels at all. Because a farmer has to remineralize only once every five or

*Williams grinder/spreader.*

ten years, Williams estimates that remineralizing would cost only about $30 per acre per year, compared to a typical cost now of $100 an acre for chemical fertilizers. And the yields are a lot higher, and there's no need to spend even more money on expensive chemical pesticides.

# How much dust should you use on farms and gardens?

Hamaker says,

> 10 tons of gravel dust per acre with minimal organic matter will ensure at least as good a crop as last year and require no additional expense for about 10 years.

The rule of thumb is about 1 ton per acre per year, if you're shipping crops off the land each year; and it can be added at five- or ten-year intervals, perhaps even longer. Hamaker says you shouldn't have to pay more than about $10 a ton at the grinder. If the dust measures out to be really fine (say, 90% will go through a 200-mesh screen), an initial application of 5 tons instead of 10 may be sufficient. Experiment. (Ten tons per acre is about ⅛th of an inch of dust. The glaciers bring 6 to 10 feet.)

"At least as good a crop as last year" means those who've been farming chemically. Organic farmers will get a much better yield with this amount of dust because they've put much more organic matter in their soil. (On a home garden scale, that's ½ pound of gravel dust per square foot. Hamaker also points out that the black soil many organic gardeners prize is laden with undigested carbon; adding the minerals supplied by gravel dust will allow the microorganisms to make good use of this organic material, with enormous increases in yields.)

If you can only get crusher screenings, and if they're ⅙ dust, for example (and you can't screen them further), add 6 times as much: it's only the dust which can be quickly utilized; the larger particles will take years to break down.

Disc the dust into the top 6 to 8 inches of soil. Mix it into the pot or planter box, or turn it with a shovel into a backyard garden.

To get *greatly increased* yields, add multiples of ten tons per acre up to 50 or more tons per acre (2½ pounds per square foot). Once you've also got plenty of organic matter in the soil and it's had time to break down and be utilized, 20 tons per acre may get you doubled yields in a few years, 30 tons tripled, and so on. There's probably an upper limit beyond which more dust is ineffective or even counter-productive, but 100 to 200 or more tons to the acre can be well utilized (that would be about 1¼ to 2½ inches of dust). If you put on much more than 30 tons to the acre, disc it in a little deeper.

For tree crops like fruit and nut trees, remineralize the area around each tree out to the drip-line, or as far as the roots of that type of tree normally grow outwards.

And the more organic matter you can get back into the soil, within normal limits, the greater will be your yields. If your soil tests as too acid (say, pH 5.5 or below), some agricultural limestone can be added along with the gravel dust (1 part to 3). The dust has a buffering effect as well, so if your test calls for a certain amount of limestone, use only about half as much.

If you're a typical farmer in today's controlled agricultural markets, once you see what gravel dust can do for your yields you might prefer to grow the same amount of food you grow now on half or a third the amount of land, selling off some land and cutting your expenses while making increased profits.

The gravel dust is *instead of* all the chemicals you may now be using, not in addition to. The acid in the chemicals will kill the micro-organisms and other soil life you're trying to rejuvenate. Moreover, the dust is much cheaper than chemicals; any money spent on chemicals will bring greater yields if spent on dust.

In fact, Hamaker once stirred some NPK fertilizer into water, allowed it to settle, and then poured off the solution.

> What was left was ground glacial gravel dust.... If a farmer uses 200 pounds of 15-15-15 NPK fertilizer, he gets about 100 pounds of gravel dust per acre. That costs no more than 75 cents. The fertilizer costs $25 to $30. What the farmer pays for is five paper sacks and some chemicals, neither of which he needs. Sooner or later the chemicals will destroy the land. Some bargain!

Hamaker thinks it is this "filler" in chemical fertilizers that is preventing the complete collapse of high-tech agriculture. (He points out that "eco-agriculture" and organic methods often add some minerals to the soil, but not in sufficient quantities to remineralize it fully.)

As the microorganisms in the soil begin multiplying and doing their thing, the topsoil will become increasingly light and aerated, holding more rainwater and not drying out so quickly in a drought. (There will be more droughts.) When the aerated zone is 18 to 24 inches deep the soil should be capable of holding all the rain that falls. (Unless we don't stop the deteriorating climate.) "It will take a decade or two for roots and earthworms to deepen the topsoil significantly below plow depth."

Gravel dust should also be added to compost, 60 to 80 pounds per ton; it will improve the aeration and help prevent rotting. Dust added to raw manure will absorb valuable ammonia that would otherwise be lost to the air and will also neutralize the smell.

The loosening and fertilizing of topsoil will be assisted by what has come to be called conservation tillage: little or no plowing. Crop residues and stubble are left on the land to return nutrients to the soil and prevent erosion. Crops are sown in shallow furrows (with light tractors), or drilled in without turning the soil. If irrigation is needed, drip irrigation is preferable; it uses less water and energy and doesn't kill the soil with evaporated salts.

A very advanced kind of no-till agriculture that produces two to three record crops a year (even without remineralization) has been developed by a Japanese wizard, Masanobu Fukuoka. It is fully presented in his book, *The One Straw Revolution* (see Appendix: *Access*).

From an article by staff correspondent F. A. Behmyer in the *St. Louis Post-Dispatch*, November 17, 1945:

> Nicholasville, Kentucky ... Albert Carter Savage stands in his mineralized garden where the lamb's quarter is head-high and the hog weeds thrive.... He came to know that the rock in the soil had something to do with the growth of plants.... For twenty

years the man applied himself with consuming fervor to the proving of what he knew to be true. There were countless experiments. . . .

There were dissenters among the state university men at nearby Lexington. . . . They shrugged their scholarly shoulders and asked could any good thing come out of the little town of Nicholasville, as skeptics once asked could any good things come out of Nazareth. . . .

Peas had been planted in January, harvested and followed by tobacco by the end of May, that in turn followed by turnips and kale with cover crops of rye and vetch. . . . That was the mineralized garden in which Albert Carter Savage walked and talked that sunny Saturday morning, speaking softly as one who walked in a temple, touching with something like a caress the "weeds" that alone remained at the end of the season, the clumps of lamb's quarter and the rows of hog weeds, snapping off their tops, nibbling them and offering them to his guest, for they were food when they grew on mineralized ground and there was healing in their leaves. Just as there was nourishment in the tops of the beets, carrots, and turnips. . . .

The man of science spoke of creation's climax when God, having formed man of the dust of the ground, breathed into his nostrils the breath of life. Daringly he said: "Man couldn't be created from the dust of the ground today because the dust doesn't contain the 29 elements recognized as required. . . ."

The banks were piled high with hundreds of tons of mineralized settlings that had been scraped by a bulldozer from the pond bottoms in dry season, enough, he said, to mineralize 10,000 acres.

Belatedly, for the walk had been long, the scientist and the wayfarer came to the house on its hill where the table was spread. Over the food from the mineralized garden and farm the scientist's young son bowed his head and prayed that the Truth might prevail and spread through all the earth.

## NOTES TO CHAPTER TWO

1. The Hamaker material in this chapter comes primarily from his book, *The Survival of Civilization, Selected papers by John D. Hamaker with annotations by Donald A. Weaver* (1982); and from a series of articles Hamaker wrote between 1970 and 1979, many of which were published in the organic farming monthly *Acres USA: A Voice for Eco-Agriculture* beginning in 1974. The book and the articles contain much more detailed information than can be reprinted here. They should be especially valuable to farmers and agricultural scientists because they contain many detailed experiments Hamaker carried out to test his hypotheses. The book also contains more background information and references on all the topics covered here. Reprint information can be obtained from *Acres USA* at Box 9547, Raytown MO 64133, USA. See Appendix: *Access* for information on *The Survival of Civilization*.

2. The Detroit Testing Laboratory can be contacted at 8720 North End Street, Oak Park, MI 48237; (313) 398-2100.

3. Addresses for Alan LePage, Dan Hemenway, Helmut Snoek, Perry and Jean Marie Spiller, and people all over the world who have been doing remineralization experiments and coordinating remineralization efforts can be found in the *Access* section at the end of the book.

4. Helmut Snoek's work was brought to my attention by Joanna Campe, who publishes "Soil Remineralization: A network newsletter." (See Appendix: *Access*.)

5. Of course it is primarily an enormous political problem, as Live Aid's failure to get much food to starving Ethiopians testifies so dramatically. It's primarily a problem of concentrated land ownership, and land reform is the only solution. That's what revolutions are usually about. Land is becoming more concentrated in the United States and other industrialized countries as well, as the farm crisis and large numbers of bankruptcies shows. For detailed evidence on the politics of food, and suggestions about what we need to do to end world hunger, see *Food First: Beyond the Myth of Scarcity,* by Frances Moore Lappé and Joseph Collins (New York: Ballantine). Lappé is the author of *Diet for a Small Planet.*

  Remineralization will undoubtedly decrease world hunger as it brings down the price of food. How much will still remain because of greed and political repression?

6. Von Liebig's remorse about the monster he had helped create, chemical agriculture, was quoted in the 1899 edition of the *Encyclopedia Brittanica*. It was removed from subsequent editions.

7. Much of the information on the harmfulness of chemical agriculture comes from an astonishingly glowing endorsement of organic farming put out very briefly a few years ago by the U.S. Department of Agriculture, "Report and Recommendations on Organic Farming." It was published under Jimmy Carter's Secretary of Agriculture, Bob Berglund, in 1980, shortly before he left office. Similar information can be found in many other books now, including Jim Hightower's *Eat Your Heart Out*.

8. These days most commercial potting soil seems to have been sterilized, presumably to kill unwanted weed seeds. The same process kills the beneficial microorganisms as well, however, and renders the soil lifeless. Plants raised in it will be undernourished, grow slowly, and be more vulnerable to insects and disease.

9. This is also partly attributable to the fact that many inhabitants of America and the other wealthy nations no longer eat significant quantities of fresh fruits and vegetables, which contain the most minerals of any foods. The methods by which vegetables are often sold and prepared in America— canning, freezing, dehydrating, and boiling—destroy up to 90% of the few nutrients that were in the chemically grown plants in the first place. A 90% loss in growing, times a 90% loss in cooking means that only 1% of the potential nutrients are available to the unknowing consumer!

   Now they're also irradiating food, to increase its shelf life. The radiation (they're using otherwise undisposable toxic wastes from nuclear plants) destroys a significant portion of the vitamins and enzymes, making the food less nourishing. This is another factor in the death of our food and hence of us. A recent article in the *San Francisco Chronicle* was humorously headlined "Keeping fruits radiant for weeks." And the powers-that-be don't even want irradiated food to be labeled as such—they know people won't buy it. Hamaker refers to all these things as "embalmed food."

10. To be fairly certain of avoiding deposits of heavy metals that might be toxic to agricultural soils, Hamaker suggests that river and stream beds that are not very close to mountains should be safe, since heavy metals tend to be concentrated in the mountains and will precipitate out in running streams. In stream beds close to mountains the gravel should be tested for heavy metals.

    The companies that are currently selling rock dust for agriculture generally rely on chemical analysis of the soil to determine which elements are missing and then supply the missing elements with a mixture of a two or three kinds of rock. They tend to get dramatically good results and should be encouraged. However, they typically analyze only for a half dozen or so of the 92+ elements, and even though their powdered rock mixtures may contain many more, there is no assurance that the full spectrum of minerals needed for healthy plant (and human) growth is present in anything approaching the right proportions. These companies can be a priceless resource now, since they already have the physical plants to grind much of the gravel dust we need quickly. But they should be gently pressed either to expand their analyses greatly, or more simply, to use a mixture of proven glacial gravel as their rock source.

*Chapter Three*

# THE POLITICAL CLIMATE

*"Breakthroughs never come from within the establishment."*

—CLIMATOLOGIST REID BRYSON,
UNIVERSITY OF WISCONSIN

The idea of a "greenhouse effect"—that large quantities of carbon dioxide discharged into the atmosphere might warm the climate—was first proposed toward the end of the last century, when industrialism was already burning large quantities of fossil fuel, especially coal.

But there has never been any agreed-upon evidence of significant global warming attributable to the greenhouse effect of the last hundred years. There was some warming from 1880 to about 1940, but there is considerable agreement among scientists that the earth's climate then cooled (or at least did not warm any further) until at least the early 1970s. In fact, during the 1970s the cooling became a matter of serious concern among many climatological scientists.

Research in the 1950s and '60s by Cesare Emiliani and then George Kukla provided evidence of the 100,000-year cycle of major ice ages and showed that we are now "close" to the beginning of the next one. Coupled with the 30-year cooling period the earth had been going through, many scientists began to express serious concern.

In 1972 a group of prominent climatologists meeting at Brown University sent letters to the governments of the world, warning that the earth was rapidly cooling and urging immediate action to avoid global disaster.

In 1974 a meeting of scholars in Bonn called by the International Institutes of Advanced Study

> reached a consensus that ... a climatically related disaster was likely within the coming decade.... There is a growing consensus that ... the current food-production systems of man cannot easily adjust.... The direction of the climatic change indicates major crop failures.... This, coinciding with a period of almost non-existent grain reserves, can be ignored only at the risk of great suffering and mass-starvation.
>
> We urge the nations, individually and collectively, to plan and act to establish the technical, social, and political means to meet this challenge to peace and well-being. We feel that the need is great and the time short....

In 1975 a meeting of 84 climatologists from ten countries (chaired by Cesare Emiliani and Nobel Prize winner Willard Libby) agreed that "because the global food supply depends primarily on climate, current understanding of climate must be vastly improved...." They pointed out that ice ages "have been the normal condition during the last several million years, with temperate climates enduring only about 5 percent of the time."

In 1979 a "Conference of Experts on Climate and Mankind" convened by the World Meteorological Organization in Geneva concluded that "there seems to be a consensus that the Earth is at the start of a potential cooling period of perhaps 10,000 to 20,000 years...."

Also during 1979, Genevieve Woillard published her pollen research showing that the transition from temperate to glacial conditions last time took less than 20 years. She suggested that the current state of the earth's forests indicates that we may already have entered that brief transition period.

And that same year, Choudhury and Kukla published research which showed that $CO_2$ can contribute to cooling by absorbing the near-infrared wavelengths that play a large part in melting snow and ice.

# Enter the
# warming theory

From 1940 through the early 1970s humanity's carbon dioxide production was doubling every 10 or 12 years, while the climate was steadily cooling.

Yet in 1957 two scientists at the Scripps Institute of Oceanography, Roger Revelle and H. Seuss, revived the warming theory of carbon dioxide first proposed in the 19th century and put forth the dramatic image, snapped up by the media and widely circulated, that a $CO_2$-induced warming would eventually melt the polar ice caps and flood coastal cities all over the world.

In 1976, after 30-plus years of cooling with the $CO_2$ curve rapidly accelerating every year, members of the National Academy of Sciences, meeting in closed session with government officials in Washington, D.C., issued a report that stated that the warming theory of carbon dioxide represented "the best model available . . . a consensus of prevailing scientific opinion."

In May 1977 the American Geophysical Union held a convention in Washington. One of the meetings was a joint presentation by Wallace Broecker, a geochemist, and William Nordhaus, a member of the President's Council of Economic Advisers, who discussed the energy and climatic implications of the recent decision by the OPEC oil-producing nations to dramatically raise the price of oil and cut off shipments to the West. It was suggested that there might be a shift toward more use of coal, a high carbon fuel that produces greater quantities of $CO_2$ than oil or gas. Nordhaus said that the government believes the climate is warming, and that it was leaning toward the warming theory of $CO_2$—though this was not "official policy."

Irving Kaplan—formerly a Navy scientist and a consultant to the

UN, the Club of Rome, and the Center for the Study of Democratic Institutions—was present at that meeting and says that every scientist he talked to after Nordhaus's speech had gotten the message: warming research would be funded by the government and cooling would not. The warming theory had become the "unofficial policy" of the government. And the government provides more than 90% of the money for climate research in the United States.

Some thought the government's interference in scientific research in many fields was becoming quite pervasive. The following is from *Sanctuary*, the magazine of the Massachusetts Audubon Society (hardly a radical organization), September 1984, quoting Orie Loucks, director of the Holcomb Research Institute at Butler University in Indiana:

> Government and industry are controlling what gets published in scientific journals by "sandbagging" the review process ... it's like the 1950s when McCarthyism was rampant and you didn't dare say certain things. Today we cannot get certain things published. ... In the past, if you had a hypothesis and a reasonable amount of evidence to support it, you could publish it. ... It starts with the big industrial lobbies. ...

The "unofficial" shift in emphasis to climatic warming was noticed as far away as England by H.H. Lamb. In a 1975 letter to Kenneth Watt at the University of California at Davis, Lamb said that even British research had been affected, and he believed the directive had come from Washington. He noted that there was no evidence that could account for such a shift. And he said he believed there were political pressures behind it similar to those which had put off research on acid rain for many years.[1]

## Congressional hearings

In 1981 and 1982 the United States Congress held extensive hearings on "Carbon Dioxide and Climate: The Greenhouse Effect," co-chaired by Representatives James Scheuer of New York and Albert

Gore, Jr., of Tennessee. According to Kaplan, the hearings were called by Gore at the urging of warming theorist Roger Revelle.

The hearings seem to have assumed without question the validity of the warming theory of $CO_2$, focusing only on issues like how fast $CO_2$ is rising, how accurate our projections are, what the consequences would be and what we can do about them. Many prominent scientists and administration officials testified, and not one reminded the committee that the earth's climate had been cooling for most of the past 40 years along with rapidly rising $CO_2$. No one even raised the possibility that $CO_2$ might lead, through various unstudied feedbacks such as increased cloud cover, to increased cooling. (Cloud cover was merely mentioned as one unknown.)

James Hansen, a well-known climatologist working at NASA, was among those who spoke only of warming. However, buried in two sentences toward the end of a paper he also submitted to the committee (Hansen *et al*, 1981) is this alternative scenario:

> ... it is not certain whether $CO_2$ warming will cause the ice sheets to shrink or grow. For example, if the ocean warms but the air above the ice sheets remains below freezing, the effect could be increased snowfall, net ice sheet growth....

Hansen apparently did not think this possibility needed to be taken seriously by the committee. In the article, he and his coauthors asserted that the ice sheets' "natural response time is thousands of years...."

There was some agreement that warming from $CO_2$ might become a serious problem at some point, and the discussion of what we might be able to do about it brought out some interesting economic and political issues. Nobel Prize winning chemist Melvin Calvin, Congressman Schueur and Congressman Carney had the following exchange:

Dr. Calvin:

> We would have to use the carbon dioxide that we produce as fast as we produce it. That means we would have to learn how to collect it in annual crops to keep it from rising ... to use the

forests and the growing plants as a source of our energy, because that cycles the carbon through each year. . . .

## Congressman Schueur:

We have two national movements in terms of energy production. The first is a sort of "stop, look, and listen" with nuclear. There has been a slowdown in nuclear, and a lot of people think we are not going to be building any more nuclear plants.

The second is a massive push toward conversion from oil to coal on the assumption that we have 500 years or so of coal in the ground, and it is here. There is an urgent national security need to free ourselves of energy dependence upon the Persian Gulf oil. . . .

So we have two national pushes. . . . Now, what you are saying is that we probably ought to reverse both of these. . . . You are talking about a change in American energy policy. . . .

## Dr. Calvin:

. . . keep in mind that when you burn coal . . . you have to produce almost twice as much carbon dioxide . . . as you do with oil, and certainly more than twice as much over the use of gas. . . . That is a big difference; that is not a trivial difference. It is a very big difference.

## Congressman Scheuer:

Professor, the Earth has enough coal under there available to last us a long time.

## Dr. Calvin:

That is the trouble. . . . My personal reaction to this is that there are ample ways to make ourselves dependent on renewable re- sources which ultimately, of course, are solar in their origin. . . . [By *solar* he means not only direct solar energy but biomass— trees—as well.]

## Congressman Carney:

You are saying that if we went to nuclear power, we would alleviate some of the problems with the carbon dioxide situation, but you are not particularly supporting nuclear power.

Dr. Calvin:

You would have other problems, much bigger ones. (Laughter) ... Let me point out to you that nuclear power produces only heat. It does not produce liquid fuel. Our country runs on liquid fuel, and you know it.... I don't know who is doing it—but the Congress is cancelling out the liquid fuel option from biomass [that is, methanol] ... and that is what I am fighting for.... That is the only way—renewable....

... you can burn coal and burn it cleanly, take away the carcinogens which it produces ... take out the ash, remove the carbon dioxide, condense it into solid dry ice and drop it in the bottom of the sea. It can be done if you are willing to pay the price ... and I think the price for that is less than the price for nuclear waste disposal on the moon. (Laughter)

When the committee eventually published its findings, in *Carbon Dioxide, the Greenhouse Effect, and Climate: A Primer,* it included this collage of newspaper headlines—all of them emphasizing warming. The tone of almost all the stories represented is most reassuring. The image of the global greenhouse was easily grasped by a

wide public, and willing media spread the scientists' fairly benign predictions of a gradually rising sea level from melting glaciers. Even the image of coastal cities perhaps eventually being engulfed and populations having to relocate to higher ground was not particularly frightening since it was set in a future beyond our lifetimes.

The impression of almost certain warming created by testimony at the congressional hearings is very different from that created by a number of papers in the *Carbon Dioxide Review,* organized by a program managed by the U.S. Department of Energy and published the same year, 1982, by Oxford University Press. Here are some quotes from that collection, edited by William Clark of Oak Ridge National Laboratory:

> ... the vast climatological differences between water in its solid, liquid, and gas phases suggest the possibility of discontinuous changes involving snow/ice albedo feedbacks, the insulating properties of sea ice, and cloud feedback mechanisms. That small changes to the radiation budget might be amplified into large climatic changes through such processes has been evident since the early models of Budyko.... (p. 28)
>
> With increased $CO_2$, moisture-rich warm air would penetrate further into high latitudes, increasing precipitation.... (p. 122)

And a veiled hint that the computer models on which warming projections are usually based may be not only inadequate but misleading:

> Global average warming is unlikely to be the most important consequence of future increases of $CO_2$. It is emphasized primarily because it is the only aspect of $CO_2$-climate change that can be modeled with some degree of confidence.... (p. 104)

# The experts

*(To the tune of O Tannenbaum)*

*Oh Climate Change,*
*Oh Climate Change*
*How can you be so stubborn?*
*You do not do what we expect*
*Our theories all are incorrect*
*Oh Climate Change,*
*Oh Climate Change*
*How can you be so stubborn? (etc.)*

–SUNG AT THE EIGHTH ANNUAL
CLIMATE DIAGNOSTICS WORKSHOP,
ONTARIO, CANADA, OCTOBER 1983

Stephen Schneider, a well-known climatologist and editor of the journal *Climatic Change,* invited John Gribbin, an editor of *New Scientist,* to review *The Survival of Civilization* by John Hamaker and Donald Weaver, "just to show how extreme the $CO_2$ debate can become.... Gribbin does a fine job in putting some perspective on this radical view, asking for 'a little restraint' by people dealing with the $CO_2$ problem so as not to 'sensationalize the issues.'"

From Gribbin's review, published in early 1986:

> Nobody with any competence in the field would look at it twice; the authors show little understanding of the Milankovitch mechanism, make no attempt to explain why the concentration of carbon dioxide in the atmosphere was less during the most recent glaciation, and perpetrate other scientific howlers. But their misguided, though clearly honest, endeavors gain credibility as one more voice among a crowd of conflicting arguments.

Two issues later one response was printed, from Pierre Lehman, an atmospheric physicist at an environmental research center in

Switzerland. Lehman protested:

> I have read the book by John D. Hamaker.... So I was curious to read the review John Gribbin made of it. The review was to me a matter of considerable puzzlement. In effect Hamaker's book is not reviewed but summarily dismissed with the statement, quote: "Nobody with any competence in the field would look at it twice." Now that's a rather harsh statement to make, even if it may be true that the book does not make much sense to the "$CO_2$ community." ... it is an attempt to say that one should look at the climatic problem in a more holistic way than has been done so far.
>
> Indeed, reading the controversy about the $CO_2$ problem one gets the impression that the arguments hurtling back and forth are no more important than the feelings of those who do the hurtling.... Hamaker ... has at least made an attempt to put the climatic issue on a broader basis not very different from the Gaia approach of Jim Lovelock.... Climate, biosphere and tectonic systems form an indissociable whole and condition each other. The biosphere and the atmosphere are interlocked in a permanent exchange of matter (carbon in particular) and energy which makes it impossible for the one not to be influenced by the other. So the soil fertility is a contributor to the climate.... Today forests are in a pitiful shape in many places despite increased $CO_2$ concentration in the atmosphere....
>
> To sum up I would suggest that the "$CO_2$-community" would not become destitute if it would give a fair hearing to so-called outsiders. The statement on Mr. Hamaker's book by Mr. Gribbin shows a surprising lack of scope and, I would say, decency. As it happens some of Hamaker's ideas have proved to be well founded, in particular his insistence that minerals in the soil contribute to soil fertility.... soil fertility is a prime concern....

Only a few months later, Gribbin talked with a reporter about some of the new research findings in climatology. Discussing the surging of the Alaskan glaciers in recent years and relating it to heavy snowfall, he said:

> This fits rather nicely with the new evidence of global warming.... The three warmest years on record are 1980, 1981, and 1983.... The change is, they say, "in the right direction and of the right magnitude" to fit the predicted carbon dioxide greenhouse effect— *and, of course, to explain the recent build-up of ice in both polar regions.* (emphasis added).[2]

This connection is shocking coming from a man who has just trashed

Hamaker's theory that $CO_2$ causes glaciation. The disparity suggests that Gribbin, like most of the other climatologists who have recognized the connection between global warming and the buildup of snow and ice, see the ice buildup only as a kind of side effect of continued overall warming. None so far have explicitly linked all the elements of the process together: $CO_2$ increase, global warming, ice buildup, glaciation, ice ages. One wonders how much the government's unofficial policy of awarding research grants only for studies of warming is responsible.

John Hamaker's theory encompasses many different fields of study—someone has said as many as 25.[3] Yet academia encourages people to specialize, to learn all there is to know about a circumscribed area, perhaps assuming that all this factual knowledge can be pooled to get the bigger picture. It doesn't always work that way.

Perhaps it is not surprising that the geological climatologists who comprise the majority of the "$CO_2$ community" have been skeptical of a theory that purports to include the health of the earth's vegetation in an explanation of the ice ages. (Their equations tend to focus on physical things, like the movements of the sun, temperature, the atmosphere, and the oceans, things that can be modelled on their multimillion dollar computers.) Given Hamaker's position as an outsider who doesn't publish in the right journals (a "catch-22"), his work was almost bound to be dismissed. It would not be easy for the scientific establishment to admit that an outsider might have solved the ice age problem.[4]

# The cover-up

It seems pretty clear that the United States government has successfully perpetrated a massive cover-up, actively suppressing a growing scientific consensus during the 1970s that the earth was cooling and later for the potential cooling effects of $CO_2$, and lending all its weight to the idea that $CO_2$ will inevitably cause the earth's climate to warm.

But why the cover-up? What difference could it make to the people in power in this country, including the industrialists behind the politicians? Wouldn't drastic climatic effects be expected either way, leading to massive social and economic problems? Wouldn't the fact that dirty fuels like coal and oil spew out lots of $CO_2$ lead to serious questions about energy policy under either hypothesis— especially when and if deleterious climatic changes actually began to occur?

The answer emerges when we compare the scenarios projected by the two different theories. The many prestigious scientists who believed that the earth was already rapidly cooling warned that *immediate* large-scale action is necessary to avoid global disaster, including radical shifts in our energy priorities.

The warming theorists debated whether the expected gradual warming was even detectable yet, predicted that significant changes would not be felt for 50 to 100 years, and suggested that at worst some cities would have to be relocated (for which there was obviously plenty of time) and some new crop varieties developed to thrive in a warmer climate.

The government, representing first and foremost the economic interests of big, centralized business—in this case, the gigantic, enormously powerful energy conglomerates of oil, coal, and natural gas—did not need more than a few moments to decide that any theory that $CO_2$ was already having undesirable effects on the climate, if taken seriously by the scientific community and the people of the world, might lead to an immediate clamor for the phasing out of dirty, carbon-spewing fuels in favor of non-$CO_2$-producing sources such as solar, wind, biomass, hydrogen, and geothermal energy. The government has never given much support to such decentralized sources of energy because centralized business and centralized government keep each other going (campaign contributions, favorable laws, and so forth).

Jim Green, on the congressional staff of the House Science and Technology Committee, made it quite explicit recently, speaking on a projected major study of the greenhouse effect by the Department of Energy:

> As far as I can tell, the bottom line for the administration is that this study falls into the category of making sure that the government stays off the back of industry.... There seems to be an effort underway to make sure that any research that might lead in the direction of greater regulation is stopped before it gets to that point.

Government money for $CO_2$ research has primarily been funneled not through the Environmental Protection Agency or even some group like the National Academy of Sciences but through the Department of Energy, which has direct control over the research priorities of most climatological investigations in the United States. The DOE —like most U.S. regulatory agencies headed by people from the industry it's supposed to be regulating—is supposed to regulate energy for the common good, but in fact gives most of its support to the most highly centralized, big business energy sources: nuclear and fossil fuels. This is in direct opposition to the clear preference of the American people, as shown in a recent NBC poll, for conservation and renewable energy sources, especially solar energy.

The "$CO_2$-community" may have been a somewhat willing victim of this conspiracy. Not only does science follow the research money, but research on a very long-range problem (50+ years under the warming scenario) is always more secure than studies of a crisis situation. And government-subsidized scientists are not usually known for sticking their necks out.

A few years ago some 33 different academic and research institutions, working on 51 different $CO_2$-related research projects, were getting money from the Department of Energy. John S. Perry, staff director of the Board on Atmospheric Sciences and Climate of the National Academy of Sciences, puts it humorously but bluntly (1984): "The Niagara of writings on carbon dioxide ... suggests that the gas is becoming an essential nutrient not only for green plants but for a large segment of the scientific community as well."

President Eisenhower reminded us of what often happens when research money is handed out by the government. In his farewell address to the nation, right after warning us against "the acquisition of unwarranted influence" by what he called "the military-industrial complex," he talked about government-sponsored scientific research:

> ... a government contract becomes virtually a substitute for intellectual curiosity. ... The prospect of domination of the nation's scholars by federal employment, project allocations, and the power of money is ever present—and is gravely to be regarded.

Some $CO_2$ research money even comes directly from the fossil fuel companies themselves. The Scripps Institute of Oceanography (connected to big money through the Scripps-Howard newspaper chain) has been in the forefront of the warming theory since Revelle made his proclamation back in 1957. (Svante Arrhenius, who coined the term *greenhouse effect,* also ended up at Scripps.) The list of financial contributors to Scripps includes AMOCO, ARCO, British Petroleum, Chevron, Conoco, EXXON, Japan Petroleum, Martin Marietta Energy Systems, Mobil Foundation, Pacific Gas and Electric Company, Phillips Petroleum, San Diego Gas and Electric Company, SOHIO, Texaco, and Union Oil Company.

The rationale is that oceanographic and geological research centers develop information useful in finding oil. But are they really going to pursue a line of inquiry so devastating to their benefactors? Other prominent $CO_2$ research institutions also get money from the fossil fuel companies. These funds are only a small part of the total budget of these institutions, but together with DOE money it may exert considerable pressure on what gets studied and what gets reported.

# The stakes

The stakes for big money are enormous. There is a huge investment in oil and natural gas facilities, and known reserves expected to last some decades more—plus, as Congressman Scheuer put it, "500 years of coal in the ground." A substantial part of the world's known coal reserves are in the U.S. All of these fossil fuels represent vast economic and political power, which is wielded by the U.S. and a few other nations.

Since the oil crunch, the World Bank—the international representative of big business interests—has been encouraging Third World countries to import coal rather than develop solar energy, as their best protection against dependence on OPEC oil. It's not hard to understand why. Exxon recently collaborated with the Colombian government to open one of the biggest coal strip mines in the world.

Other major industrial sources of greenhouse gases— garbage dumped cheaply in open landfills, raw sewage, unrecycled animal manures from giant centralized feedlots, chemical fertilizers (also made from oil), industrial refrigerants, and so on—are all an integral part of today's highly centralized, oil-based, capital-intensive industrial system.

To reduce them substantially we would have to begin returning to an organic agriculture (which employs more people), stop eating so much meat (which will help us feel better and live longer, not to mention the animals we eat), recycle animal and human wastes and garbage (which will enrich the soil and thus provide us better food and faster-growing trees), and grow and process food locally to minimize the need for refrigeration (which will revitalize our local economies)—all things many of us would like to see for a lot of reasons, but which would reduce the enormous profits of the people who essentially own this country, and most of the world.

# *Nuclear power tries to get its radioactive foot in the door again*

Nuclear power figured prominently at the hearings. The $CO_2$ debate provides an opportunity for the dying nuclear power industry to try to get its foot back in the door, since whatever terrible things you can say about nuclear reactors, they don't produce $CO_2$ (except while they're being built). Perhaps the nuclear industry was a prime mover in the behind-the-scenes maneuvering that led to the government's "nonofficial" support of the warming theory. The nuclear industry moguls might have even more to gain than the fossil fuel czars. And they would have supported the $CO_2$-warming idea rather than cooling because it seems more plausible at first glance, and more obviously the result of fossil fuels, their closest competitor. A Swiss nuclear power plant builder told a climatology professor from a major American university that his country was giving financial support to research on $CO_2$, because as soon as they could show that warming was going to be a serious problem it would clear the way for Swiss nuclear plants.

If the nuclear power industry had been bigger and more powerful than the oil, coal, and gas industries, there is no doubt that $CO_2$ research would be a government priority even now. But since fossil fuels have more political clout than nuclear, the Reagan administration has attempted to drive even the warming theorists out of sight. Congress is keeping $CO_2$ research alive, but the Department of Energy has managed to reduce the program to what one observer has described as a "severely neutered" remnant of its former self. (The *Global 2000 Report to the President,* commissioned by Jimmy Carter before he left office, warned of catastrophe from many things that Hamaker also talks about—loss of forests, desertification, loss and deterioration of the earth's topsoil, and increasing $CO_2$ in the atmosphere. One of the first things the Reagan administration did was to fire its authors.)

The long-range, gradual scenario provided by the warming theorists also gave the political-industrial complex the opportunity to give the press and public great hope that new, scientifically discovered high-tech solutions to these future problems would be forthcoming. Thus congressional hearings were told that new techniques of genetic engineering might be able to produce crop plants that would thrive in a warmer climate (with enough funding). This supposed link to future climate problems provided another rationalization for high-tech industries which many scientists and members of the public have questioned the safety of and need for.

It seems that the government's support of the warming theory backfired a little, however. The widespread press coverage of the "greenhouse effect" and the graphic image of sea level eventually rising and engulfing our cities, however far off, was just horror-filmish enough to get people's attention. The warming theory, mild as it is, gave people another reason to oppose our continued reliance on energy sources that pollute the air, keep us dependent on other countries, and threaten to involve us in the volatile Middle East.

Not enough people so far. But there have recently been signs that some people are beginning to become aware, perhaps subconsciously, that something quite different may be happening. The dripping letters are from a recent ad by the New York Museum

## "1986 Yearbook"
# SENIOR PICTURES

**LAST CHANCE !**

of Natural History, publicizing an exhibition. The cartoon is from a recent issue of the *Daily Californian,* the student newspaper at the University of California at Berkeley.

So we find ourselves in a horrible situation, facing the possibility that we are in the last five or so years of our warm interglacial period and about to enter the next ice age, with nowhere to turn. Our own government is not likely to help us—at least not until it is too late—because apparently it is working for someone else.

Pulitzer Prize journalist Ben Bagdikian puts it this way:

> ... it is more difficult than ever for society to hear minority voices in the majority thunder. And the last quarter of the twentieth century confronts potential errors of such catastrophic magnitude that a misled civilization conceivably will not have the luxury of looking back.

## NOTES TO CHAPTER THREE

1. In the 15 years from 1971 to 1986, some 3000 studies on acid rain were published (from *Harper's* Index), but very few major steps were taken actually to do something about the problem. (Requiring catalytic converters on cars was a rare exception.) It is clear that after a point, more research is commissioned *in order to postpone taking action*.

2. The Gribbin interview was published in *The Guardian,* October 15, 1986. Only a few years before, Gribbin (1982) published a book that explicitly recognized the serious limitations of current scientific approaches to the greenhouse question. Speaking of the general circulation models (GCMs), he wrote:

   > Perhaps most serious of all, no GCM yet developed deals adequately with the oceans. Sea surface temperatures are set in the models, but usally do not change in feedback with other parameters. This is a very crude approximation to reality for a planet whose surface is 70 percent covered by water.

3. Some of the academic fields included to some degree in Hamaker's grand theory are paleontology, palynology, climatology, volcanology, glaciology, geology, geography, seismology, meteorology, forestry, biology, botany, paleobotany, physics, plant and human physiology, soil science, microbiology, and engineering. Specialists in each field seldom stray far from its usual relatively narrow boundaries.

4. Over the past two years I have asked dozens of climatologists to review a scientific paper I wrote on this material and to give me their comments and criticisms. Many of them did. It is interesting, however, that almost none of those who are committed to the Milankovitch theory (that the ice ages are caused by minute variations in the earth's orbit) were willing even to respond, including some of the most prominent men in the field: Shackleton, Pisias, Imbrie, Broecker, Emiliani, Jones, Wigley, Pittock, Ruddiman, Kaminsky, and Lazarus.

   Kukla responded by saying simply that the theory I am presenting is wrong, with no explanation. McIntyre said he had not received anything and never reviews books. Henry Diaz felt the theory was "an amalgam of various facts, wild speculation, unwarranted pessimism." John Gribbin replied, "I respect your right to write on anything, but the enclosed is about as accurate as I would expect a book by myself on clinical psychology to be." (This was a few months after his published explanation of ice buildup as an "obvious" consequence of global warming, cited above.)

   Hermann Flohn: "I am virtually unable to follow such dangerous—and indeed ridiculous—doomsday prophecies.... which could seduce simple-minded persons and lead them into unfounded hysteria.... [Mr. Hamaker's] speculations are utterly primitive...." Jim Kasting: "I am familiar with John Hamaker's ideas and I must inform you that I regard most of them as silly." J. Murray Mitchell: "What motivates supposedly educated people like yourself to climb on such absurd bandwagons?"

There were a few exceptions, some of them noted on the cover. Sir H. H. Lamb, dean of climatologists, now semiretired from the University of East Anglia in England, wrote:

> I share the skepticism that you and others express about the many overconfident and overpublicized forecasts of $CO_2$ warming. And I fear that the sciences of meteorology and climatology may be brought into grave embarrassment as a result. The tremendous outpouring of scientific papers since about the mid-1970s surely betokens the spending of really big sums of money by vested interests, selectively putting money into just those research teams which are judged likely to produce the desired results. This threatens to distort the general perception of our present climatic situation....

George Woodwell wrote, in response to my request for a possible quote for the book: "While I wish to encourage you in your bold venture, I do not wish to be quoted as you propose."

One of the Milankovitch theorists who didn't respond, Wallace Broecker, recently published this impassioned warning (*Nature*, July 9, 1987, p. 123ff):

> If, as the climatic record in ice and sediment suggests, changes in climate come in leaps rather than gradually, then the greenhouse buildup may threaten our food supply. To date, we have dealt with this problem as if its effects would come in the distant future and so gradually that we could easily cope with them. This is certainly a possibility, but I believe that there is an equal possibility that they will arrive suddenly and dramatically.

The main point of his article, paradoxically, was a call for long-term research funding, instead of "legislatively imposed five-year reports...."

Stephen Schneider, editor of the journal *Climatic Change*, responded with lengthy and considered comments, including these remarks:

> First of all, I applaud all your hard work, literature searching, and dedication and agree in principle that "soil remineralization," halt to deforestation, reduction of inefficient fossil (and other) fuel uses and rapid development of renewable energy supplies make good sense *regardless* of whether the greenhouse process effects prove true or not (what I described as the "tie-in" strategy in *The Coevolution of Climate and Life*). However, I was in far less agreement with your long chain of connected assumptions that start with more $CO_2$ and end up with rapid shifts to the next ice age. You put too much faith in the precise

dating of sediment cores ..., make too much of short-term, regional trends in winter temperatures, and don't present any evidence of glacier growth (mountain or otherwise) over the past few decades. ...

In summary, I agree that the ice age/interglacial story is not a solved problem, despite some overly enthusiastic Milankovitch supporters, but neither do I find much credence in the Simpson theory, e.g., can it survive the obvious criticism that the seasons work? I'm sure the Institute for a Future has a future, so please keep up your iconoclastic role; it is good for the field. ...

My reply included the following:

I was surprised to find you discounting the sediment core data that you had only recently referred to as the best evidence we have of climatic change. In any case, I was not putting any particular faith in it, I was just showing that the theory being presented could explain the available data if asked to. Now I come across a series of articles on the Vostok ice core ... which seem to validate the deep-sea core data independently, finding a very similar curve of both temperature and $CO_2$—and moreover a $CO_2$ record with less assumptions needed between evidence and projections than the deep-sea record.

I feel you are unfair to characterize the half century of data from most U.S. regions, and the century of data from central England, as "short-term trends" in winter temperatures. Since we don't have much going back beyond such time frames, perhaps you are asking the impossible here. ...

A very recent article by Bradley, Diaz, Eischeid, Jones, Kelly, and Goodess ... provides additional confirmation of the theory I presented, and I will include it in my paper.

As I noted, you wrote that "about a 10% sustained change in cloud cover ... could bring on ... an ice age." You note in your remarks on the paper that the key is sustained. What is the marked increase in precipitation over the last 30 to 40 years, noted by Bradley et al., if not a sustained increase in cloud cover? They don't provide precise figures on increase in the precipitation index, but inspection of their graphs suggests that it has been at least 10% since about 1950, in the mid- and higher-latitudes, autumn through spring.

You suggest that other explanations for the succession of tree life through the interglacial are at least as plausible—but neglect to say what explanations. I presume you are referring to a cooling climate. But both Andersen and Woillard stated that the retrogressive succession of tree life is independent of climatic changes, especially the rapid dieback toward the last few years of the interglacial. Do you have something else in mind?

Another recent article which seems to lend additional credence to the Hamaker theory I have presented is that of Roeckner et al. ... This seems to be a very strong confirmation/support of the theory I have tried to present, don't you think? ...

Finally, I feel your concluding statement, describing all this as "a long chain of uncertain bits of evidence," is quite unfair. Most of the connections that make up the theory seem to be quite well sustained by scientific evidence....

I must remind you that ... our very survival may be at stake now. The Sahel drought has been very severe, with much loss of life. The drought in the southeastern states of the United States was also very severe last year. Parts of Canada and the USSR have lost their ability to grow food. United States farmers were not sure their crops were going to sprout this year, [1987] because of widespread drought. There is a great deal at stake in our theories. I trust that the fate of the earth, and of the people you love, is more important to you than whether you are right, what your status is in the profession, and how large your next research grant or institutional budget will be.

Schneider is head of Interdisciplinary Climate Systems at the National Center for Atmospheric Research in Boulder, which has a budget of $30 million to $40 million a year.

*Chapter Four*

# STOPPING THE COMING ICE AGE

*"Blackbird singing in the dead of night,
Take these broken wings and
learn to fly;
All your life—you were only waiting
for this moment to arise."*

—JOHN LENNON AND PAUL MCCARTNEY

The big chill is almost upon us, and our lives are about to change—maybe shorten, but in any case become much more real. More physical. More emotional. We have been asleep too long.

We can deny it, repress it, pretend we don't feel what is happening. But that will take even more energy than opening to it, welcoming it even, as the salvation we have longed for. We didn't think it would take this form. We expected a messiah, the voice of God, angels. What we get is reality, nothing more. One of the first laws of physics, which we have tried to avoid for so long: for every action there is an equal and opposite reaction.

And we get ourselves, as we are, to work with.

> *"Everybody talks about the weather but*
> *nobody does anything about it."*
>
> —Folk Saying

What do we have to do, and when do we have to do it?

The end of the warm interglacial period is being accelerated greatly by our own activities—our clearcutting of the forests, our burning of ancient fossil fuels, our release of greenhouse gases from our agriculture and our industry. If it were not for us, the next ice age might be centuries away.

If we were instantly to stop all our fossil fuel burning, our tree cutting, our industry, the ice age threat might subside immediately, and we could take our sweet time remineralizing the earth (in other words, leave it for somebody else to do). But we're probably not going to stop all those things next week, unfortunately.

What we can and must do is this:

- Stop the wholesale slaughter of trees very soon, within a matter of months; clearcutting must be absolutely stopped as soon as possible.

- Remineralize enough of the earth's forests quickly enough that their renewed vigor—within one to two years—will begin to consume the $CO_2$ from any temporarily continuing fossil fuel burning.

- At the same time, immediately begin phasing out fossil fuels as much as possible; temporarily scale back our industrial activities to the minimum necessary for our *subsistence*, and institute and accept the strictest possible rationing of fossil fuels; and where some continued fossil fuel burning is *absolutely unavoidable, immediately* phase out coal and oil in favor of natural gas.

- Temporarily reducing our industrial activites will also help reduce the emission of other greenhouse gases; we need strict controls on them, too, while we develop environmentally safe substitutes.

- Quickly return to an organic agriculture on remineralized soil. This will not only give us more delicious, more nutritious food, it will reduce emissions of carbon dioxide at several stages, and nitrous oxide, as well as developing much healthier and more abundant crop plants which will further bring down $CO_2$.

- Quickly begin planting billions of new fast-growing trees all over the world. When these trees grow enough to begin to be harvested in three to four years, we can convert their wood to methane and alcohol as an alternative to fossil fuels, and begin phasing back in more of our industrial activities—which can increase to "normal" levels if we still want them to as more wood-based fuel becomes available. Or we may have found by that time that there is a better way to live.

We are in a race against time, against the spreading death of the world's forests, which may soon reach a point of no return. And against volcanic eruptions that pour great quantities of $CO_2$ into the atmosphere, together with sulfuric and other acids, which further kill the earth's vegetation. The increase in volcanism is caused by an increasing build-up of snow and ice over the polar regions, which presses down through the earth's thin crust on the molten fluids underneath it.

At some point the feedback system of volcanism to $CO_2$ to differential greenhouse to ice to volcanism will become self-per-petuating—requiring no further inputs of $CO_2$ from dying vegetation or human activity to continue for tens of thousands of years. At that point nothing we could do would make any difference, and the earth would be committed irrevocably to another ice age lasting some 90,000 years.

We do not know exactly when these points will be reached. But think of all the volcanoes that have erupted in just the last few years—Mount St. Helens, El Chichon, Mount Etna, Mount Luzon, Kilauea, Mount Mihara, etc. Think how many forests are dying, from acid rain, from cold winters and hot, dry summers, from blights. The point of no return may be here *very soon*—before we know it.

# Stopping the clearcutting

*"The forest is a peculiar organism of
unlimited kindness and benevolence
... It affords protection to all beings,
offering shade even to the axeman
who destroys it."*

—GAUTAMA BUDDHA

How many hamburgers is your life worth? They may be cutting down much of the Central American rainforest for you.

Even if we don't eat greasy hamburgers, or meat of any kind, we can get our governments to make it illegal to import beef, to pass a law with teeth in it. We can picket fast-food restaurants, boycott them and their corporate owners, and find other creative ways to get the facts to people. (Some fast-food restaurants deny they still use Central American beef, but how can we trust them? Ninety percent of Central American beef is eaten in the United States. Half the clearcutting of Central American rainforests is for cattle ranching for export. Burger King, owned by Pillsbury, has admitted they've been using Central American beef;[1] so does Campbell's, which makes canned soups and Swanson's TV dinners; so does Big Boy restaurants, owned by Marriott. And all this is probably just the tip of the iceberg.) You can also boycott tropical hardwoods, such as mahogany and teak. But we have to stop cutting every kind of lumber now, for the next few years.

The rainforest countries of the world have to take responsibility themselves to stop the madness, and the rest of us have to help them. Somehow we have to convince them that "development" is not the panacea they've been led to believe—perhaps by letting them see what we in the "developed" countries have done to our environment, and the kinds of pressured, tense, monotonous lives technology often leads to, glamorous television commercials notwithstanding.

The rainforest countries have another, undeniable self-interest in maintaining their forests: as they cut them down, rainfall decreases, bringing heat and drought and destroying agriculture in the whole region. This is an educational job that urgently needs to be done.

Apolonildo Brito is a former Amazon frontier pilot who has become very angry at the destruction of his country's land and people,[2] and is doing something about it. He has started a magazine, *Enfoque* (Focus), which is written for the people of the region rather than for specialists or government leaders. Brito used to be a government adviser himself: "Then I understood that the top politicians are compromised with big business. They get finances for their pockets and their political campaigns."

*Former rainforest land that has been denuded for cattle grazing.*

He describes how the massive destruction of the rainforest often occurs:

> Businesses or wealthy individuals buy up vast tracts of land for speculation, preferably in areas marked for development projects. Because the law requires that at least one-third of the property be put to use, the owners set fire to the forest and declare it cattle land.

Brito does not think it's hopeless. "I think we can make a difference. Many students and some mayors are getting interested. The Governor of Amapá has ordered a thousand copies."

One partial solution that has been proposed is for the 17 nations that contain 90% of the world's tropical rainforest to form an organization like OPEC for timber—the Organization of Timber Exporting Countries, OTEC. By unionizing, so to speak, they could raise the price of timber 50% and earn the same income with only half the tree-cutting. *Controlled* cutting of timber would then be more profitable than the other uses to which clearcut rainforest lands are put when the trees have been destroyed.

With an adequate economic incentive to protect the forests, less persuasion would be needed. Money might even be found for reforestation. A similar organization is needed for minerals, which big money lusts after even more than wood. Oil exploration has also destroyed large tracts of the rainforest.

When the Australian government decided to log the Nightcap rainforest, many Australians got angry—and got organized. People nonviolently blockaded the bulldozers with their bodies and climbed into the trees and stayed there. They held hands and sang songs. Some buried themselves up to their necks with concrete blocks attached to their feet. It worked. The government changed its mind and decided that the rainforest was precious and must be protected.

*Rainforest demonstration at Citicorp Bank, San Francisco, 1986.*

In Colombia, Margarita de Botero turned her country's own environmental protection office into a militant, highly effective organization. As its director, she organized most of Colombia's municipalities into green councils, with decision-making power. She provided them with tools, seeds, and information on how to set up greenhouses. Entire hillsides that had been stripped bare began to show the bright green of newly sprouted seedlings. Small dams were built and rivers shored up. Lawyers taught council members environmental law and how to enforce it. A landowner who had cut off a nearby town from access to water stood trial and went to jail. Botero led a struggle that eventually stopped a $200 million hydroelectric project, including a proposed dam that would have flooded thousands of acres of forests.

*"Say you're a feisty little band of freedom fighters bravely attacking the Marxist strongmen who have taken over your nation and forced the peasants to plant and harvest their own crops.... And say you're running a little low on cash. No problem! Bring your provisional leader and your wish list down to me, Honest John Poindexter, here at House O'Bucks ...*

*And terms? We've got 'em! You
pay nothing down until your army
takes over the country. Then, all you
have to do is let us put American
missiles anywhere we want and allow
our multinational corporations to
deplete your natural resources . . .*

—COLUMNIST JON CARROLL

We have to get back control of our rich, powerful governments
which, through organizations like the World Bank and the International Monetary Fund, have been pushing the less "developed" nations to industrialize as fast as possible—for the benefit of the
rich nations.[3] (*Development* is such a loaded word; how can you argue
with "progress"? What if we called it enslavement to the clock, or
indoorism, or entertainment-addiction? Ivan Illich points out that if
we counted up all the time we really spend on our cars—not just
driving them but the time we spend working to pay for them and for
insurance premiums, gas, service, parking, and tickets—and divided
all that time by the distance we drive, it would average out to about
5 miles an hour, about as fast as we could walk. One of the main
reasons we don't just walk is because driving and fancy cars have
more "status," and because our work is now usually far from our
houses—which is what a lot of "development" seems to be all about.)

The reason so many "Third World" countries are defaulting on
the loans they took for development is that they really didn't need
them and couldn't afford them. But now they've got these huge debts
and interest payments, so they're under constant pressure from
these same banks to continue destroying their environment so they
can earn enough money in foreign trade to pay off the banks.

Conservation International, a nonprofit organization in Portland,
Oregon, has been very concerned about the destruction of the
tropical forests. Peter Seligmann, executive director of CI, said that
many countries are using up and destroying their natural resources,
and thus their economic potential, trying to pay off their debts. With
a $100,000 donation from the Frank Weeden Foundation, CI offered

to pay off part of Bolivia's debt if the banks would reduce it substantially and Bolivia would in turn protect a large portion of its Amazon forest lands. The banks gave Bolivia a $650,000 reduction in its $4 billion external debt for CI's $100,000 cash contribution (an 85% discount), in exchange for which Bolivia set aside almost 4 million acres of forest and grassland where economic development will be severely limited and the habitat of traditional Indians and native plants and animals protected.

This kind of project can be a model for others on a much larger scale. The banks are worried that their debts will be written off eventually, and are apparently ready to make serious deals to get *something* back on their money. The CI's $100,000 protected 4 million acres, which is 6,250 square miles. Something like 4,800 square miles of rainforest are being destroyed every month. So protecting all of that rainforest, at something like the same rate, would cost only about $77,000 a month, less than a million dollars a year! Even if it cost twice that, or more, the governments of the world's industrialized nations wouldn't even have to think twice about amounts like that. They probably misplace that much every year.

It's only a question of motivation. Can they put their greed for cheap raw materials aside for a while and recognize the fact that we are now at the top of the endangered species list ourselves?

But we haven't got time to wait for governments now. We can probably save most of the rainforests ourselves! At the present rate of destruction, the world's rainforests will be almost completely gone in about 30 years. If it costs a million dollars a year to make enough deals to protect the world's rainforests, perhaps most of the remaining rainforests could be saved for about $30 million—an enormous sum of money, until you remember that the Live Aid and Band-Aid concerts have already shown that we can raise that kind of money in one weekend! (Live Aid raised $82 million.)

Similar amounts of money might remineralize a million acres of forest, or get millions of tree seedlings planted. We can't do the whole trillion dollar job ourselves, but we might be able to buy enough time to get the world's so-called leaders off their asses—or replace them.

Wouldn't it be great if music saved the world?

Forests in the Third World are also being destroyed by poor peasants, but at a much slower rate, and much less cause for *immediate* alarm. Slash-and-burn agriculture is often practiced by native peoples, usually out of desperation because every piece of more reasonable land has been taken away from them. As we have seen, the cure for slash-and-burn, as for rainforest-hamburgers and so many other outrages, may be nothing less than revolution. (In Guatemala and El Salvador, for example, 2% of the population controls more than 80% of the farmland. The situation was similar in Nicaragua before its revolution.)

Many trees in the less "developed" countries must continue to be cut and burned for firewood. Here the main pressure is increasing population, though it is not increasing as fast as it was a few years ago thanks to birth control and economic reforms. Population has decreased wherever birth control methods and education have been made available. (Reagan withdrew U.S. support for global population control efforts.) And people tend to have more kids the poorer they are, hoping for some security in their old age. Giving them more of a stake in things takes the pressure off. Here again, more equitable distribution of wealth by available means would seem to be a big part of the solution.

The overdeveloped countries are also destroying their own forests. From a recent *New York Times* article (November 1986):

> The Agriculture Department today unveiled a proposal to nearly double the timber harvest from the national forests by the year 2030. Department officials said the increased timber production would be necessary because of population growth ... the plan ... also provides for increased mining and grazing in the national forests....
>
> R. Max Peterson, chief of the Forest Service, an arm of the department, criticized conservationists who wanted to reserve more forest land as wilderness ... Mr. Peterson said assertions by conservation groups that the spreading road network and timber harvest would devastate the national forests were "nonsense." "There are already 32 million acres of wilderness" desig-

nated in the national forests "and now they want more. . . ."

Peter Kirby, national forest expert for the Wilderness Society, a conservation group, said . . . the road construction proposed for the forests, "enough to get to the moon and back," would lead to "the destruction of millions of acres of wilderness."[4]

Big money has no more compunctions about destroying its own nest than it does others'. A buck's a buck. Unfortunately, big government usually seems to listen to big money—money talks. (Or as Dylan says, "money doesn't talk it screams." Maybe we'll have to do some screaming of our own.) Brock Evans, vice president of the National Audubon Society, said the Bureau of Land Management plans to cut down all but 2% of the old growth forests in America, despite its irreplaceable beauty and the recent discovery that it is an indispensable habitat for many forms of animal and plant life. "Trees like this exist nowhere else in the world but they keep selling it for logging. . . ." Maybe a lot of people can't stand the deep quiet in such woods, after so much radio and television, so much programming of all kinds.

We highly developed folks could also begin saving much of our forests simply by cutting the trees we take in a saner way. Ray Raphael, who grows some timber himself, has written a wonderful book about forestry called *Tree Talk* (1981) which has much to offer us in this global crisis. It looks at the way American forestry is destroying the landscape, and examines the alternatives.

Clearcutting, for example, causes soil erosion and flooding. It is often accompanied by burning to remove brush and stumps, which releases more nutrients into the air (not to mention $CO_2$ and other gases) and destroys the soil microorganisms that keep the soil fertile. (The U.S. Forest Service recently set fire to 500 acres of dense brush to see if the smoke from a nuclear war would screen out the sun and bring on a "nuclear winter." Asked how setting a fire would test such a global theory, the scientist in charge said "It's impossible to say . . . it's a piece of the puzzle.")

The types of brush that naturally develop after a fire often have the ability to fix nitrogen and refertilize the soil—yet they are typically considered "weeds" by logging companies and killed off with poisonous herbicides, which further starves and pollutes the land.

Clearcutting is done by people interested only in short-term profit. Since it takes 35 to 50 years for a new stand of trees to grow to timber size, it's beyond not only the attention span but also the life span of most of the people making the decisions. Forest sections are cleared of all their trees and planted uniformly with a single species because it's simple and easily comprehensible; you can program it into a computer and forget about it. No matter that single species forestry, like monocrop agriculture, is much more susceptible to devastation by insects and disease, leading to massive spraying of poison, more resistant insects, and on and on.

The dying of America's forests is being accelerated by such practices, which are fostered by the Forest Service in their zeal for "revenue." Their destruction of the land may not even be profitable. The Forest Service claims their lumber operations made $232 million in 1985, but the General Accounting Office, by including such additional costs as fire protection, pest management, and administrative expenses, says that the Forest Service *lost $621 million* in 1985 on timber and mineral operations, mostly timber.

And more than likely the people who make all these decisions are many miles away in some office or other, and have little identification with or feeling for the land. Like many professionals in America who work for large companies, they are usuallly transferred from one place to another every few years and have little sense of place and rootedness. The people who do the actual cutting and hauling under the present system also move from one job to another, to keep up with the specialized work.

Rudolf Becking, professor of forestry at Humboldt State University in Northern California, reminds us that there is another way. From *Tree Talk:*

> I received my training in ... Switzerland ... the Couvet forest. I became intrigued with the philosophy they had there. Their basic theory is that the forest is a community of trees. ... Experienced farmers were elected by their community to designate which trees would be cut this year and which would be cut next year, and so on. These farmers had no university training but they were in tune with the environment. ...

They carefully measured the rate of growth and the changes in the forest over time.... In all-age management you thin young stands out, harvest a few big trees, and create a space for the young stands to grow. You work in all size classes.... The advantage of this is that you can more readily balance your books. You get a repeated income ... not just one lump sum at the end.

The forester is involved in all stages of succession at the same time, as are the worker, the tractor driver, and the logger.... There is no pecking order. There is no status symbol for who takes out the biggest logs.... Some of these people always work the same tract. When a forester gets to a certain tract, he hires a certain guy to cut it, because that guy has been doing it since he was a small boy. A tradition has developed.... you have a commitment to a specific piece of land. And specific trees. They say, "Don't touch this tree because I know the old guy who planted this tree." ... It's quite a feeling. These guys are very careful. When they log, they know exactly what they're doing.

The forester has not only to mark the timber ... he marks which direction it has to go.... In Europe, you *compute* the force ... the force for a tree of this volume when it hits the ground. That way you get an idea of how much breakage you will get. I tried to introduce tree falling into the curriculum here, but I got into all kinds of trouble because of liability....

Certain trees that are too big-crowned are earmarked, and then the faller will have to climb the tree. He will saw off the branches and actually lower the branches by rope, so they don't do any damage. He doesn't let them fall lest they break some regeneration. Then once the branches are off, he will drop the tree like a pencil into the stand.

... the equipment is confined to the roads. The main tractor is not allowed to go into the stand per se. It can only travel the skid trail.... The tractor travels the skid road backward, so it doesn't have to turn around and create a tremendous circle.... Also, in Switzerland they do it over snow, so there's no damage to the soil. They wait until the snow hardens a foot or more and then they skid over the snow on sleds....

A tradition develops of working on the same land for generation after generation. There is more interest in keeping the land productive.[5]

The woods are cut for our needs—lumber, paper, firewood. Besides doing everything we can to stop obscene timber and agricultural practices and to regenerate the earth's forests, how much wood and paper can we do without for a few years?

Can you put off building a new home, room, fence, deck or hot tub for three or four years? Can you share magazines and books, buy the newspaper at most once a week, and use the library more instead of buying so much stuff to read during the next few years, until a vast new crop of trees starts maturing? Maybe if we stop reading and watching TV so much and get outside we'll *see* this beautiful world and find a way to save it. (You won't miss much on television or in the papers, I promise. I'm telling myself that too, of course.) We may also find out that we live in the real world—the one where food comes out of the ground—and not the one we see on television.

Can we buy recycled paper to write on, and recycle bags and boxes? Can we do without many of the "convenient" paper products we've grown so accustomed to—the paper plates and napkins, the bags for every single thing we buy (instead of our own shopping bag, large purse, or backpack), and all the food in throwaway packages instead of bulk? Starving will not be very convenient.

Can we wear warm clothes in the house so we can keep the (fossil fuel) heat turned down or off and not build those millions of (wood) fires for awhile?

John Hamaker once wrote an article called "Life or Death— Yours." Can you stay conscious, and remember that every choice we make now has enormous implications?

## *Remineralizing the forests of the earth*

> *"You ever notice how trees do everything we do to get attention? 'cept walk."*
>
> —ALICE WALKER, *THE COLOR PURPLE*

*"The more I am acquainted with agricultural affairs, the better I am pleased with them ... I can no where find so great satisfaction as in those innocent and useful pursuits ... I am led to reflect how much more delightful in an undebauched mind, is the task of making improvements on the earth, than all the vainglory which can be acquired from ravaging it."*

—GEORGE WASHINGTON

We've got a big job. John Hamaker calls it the greatest human effort ever undertaken. It's certainly right up there with wars and nuclear arms races in the amount of money, effort, and organization that would be involved.

We have to begin by spreading 3 tons of finely ground gravel dust on almost every acre of some 9 million square miles of forests and jungles: 5.7 billion acres, 17 billion tons of dust. Rock around the clock. (In areas where the soil is already very acid, one part limestone should be added to every three parts dust.) And more dust on millions of square miles where forests *could* grow, and then plant them. Wetlands—marshes, bayous, and swamps—should also be remineralized.[6]

The first pass will stop most of the dying. Then we have to go back and do it again and again, to the limit of our vision and will, until we have spread enough gravel dust to completely rejuvenate the world's vegetation, and it brings down the excess $CO_2$ in the atmosphere. Helmut Snoek, the Bavarian scientist who has experimented with remineralization for almost 30 years, says, "In all cases where we have applied rock dust on areas of damaged forest ... forest-death was over—it didn't exist anymore!" He cites the more than 50 years of research at the University of Zurich.[7]

Thousands of grinders will have to be built, to minimize the expenses and fossil fuel demands of unnecessary transportation of rocks and dust. But we have to stop all construction for perhaps a year so we can use cement plant grinders exclusively for producing finely ground gravel dust, until enough new rock grinders can be built. We can also use natural deposits of glacial silt (loess). There's an enormous one in Utah, and Hamaker says local well-drillers all over the world will know where there are others. (Before using an untried silt deposit, its fertility as a soil additive should be tested with fast-growing radish seeds in small pots.)

To rejuvenate the forests quickly, we also need to build up the organic matter in their soils. The sludge left over after city sewage is treated is ideal for this. It can be mixed with the gravel during the second pass—put through the grinders along with the gravel, to reduce it to very fine particles that will immediately be highly active biologically.

And if the water leaving sewage plants contains plenty of gravel dust, the explosion of well-fed microorganisms which results will help clean up our rivers and harbors.

The way to purify our drinking water naturally—cheaply, and without any toxic chemicals—is to let it run into a reservoir, where it is mixed with some gravel dust and let stand for 6 to 24 hours. The microorganisms in the water will feed on the rich minerals in the rocks and multiply greatly. Then they will biodegrade all the organic matter in the water, combining it into granules that will settle out at the bottom. This is repeated in a second reservoir which is well aerated (the digestion of organic matter is an aerobic process). After about a week, says Hamaker, "the water will be of the same quality as that of any mineral-cleaned mountain stream."

(Putting chlorine in our drinking water kills all the beneficial organisms along with the potentially harmful ones; since we, like plants, need helpful microorganisms to digest our food, drinking chlorinated water interferes with our own ability to get nourishment from the food we eat. Hence so many overweight people, trying to get enough to eat? Hence so much acid indigestion in the over-developed countries?)

How much will it cost to remineralize all the arable regions of the earth? Probably on the order of a trillion dollars or so, give or take a few billion.

Can we afford it? Well, that's about what the world now spends on weapons and military activities—*every year*—at the rate of *a million and a half dollars a minute.* The U.S. alone spends a trillion dollars on military hardware and activities every four years now. The MX missile system would cost about $50 billion. Trident submarines cost over a billion dollars each, and they want to build 30 or more of them. So do B-1B bombers, and they'd like to build a hundred of them. The Soviet versions would cost about the same. You get the idea.

Remineralization will not need submarines or missiles, but it will need planes, helicopters, and blimps, and lots of them. Every available military and passenger plane will have to be borrowed. Air travel will have to be for emergency only or rationed very carefully for 2 or 3 years. New helicopter-blimps may have to be built to carry enormous loads of gravel dust without continually refueling. Thousands of planes will have to begin flying full time if we are to have any hope of succeeding.

Gravel dust can also be blown onto forest lands from thousands of trucks; existing lime blowers can be used. Dust from glacial rock and stone can be distributed by people on foot, horseback, and bicycle: everybody must get stone. Snow blowers and leaf blowers might be modified, but many hands and buckets will work well too. (By hand, finely ground gravel should be spread on forest soils at the rate of about ⅙ pound per square foot, especially out to and around the leaf circumference of trees.) Efforts of government at all levels can be supplemented by locally organized volunteer activities. What is needed is some organization in each region to get things done and keep track of what still needs doing.

Remineralizing croplands and recycling farm residues in tropical areas will keep the soil fertile year after year and end the need for slash-and-burn agriculture, with its vast uncontrollable fires.[8] And we must stop spraying the forests with deadly poisons to try to control the present blights—it is doing more harm than good. Masanobu Fukuoka has tried to make this clear to the leaders of Japan, where the old-growth pine forests are all dying, but to no avail. (There is the haunting image of an old and once-beautiful pine

*Maria Felsenreich (her name means "rich in rocks") spreading rock dust by hand on her woodlot outside Vienna. She has been one of the foremost proponents of remineralization in Europe.*

in a temple garden in Kyoto, dying of pine blight; it had been completely wrapped in white bandages, a bottle containing a liquid was strapped to its side, and a feeding line ran beneath the bark. It was not expected to live.) Fukuoka calls spraying poison "expanding the darkness within the cave by chipping away at the walls." It is no different from chemotherapy and radiation as treatments for cancer, instead of cleansing and rebuilding sick bodies with optimal nutrition.

The trees, bushes, weeds, and grasses have become our best friends now, our most important allies. If we feed them well they may save our lives.

*"In a real sense, all life on earth is locked in the minerals ... through weathering, nutrients essential to life are made available. ... Even life in the seas awaits nutrients that are released by weathering on the land then carried to the sea by rivers."*

—HENRY D. FOTH
PROFESSOR OF SOIL SCIENCE,
MICHIGAN STATE UNIVERSITY

We also need to remineralize the coastal waters of the world out to the edge of the continental shelves. Given the rich mineral nutrients in glacial gravel dust, many forms of shelled sea life, from microscopic to sizable, will thrive and multiply. As they do, they will extract carbon dioxide from the sea to build their calcium carbonate shells.

When each generation of shellfish dies it takes the carbon in its shells to the bottom of the ocean with it, where it remains for eons—until some time in the far distant future when upheavals build new mountains with it. As the ocean's carbon is removed in this way, the ocean absorbs more $CO_2$ from the atmosphere. Thus our cousins in the sea will also help us bring down the $CO_2$, if we feed them.

But if they are to do their part, we must stop poisoning them with toxic substances of all kinds spilling out from our industries, even the poisons we stupidly put on our food crops, deadly pesticides and herbicides which run off into the streams and the coastal waters. We are quickly finding out now that everything is connected to everything else.

# Renewable energy

*"Here comes the sun.*
*Here comes the sun, I say,*
*It's all right."*

—THE BEATLES

Ninety-eight percent of the world's energy now comes from fossil fuels, only 2% from other sources (primarily hydroelectric and nuclear). Much of the world's fossil fuel is burned in the United States, so let's talk about the U.S. situation as one example.

Amory Lovins points out in his landmark book *Soft Energy Paths* that more than a third of all energy use in the U.S. is for space heating and cooling and hot water. (In Europe it's close to half.) In most climates of the world these things can be done with solar energy alone.

Total or partial solar heating is working in countries close to the latitude of Anchorage, Alaska—like the Netherlands and Denmark. Simple solar energy systems can provide total heating and cooling anywhere in the U.S. Fossil-fuel-generated electricity is often used for these purposes—and *two-thirds of the energy is wasted* when coal and oil are used to generate electricity, much of it in long-distance transmission. (More than 55% of the electricity generated in the U.S. comes from coal, the dirtiest fuel of all.) Lovins says that relatively small temperature changes, less than 100 degrees either way, are best created from more appropriate, local energy sources like solar energy, wind systems, and so on.

Only 4% of all electrical use in the U.S. is for all these things:

lighting, electric appliances, telecommunications, and electronics. Another 4% runs industrial motors. All these things could most efficiently be done locally with solar photovoltaic cells and solar-thermal plants. The technology is already here and on-line.

Solar One has been generating 10 megawatts of electricity from focused sunlight (using superheated steam to drive a turbogenerator) at its facility near Barstow, California for the past four years. SolarPlant 1, completed in 1984, incorporates a revolutionary new breakthrough in solar technology: mirrors made inexpensively from a thin aluminum-coated polymer film instead of ground glass. The lightweight, easily replaceable mirrors are grouped into parabolic structures that look like satellite antennas, which can be spread out over any kind of terrain including hillsides. Generating electricity from coal costs about 2.3¢ a kilowatt-hour, from gas 2.9¢, and from oil 5.6¢. SolarPlant 1's electricity costs only about 2¢—the cheapest of any energy source, totally nonpolluting, and there is an indefinite supply that doesn't depend on world politics.

New breakthroughs in more efficient solar cells, price-competitive with other sources of electricity, will be here soon (Stanford has already developed superefficient cell technology), and more government funding in this crucial area—say, one-tenth of the billions the U.S. government has put into research and development for nuclear plants—would help a lot. (The Reagan administration drastically cut back on funds for all the clean, renewable energy technologies, to support its friends in Big Oil and nuclear power.)

Wind systems can also generate local electricity quite well:

> Denmark once had about 100,000 wind machines supplying local electricity, but cheap oil and some powerful institutions put them out of business.... Similar stories could be told in the Netherlands and in the Great Plains of North America.

Lovins points out that "at high latitudes the wind blows mainly in the winter when heat needs are greatest and sunlight is scarcest." Electricity can also be generated locally and with no $CO_2$ or other pollution by tapping the movement of ocean waves and tides. Some 450 miles of wave power collectors alone could supply all the electrical needs of Britain, Scotland, Ireland, and Wales. And electricity can now be generated from temperature differences between different layers of the ocean, at a price already close to that of electricity from \$20-per-barrel oil.

All these forms of renewable energy require energy to manufacture, however—fossil fuel energy—for extraction of minerals, refining and other industrial processes, transportation of materials, and so forth. Can we afford to burn up this energy and produce additional quantities of $CO_2$ and other greenhouse gases, even to bring lots of renewable energy systems on line? Perhaps the additional greenhouse gases produced in this way will tip the climate over the edge, past the point of no return, and the nonpolluting benefits of solar and wind systems will come too late.

I don't know the answer to this question. Because the state of our climate is so uncertain now, there probably is no answer. We can consider the fact that every energy device has an "energy payback period," the time during which the energy it produces equals the energy which went into it. For most of these solar and wind systems that period probably ranges from one to three years or so. It can be estimated by comparing the cost of the system to the number of months or years of fossil fuel energy it can be expected to replace.

If we were to insist on only the most efficient systems, those that are so well designed that they can pay back the energy which went into them in a year or less, for example, perhaps we might safely introduce them—on the assumption that even conservatively, we probably have at least two or three years before the point of no return could conceivably come, so that such a system would have a net positive effect on the amount of greenhouse gases in the atmosphere. Passive solar space heating—large double-glazed windows, simple attached solar greenhouses, black-painted water-filled drums, and rock or concrete walls to retain the sun's heat and radiate it back slowly at night—probably makes a lot of sense now.

But there's really no way to tell how long we have, at least at this point. Cutting down one more tree to build a greenhouse might be all it takes to push us over the edge. Maybe a crash program of very focused scientific research can give us some additional answers to questions like this.

That leaves transportation. What could we possibly find to substitute for all the gas, oil, diesel, and jet fuel we burn to run our cars, trucks, buses, trains, and planes?

Methanol. It comes from a number of sources, but we're going to have to get it mainly from trees—the billions of *new, fast-growing* trees we plant on *remineralized soil* in the next few years. The trunks are converted to wood chips, which are fermented to make wood alcohol (methyl alcohol, or "methanol" for short.)

Methanol is an *amazing* fuel. It is a more efficient fuel than gasoline, yet has a high octane rating. It burns best with a very lean

*Methanol cars developed by the California Energy Commission under Governor Jerry Brown.*
PHOTOS: CALIFORNIA ENERGY COMMISSION

mixture—lots of air and little fuel—and will cost less to run on than gasoline. While idling, methanol engines use only *half* the fuel of gasoline engines. Methanol burns *much cleaner,* so emission control systems don't cost as much. And it burns *cooler,* which brings down the cost of cooling systems. So the same power can be delivered with less expensive engines, reducing even the cost of new cars.[9]

Methanol engines put out less carbon monoxide and nitrous oxide and no sulfur dioxide. And they don't put out any smoke! You'd never have to gasp for air behind an old car, a truck or a bus again. Diesel trucks, buses, and trains will run even more efficiently on methanol (with a simple spark-ignition system added), and they'll have even more torque and power for big loads. We'll be able to breathe the air in our cities again, even in Los Angeles! We'll be able to see the mountains and the blue sky. And we can get rid of those stinking diesel cars, which we should have outlawed long ago.

The long gas lines and rationing we suffered in the 1970s resulted from very minor shortages—only 3 to 5%. Methanol would guarantee all of us reliable long-term supplies, energy independence, and stable prices. And we could stay out of the volatile Middle East with its potential for nuclear war.

Methanol is such a clean fuel that it dissolves in water. A methanol spill would quickly disperse to nontoxic concentrations. So no more massive oil spills that kill so many wild creatures and ruin so many beaches. And no more need for offshore oil platforms, or drilling in Alaskan wildlife refuges. Ocean shipping itself would be greatly reduced, since most production would be domestic, even local. And local production means less shipping, handling, and pipeline costs, therefore cheaper prices at the pumps. Conversion of existing cars could be done for around $200.

Experiments to improve the combustion efficiency of methanol fuels are still going on. Higher efficiencies have even been obtained by adding water! Since methanol still burns when mixed with 74% water, who knows how far we can go on how little money?

In Brazil they're running millions of cars on ethanol—ethyl alcohol—made from sugar cane. They wanted to be energy independent and keep their money at home. Chrysler, GM, Ford, VW, and other manufacturers are all making cars in Brazil that run on ethanol alone. (Brazil is also running some of its diesels on vegetable oils, which Rudolf Diesel himself thought might be the wave of the future. Vegetable oils are better than petroleum diesel fuel in that they recycle carbon every year, but they produce almost as much smoke. Methanol is a much cleaner fuel.)

America has imported enough ethanol in the last ten years (adding it to gasoline to make gasohol) to reduce its oil imports by a hundred million barrels. (Brazil recently started adding a little gasoline to its pure alcohol fuel—not for fuel efficiency but to keep people from mixing it with fruit juice and ice and drinking it!)

Even as this is being written, methanol and other alternative fuels are becoming news across America—as a means of coping with mounting air pollution. The federal government announced it would buy at least 5000 "flexible fuel" vehicles that can burn alcohol fuels and compressed natural gas as well as gasoline. All three major American auto companies are developing flexible fuel vehicles. The governor of Iowa said he would order the use of ethanol-blended fuels in all state cars, as a means of increasing the market for Iowa's corn. California has arranged to have methanol marketed at 75 stations within the next three years. And Colorado mandated the use of blended fuels in the Denver area to deal with intolerable carbon monoxide pollution during cold weather.

Methane gas from the trees we plant can be pumped through existing natural gas lines and will cook our food, provide backup heating and cooling for our homes and workplaces, run industrial plants, and generate electricity. Using fast-growing trees, enough methane to fuel all the present electrical generating capacity in the U.S., for example, could be obtained from fast-growing trees planted on the equivalent of a square 500 miles on each side. With remineralization, this square might be brought down to 250 miles on a side. And with increased efficiency in converting wood to fuel developed through more research, the equivalent square might eventually be only 145 miles on each side. Of course the stands of trees would be spread out across the country and across the world, to minimize transmission costs and multilevel profit taking. And to keep power—all kinds of power—as close to home as possible.

It will take at least six years to get enough new tree growth to replace all our coal, oil, and natural gas with methanol and methane fuels. Meanwhile, we have to start phasing out high carbon fuels immediately. How are we going to accomplish this?

John Hamaker points out that one of our priorities has to be to begin using all the dead trees in our forests for energy now—burning them in our fireplaces instead of using gas or oil heat, making methane and methanol with wood chips made from them, and so on. They will be decomposing and giving off greenhouse gases anyway (though at a slower rate—but we have to keep warm in the winter).

We can also begin immediately converting plants that burn the dirtiest fossil fuels—coal, coal-derived synthetic fuels, and heating oil—to natural gas, which is much cleaner. Every ton of coal that's burned adds 2 tons of $CO_2$ to the atmosphere!

And we can immediately start running our cars on natural gas— which is just the gaseous form of methane (methanol is the liquid) and produces considerably less carbon than gasoline—and keep on until the new trees mature and large quantities of tree methanol become available in a few years. The technology is already here— fleets of government cars have been tooling around on natural gas for years. (It's often liquified to make propane.)[10] Natural gas now sells for the equivalent of $8-a-barrel oil, *less than half* the current price of oil. Propane is 20 to 30% cheaper than gasoline and has a high octane. But our main consideration has to be our survival now, not price. So we have to cut back greatly even on our use of natural gas during this most critical period.

American farmers are now burning enough straw on their fields— 200 million tons of it each year—to provide all their own electrical and natural gas needs from it if it were converted to ethanol.

Farmers can also grow corn to produce ethanol, and sell it at a price comparable to gasoline. Ethanol was widely used in the U.S. before cheap oil replaced it. The major selling point of this alcohol fuel was the increased power it provided. With remineralization, ethanol should be much cheaper than gasoline. (What's left after ethanol fermentation of corn is high in protein and corn germ and can be added to cheaper feeds and fed to animals.) Many farmers in the U.S. are paid not to grow crops, in order to keep prices up—they simply have too much capacity. But if we remineralize all our soils we will soon have many times the capacity and can use the excess yield to grow fuel crops so we can get rid of all the dirty fossil fuels and bring down the $CO_2$. The federal government now has millions of dollars available for low-interest loans to set up systems for making alcohol fuels.

Hamaker estimates that all our petroleum fuels could be replaced by alcohol made from crops grown by farmers, not even counting the billions of new trees we're going to plant and use for fuel. And still there would be enough food-producing capacity, on remineralized farmlands, to end hunger on earth several times over. (Though hunger is primarily a political issue, not a question of food production: the rich in every country try to take away as much of the peasants' land as possible and put them to work at starvation wages growing profitable export crops like coffee, sugar cane, and rubber. That's really what most revolutions are about, redistributing land and power back to the majority of the people. If you have the opportunity, you might want to vote for people who understand this—or get even more involved in helping bring about change peacefully.)

And consider this: trucks use *4 to 6 times as much fuel*, in miles per ton of cargo, than trains—and produce that much more $CO_2$ and pollution. Let's bring back the beautiful trains. American railroads can handle three times as much cargo as they do now without increasing the physical system. And we can have much more efficient machinery in every area of life, to do more with less fuel. (The Reagan administration rolled back the mileage standards for cars and vetoed a congressional act requiring more efficient appliances.)

It's all political. We have the technology and capacity to create a paradise here, if we use our heads and distribute power more equally. *This land is your land, this land is my land.* . . .

(Other renewable fuels are coming in the probably not-distant future. Lee Spano and his colleagues at the U.S. Army Natick Laboratories in Massachusetts found a tropical fungus that can turn waste paper first into sugar and then into ethanol; he said Pentagon documents worked especially well, turning into pure sugar in just a few hours of digestion. Donald Krampitz and his associates at Case Western Reserve University in Cleveland have developed a method of using blue-green algae and bacteria to produce hydrogen gas directly from sunlight, which can be stored and used to power engines and generate electricity; they think the efficiency can eventually be brought up to 10%, which would mean that most of the world's energy might be produced in this way; unlike fossil fuels and even wood-based fuels, which are hydrocarbons, pure hydrogen doesn't emit any carbon dioxide at all. But we have no time to wait.)

# Conservation and the great voluntary cool-down

*"They exchanged love's bright*
*and fragile plan*
*for the glitter and the rouge,*
*and in a moment they were swept*
*before the deluge."*
—JACKSON BROWNE

If we want to survive, all these eventual conversions may not be enough to bring down the $CO_2$ in time to stop the cycle of forest-death, ice buildup and volcanic eruptions from reaching the point of no return. If we really want to survive, we also have to substantially reduce our continual burning of fossil fuels almost immediately during a 3- to 4-year transition period—until the new rapid tree growth effectively sucks up the excess $CO_2$.

How? Conservation, for one thing. Simply insulating buildings would free the U.S. from fuel needs equivalent to *all* its current oil imports.[11]

Recycling every conceivable recyclable material—including metals, glass, plastics, wood, paper, lubricating oil, equipment, and clothing—would accomplish similar wonders in saving energy at many stages of initial production (extraction, transportation, processing, manufacturing). It is estimated that up to 80% of our wastes could be recycled! (Japan is said to recycle 50% of its metals, glass, and paper.) And recycling can create many more jobs than landfilling or incineration. But recycling has received no government support, even as landfills are filling up and transportation costs soaring.

And we need to cool down every activity that fossil fuel is burned for, including nonessential industrial production and transportation of goods, driving, nonessential heating and cooling, and unnecessary gas and electricity use. Energy of all kinds will have to be carefully *rationed* for the next three to four years if we want to maximize our chances of surviving. (I know, it's a horrible thought. I don't like it either. But if we don't start rationing fuel now, we may soon have to start rationing food.)

But we can't wait for governments to act now. *You* can directly affect the amount of $CO_2$ and other greenhouse gases that will be pumped into the atmosphere in the next 3 to 4 years, by not buying any new things you don't absolutely need—because making and shipping almost everything burns fossil fuels. You can still buy, though: anything that's used, and available nearby. This is going to be a great time for flea markets.

Rather than talk about what we might have to give up, let's ask what the *necessities* are, what we absolutely *need* to get through this brief transition period. Food and shelter. Fuel to cook with, running water, lights, heat. Anything else that's absolutely essential?

Radio and television broadcasting doesn't take that much electricity, and stereos and TV sets don't use much, so most of us can probably spend our free time pretty much the way we have been. Libraries and video stores will still be there with their treasure troves, and we can keep taping music off the radio. Movie theaters can probably stay open, at least on reduced schedules, with popcorn and everything.

But do we really need new cars, lots of new clothes, electronic toys, trips to Paris, aftershave lotion, perfumes, beauty creams, new furniture, car phones, and so on? Can we get by for a couple of years with fresh foods, simple foods, instead of status or convenience foods that require energy-guzzling amounts of processing, packaging, refrigeration, or freezing? Can we take a vacation from compulsive consuming, kick the habit for a little while, before we get consumed ourselves?

Most of us in the overdeveloped world have gotten so lost in our artificially created environments that we don't even experience the real world any more. Maybe this break from our usual routines is exactly what we need for our own sanity, our own growth. Most of us have a need to move around. If our driving had to be cut way back, wouldn't we start bicycling a lot more, walking, roller skating, hitching rides...? And wouldn't we start seeing the world in a new way, more close up and real?

This may also be the opportunity many of us have long needed to rebuild our tattered community life. Fiercely pursuing our own desires and self-interest, we have lost one of the most precious potentialities of our existence: sharing ourselves with others, our brothers and sisters on this planet. To gain some genuine security now, perhaps we would be willing to give up some of that pseudo-security we have built around ourselves—of closing the door and turning on the TV while the real world falls apart around us. Meeting new people and working together cooperatively to turn this around may be scary for some of us at first, but it's what we're really here to learn. (Trust me.)

But it doesn't have to be all work. This is the perfect time for *games,* too! Pickup games of basketball, soccer and touch football, bridge, poker, Monopoly, Trivial Pursuit, new games, old games, games to have fun, take our minds off the crisis for a while, let go of our tensions and meet some new people. I'm telling you, this could be the greatest time of our lives. (Crises are always more interesting, especially if you survive them.)

If we cool things down for a while so we can go on eating, and we temporarily cool out most of the industrial production and transportation of goods that are not really essential for life, this will mean a temporary suspension of millions of jobs for a few short years. How will so many of us get by without money?

The global effort to remineralize and reforest the earth will create millions of temporary and many permanent jobs. Some of us may have to get out of our offices for a while and do some work in the great outdoors. We may resist, yet be very glad afterwards that wc had thc opportunity to do something different. All of us resist change. Our jobs, too, can become a mindless addiction, something that we hate but won't voluntarily give up because of fear of the unknown. (Two-thirds of the people in the U.S. say they wouldn't choose the same kind of work over again. Almost half admit they feel "trapped" in their jobs.)

In a country like the U.S. with something like 110 million working people, Alden Bryant has estimated that as many as 20 million new jobs may be created by this vast environmental enterprise: collecting, quarrying and grinding gravel, transporting dust, remineralizing soils, growing and planting tree seedlings, developing and constructing renewable energy systems; temporarily expanding natural gas production, producing fuel crops and the fuel from them, and revitalizing local and regional agriculture. The people who most quickly need to be retrained and transferred to these new jobs are those who are currently working in coal mining, petroleum transportation and refining, pesticide manufacture, and the manufacture and distribution of nonessential goods of all kinds. As much as one-quarter of our total GNP may have to be allocated to this effort during the next few years.

We have to declare a *global emergency* and create the institutions we need to get us through this period. Institutions like a guaranteed minimum income for everyone, enough to buy food, pay reasonable rent and meet other basic necessities. Institutions like an intensive revival of local agriculture, which will provide new jobs, build up local economies, minimize the use of fossil fuels in moving, refrigerating, and packaging food, and bring our food production close to home where we can keep an eye on it. Institutions like well-organized networks of voluntary support at local and regional levels, to ease this crucial transition for everyone.

It means seeing the environmental crisis as comparable to a major war or depression, in which no sacrifice is too great for the common good, no idea too radical if it gets the job done. Americans, for just one example, have done equally remarkable things before— creating federal jobs for millions of people during the depression (often for conservation work), mounting during the war the biggest industrial effort the world had ever seen, coordinating battles on an unprecedented scale, getting millions of women to work in factories for the first time, and so forth. We are quite capable of making such massive changes if we decide that we need them for our own survival. (Hamaker has suggested that an existing organization highly experienced in technology, such as NASA, be given overall responsibility for coordinating the program. I think that a better case could be made for creating special organizations in each country, of people who are known to be both highly qualified and dedicated to the values involved, and giving them the necessary powers to do the job. After the avoidable space shuttle tragedy, I don't trust NASA to run this—but they could help map the problem and help monitor the global effort. And of course the UN can play a central role in helping organize this worldwide effort.)

The oil companies don't have much to lose, because most oil will be gone in 10 to 15 years anyway.[12] But they'll probably fight us. And we may have to work pretty hard to get our governments to recognize the crisis for what it is, and begin creating the institutions we'll need to make it through. Maybe we'll have to do much of the work at the state and local levels—states can be pretty powerful beasts when they get aroused.

But we can't afford to leave the discussion and planning up to government officials, at any level. We should also create $CO_2$ Councils at every level, whose members include representatives of labor, industry, environmental groups across the spectrum, citizens, consumers groups, and government. The $CO_2$ Councils would participate in making policy decisions and would help coordinate planning nationally and in their regions and localities—they would stay on top of things and report back frequently to their constituents. States and individual cities could create their own $CO_2$ Boards, to work with the Councils in making and carrying out relevant policies under the direction of state and city governments.

Ideally we'll create autonomous policy-making bodies—called something like Public Energy Boards—which would be appointed in the U.S., for example, by Congress and the president nationally, and elected within each region and locality (called, perhaps, Public Energy Regions and Districts). Modeled on a highly successful regional administration like the Tennessee Valley Authority, the Energy Boards would organize the remineralizing of forests and planting of trees in their respective areas; set priorities for fuel and electrical energy allocation during the next few years based on societal needs, the energy efficiency of users, and employment; and carry out research and development on safe renewable energy systems, especially solar photovoltaics.

Rather than simply dividing up the country geographically, the Energy Districts might be created to match natural bioregions— common watershed areas, climatic and vegetation regions, and so on. (Thus, for example, Northern California has more in common climatically and botanically with Oregon and Washington, Southern California with Arizona and New Mexico, than they have with each other.) Renewable energy is primarily regional and local rather than centralized, and such things as flood and erosion control and choice of trees to plant can best be done within bioregions that share a common geographic environment.

At the most local level, Energy Boards and Councils may help facilitate community owned solar, wind, and alcohol-producing energy facilities. These could be run by boards that included some representatives elected by the community and some of the technicians and workers in the plants, who are close to the day-to-day operations. Representatives of the workers should also participate in the detailed management of the plants.

# Bringing down the
# other greenhouse gases

## METHANE

- *From huge cattle feedlots and human sewage wastes.* We have to recycle the manure and sewage and use it to fertilize the farmland. Mixed with gravel dust it doesn't smell, and it makes a most powerful natural fertilizer to replace simplistic chemical concoctions.

- *From garbage.* The famous garbage barge that nobody wanted made a lot of us more aware of this problem (New York's sanitation commissioner Brendan Sexton said the incident was a warning: "People have to remember this is just the tip of the iceberg. New York City could fill a barge like this eight times a day."). Instead of burying our garbage or dumping it in the ocean, where it continues to decompose and give off methane and $CO_2$, or worse, incinerating it (which not only produces all the $CO_2$ at once but also distributes noxious emissions including heavy metals over a wide area), we should remove the heavy metals, plastics, and other contaminants and then use it to enrich farm and forest soils. Along with gravel dust, it is the richest and most precious substance on earth for that purpose. Any organic garbage (including paper) that isn't recycled can first be "digested" to produce methane gas as a source of energy. (It can be pumped through the same pipelines we now use for natural gas; it will be even cheaper than natural gas; and in some states, methane gas from garbage alone can supply 25% of all the gas now used.) The residue can then be cleaned of heavy metals and other contaminants, mixed with gravel dust, and used to fertilize forest woodlands.

- *From burning of wood and vegetation.* Most of this is clear-cutting, which has to be stopped immediately; more resources have to be put into stopping forest fires as quickly as possible; and wood stoves should be used as little as possible for the next few years (and with catalytic converters if they must be used).

- *From dying vegetation, including forests and chemically-farmed lands.* This can be quickly reversed by remineralizing.

- *From coal and gas mining.* We have to phase these out as quickly as possible, especially coal.

## NITROUS OXIDE

- *From cars.* Catalytic converters help some, but not enough. Nitrous oxide is one of the most deadly emissions because it reacts with water to form nitric acid, which causes acid rain and further destroys the planet's already fragile vegetation. Methanol plus catalytic converters will control most of the nitrous oxide. Eventually we may decide to build car engines that use methanol to produce steam power, the same power that ran the railroads and the great ocean liners in the good old days. This will bring the combustion temperature down from the many hundreds of degrees of internal combustion engines to the boiling point of water, 212°F, and wipe out just about all the nitrous oxide emissions and probably many other air-polluting gases.

- *From chemical agriculture.* Much of the nitrogen in chemical NPK fertilizers escapes into the air to become a greenhouse gas. The solution here, as described in detail in Chapter Two, is a quick return to an organic, chemical- and poison-free agriculture on remineralized soil. If governments will only provide the transportation and storage and will distribute it fairly, the agricultural countries of the world will be able to produce so much extra food that nobody on the planet will ever have to go hungry again.

## CARBON MONOXIDE

- *From cars.* Current knowledge can build a catalytic converter to knock out 95% of the carbon monoxide emissions of methanol; concentrated research effort in this area can probably bring it down much further.

- *From burning wood and vegetation.* As above.

## INDUSTRIAL CHLOROFLUOROCARBONS

The U.S. banned them from spray cans because they destroy the ozone layer of the upper atmosphere, which protects us from ultraviolet light and cosmic rays, both of them carcinogenic; other countries should follow suit immediately. In refrigeration and other industrial processes, we should require CFCs to be recycled starting now and forbid any new manufacture of them. Alternatives are available already, some of them at comparable cost, and new research will bring the price of alternatives down soon enough. Fluorocarbons as an ingredient in plastics should be banned for now.

The U.S. uses something like half of all the energy in the world. We don't even have to wait for international agreements to act decisively and begin solving this terrible problem immediately. But everyone will have to act soon if we are to succeed.

# *The great tree-planting*

*"Every valley shall be exalted."*
—FROM HANDEL'S *MESSIAH*

*"We are confronted with insurmountable opportunities."*
—POGO

*"I believe that the trees I have planted
have given me ten years of new life.
They are transforming the land and
me at the same time. In as much as I
can help one or a few children experience this, I will feel as if I have done
something worthwhile in my life."*

—Pulitzer Prize Winner Rene Dubos

Besides their irreplaceable ability to bring down $CO_2$, trees provide
us with many other priceless benefits:

- *Food.* Because of their deep roots and masses of foliage, trees
  can produce more food per acre than any other agricultural
  crop. The best cereal crops can produce 2 or 3 tons per acre,
  while some trees can grow up to 20 tons per acre of high
  protein nuts or beans.

- *Rain.* Trees hold water in the soil, gradually evaporating it
  back into the air. Life-giving rain is always greater where there
  are many trees; cut down the trees and you get deserts.

- *Soil.* Trees hold the soil against erosion by wind and water.
  Their deep roots help break up bedrock and bring up nutrients
  and water to the topsoil.

- *Oxygen.* While taking in masses of $CO_2$, trees give off great
  quantities of oxygen, purifying the air around them. In cities,
  trees even draw pollution out of the air and hold it on their
  leaves.

- *Shade and shelter.* Trees protect the area around them from
  extremes of wind and temperature; sheltering croplands, they
  increase agricultural productivity.

- *Habitat.* Trees nurture and protect birds, animals, insects, and
  other plants.

- *Materials*. Rubber, cork, gums, resins, waxes, soaps, oils, fibers, and lumber come from trees. The synthetics that can be made from oil can also be made from trees. Paper is usually made from trees, but better paper can reportedly be made more efficiently from crops such as hemp; and of course wood, for building human-scale structures with.

Trees are also among the most beautiful of life forms on earth, don't you think? Would you have any objection to having a lot more of them around?

We have to plant hundreds of millions of acres of fast-growing trees on remineralized soil. When and if we are able to bring the $CO_2$ in the atmosphere back down to where it was a hundred years ago, keeping it there—between about 260 and 280 parts per million of air—will keep our climate comfortably warm indefinitely. The tropics won't be excessively hot and dry, the higher temperate zones won't have severe winters.

Philip Abelson wrote in a *Science* editorial a few years ago that "with good management and superior choice of vegetation," the amount of carbon dioxide stored in the earth's vegetation "might be increased fivefold or more. The product would be sufficient to sustain a prosperous civilization.... The process of providing adequate energy need not lead to catastrophic consequences."

On remineralized soil, this estimate might be increased to twentyfold. [13]

We need to plant fast-growing trees—poplars, cottonwoods, acacias, eucalyptus, maples, willows, birches, locusts, alders, planes, southern beeches, ash, guayule, yucca, and so on—different trees in different parts of the world. Native species preferably, trees that will produce 8-inch diameter cordwood in about four years. Some types of fast-growing trees produce food (hard wickla), some produce animal fodder (leucaena-leucocephala). Where there is a choice, mixed species (to minimize disease) of fast-growing trees with the largest leaf size should be planted, since they are capable of absorbing $CO_2$ most rapidly.

Poplar trees are said to be one of the best choices here. Like some other varieties, when they are cut down they sprout again from the stumps, so they don't have be replanted for many, many years. In some countries the same poplars have been harvested as many as 50 times. (Cut every four years, they wouldn't have to be replanted for some 200 years.) And there are different kinds of hybrid poplars that are adapted to nearly every soil and climate condition (except ice ages). The trees can be used to produce methanol, methane, particleboard, paper, and firewood.

Many arid and semi-arid lands, once remineralized, could be forested with drought-resistant trees—especially those that produce a valuable crop, like pistachio nuts and jojoba oil. In this way, whole ecosystems can be regenerated, stopping and reversing desertification. Desert areas have already been reclaimed in this way, rain following the trees. Scientists at the Royal Botanical Gardens near London have developed a collection of 5000 plants they call "green glue," which are especially effective in stopping desertification. To come up with this list they studied more than seven million plant specimens over the past 150 years.

John Hamaker says,

> ... we must plant enough trees to furnish annual needs for fuel. If it takes 6 years for the tree crop to mature to useful size, 6 times the annual number of trees must be planted. Only the trunks of ⅙th of the trees are used each year. The branches go back into the soil as well as the wood ashes which contain the minerals. In addition, 6 years of growth of leaves go back into the soil. If the soil is kept well mineralized all the residue will be quickly moved into the soil. Chopping the branches into small pieces and mixing them into the soil will expedite the action of the soil organisms. So the soil and the standing wood plantations constitute huge reservoirs for the $CO_2$ in the air. A quantity of $CO_2$ equal to that resulting from the burning of tree trunks simply recycles back ... and does not increase atmospheric $CO_2$.
>
> The clean-burning forms of wood energy are alcohol and methane gas. When they burn they give off water and $CO_2$ and almost no contaminants. The residue from these biological processes contains the minerals and some top-quality organic compounds which should go back into the soil to maintain a vigorous growth in the wood plantation.

How are all these trees going to get planted?

Hamaker suggests that every generating plant (funny how we call them plants) that now produces electricity by burning fossil fuels be required to establish tree plantations big enough so that within four years they can switch completely to wood-derived methanol as their source of fuel, and continue on a renewable basis from then on. He says they should also be required, starting right away, to use any waste heat "in extensive greenhouses so that the local requirement for vegetables can be met without expending the fuel to bring them from Florida, the Rio Grande Valley, Mexico, or California." (And the fuel to refrigerate them at every point along the way. Local vegetables can more easily be picked to correspond with local demand, and so not even need much cold storage.)

The biggest part of the worldwide remineralizing and replanting must of course be done by air. Vast areas of forest and jungle have no roads. Hamaker suggests that air travel must be "cut to necessity only" and that 90% of the world's aircraft must be stripped of excess weight and refitted for remineralization and reforestation. It is a process that may take years to complete, and it must be done as rapidly as possible to maximize our chances of survival.

Airborne work must be supplemented from the ground. Richard St. Barbe Baker, founder of Men of the Trees, suggested many years ago "that all standing armies everywhere be used" for reforesting the earth, an idea that could not be more appropriate today. Organizations like the Civilian Conservation Corps, created by the U.S. government during the Great Depression to do some of the earliest large-scale ecological work, need to be created everywhere. They can provide healthy outdoor jobs for many of the people whose jobs require too much fossil fuel energy at present, and who we need to find something else for until non-life-threatening sources of energy come on line in a few years.

Charles Peaty, founder of Men of the Trees in West Australia, invented a machine that can be towed by a small tractor and which enables two people to plant 500 trees an hour. Devices like this, especially small hand-pulled ones for millions of hands around the world, will be very valuable in making the work easy and getting the job done quickly. People in cities and towns can take responsibility for remineralizing and replanting their surrounding areas. A few

years ago the Australian National Railway decided to let people
travel free to plant trees in one region.

A big job. It will be the biggest job, the biggest reason, the
biggest party the world has ever seen. And maybe it'll bring us
together and stop some of the madness.

Once the forests are all planted, who will look after them and make
sure they are logged right and cared for?

Ray Raphael has an idea. From *Tree Talk:*

> Presently, loggers and timber owners are paid according to how
> much timber they extract from the forest. What if the forest
> owners and the workers were paid instead according to the growth
> rates of the standing trees? ... The determining factor in timber
> management should not be the quantity of wood *harvested* in any
> given year, but rather the quantity of wood that the forest is
> actually *producing*.
>
> Imagine three or four families caretaking about two thousand
> acres of wooded land on a long-term basis, perhaps for a decade
> or two, perhaps for life ... their salaries are based on the timber
> that is presently growing on their land. The greater their growth
> rates, the more money they receive....
>
> Why not base their salaries also on such nontimber variables
> as the extent of their fisheries and the quality of their water?
> ... This means that they will take special care in their logging
> operations not to damage the land or the residual trees. It means
> they will try to minimize erosion, for the topsoil is their bread and
> butter. Every cubic yard of dirt that washes away means less
> timber—and less money—for the stewards. If the soil settles into
> the streams, so much the worse.... They must also provide
> trails, campsites, and perhaps even hostels to accommodate vis-
> itors to their domain, for even recreational opportunities should
> be figured into the complex formula that determines their pay....
>
> To succeed, each must have an intimate knowledge of his own
> particular place.... The stewards are *landed foresters*.... For the
> individual workers, landed forestry would mean year-round job
> security rather than seasonal and/or migratory employment. Their
> jobs would be varied and challenging, rather than repetitive and
> boring ... tree fallers and brush cutters wouldn't get white thumb
> from handling a chain saw day after day, nor would planters get

tendinitis, nor catskinners develop kidney ailments.... The landed foresters would function as autonomous professionals, not as cogs in a bureaucratic wheel....

In a society with a desperate need for wood fiber, it makes no sense to be cutting down the trees before they reach their peak productivity, but this is precisely what the timber companies are doing. It makes no sense to allow perfectly good growing land—the space between planted seedlings—to lie fallow for a decade or more. It makes no sense to destroy the biomass with herbicides, not utilizing it for energy production or other purposes. It makes no sense to plant pure stands of timber when mixed stands will grow more vigorously....

Indeed, it makes no sense to rely exclusively on energy-consuming techniques of forest management.... It makes no sense to replace men with machines at a time when high unemployment is becoming a built-in feature of our economy....

The timber companies, of course, have different ideas of what makes sense and what doesn't.... In order to return a quick profit on their investment, timber companies short-circuit high interest rates by cutting adolescent trees.... To avoid high labor costs, they take the human presence out of the woods.

The public sector, however, is unblinded by the profit motive. The government can allow itself the freedom to maximize production instead of profit, to maintain a healthy and stable forest ecosystem, and to think of people as something more than "high labor costs." In fact, governmental policies are often quite admirable. The stated goal of the Forest Service is to practice multiple-use, sustained-yield forestry.... The government happens to own a considerable portion of the means of production for the forests products industry: over a quarter of wooded land, and over half of the standing sawtimber....

Ultimately, the jobs created by a landed foresters program would be more numerous and more satisfying than the jobs that the program would replace. But the problems of transition remain: the inertia of the status quo is often overwhelming.

**FIGURE 14**

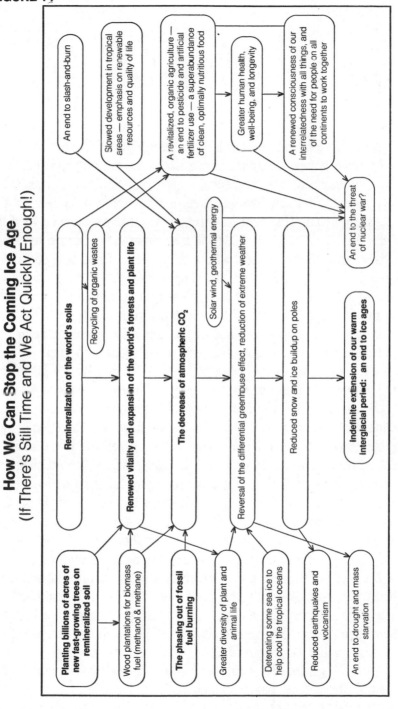

How We Can Stop the Coming Ice Age
(If There's Still Time and We Act Quickly Enough!)

# Other ideas

What other ideas can we think of to bring down $CO_2$ and the other greenhouse gases, decrease the tropic/polar temperature differential, and otherwise stabilize our deteriorating climate? Certainly the world is ready for anything creative that anyone can come up with.

Another thing Hamaker has proposed is that we blow up sections of the Antarctic ice shelf. This will free them to be carried by ocean currents toward the tropics, where they will melt and help cool down the overheated tropical oceans, decreasing poleward precipitation somewhat. Towing icebergs to tropical waters, however, would take too much energy, producing too much additional $CO_2$.

It has been suggested that we put up giant mylar or aluminum foil reflectors in the sky, each say 50 miles square, to focus more of the sun's heat on the growing glaciers. It sounds like a good idea until you realize that even such a huge reflector would look like just a speck in the sky. Even if you could build one 500 miles across, which we may not even be capable of now, the additional light probably wouldn't melt polar glaciers at all, given the fact that 80 to 90% of the sun's energy reaching the glaciers is reflected back into space because of their whiteness, and they have an abundance of cold to overcome before they would begin to melt. And think of all the $CO_2$ the rockets would put into the atmosphere getting such a huge reflector up there. All space activity should be put on hold for the next few years until we get our only environment under control.

Spread carbon black on the polar ice sheets, to lower the albedo, absorb more of the sun's heat, and melt the ice? It would probably melt a little, then get mixed in with the slush and lose its dark absorptive power. And you couldn't do it too often because of all the $CO_2$ that would be produced by the planes that spread it.

Melt the glaciers with nuclear plants? We don't have enough time to build them, the pipes and hoses would probably freeze, you couldn't build enough in 20 years to melt enough glaciers, the radiation from accidents and earthquakes would probably kill us if the ice age didn't, etc.

Use more nuclear energy right now, instead of fossil fuels? Nuclear energy won't run our cars and trucks (alcohol will); we're using just about as much of it as we can produce now; it's too dangerous, etc. Nuclear fusion? It's not here yet; it also produces undisposable radioactive wastes; an earthquake might radiate a whole region; and so on. Nuclear plants also won't consume the excess $CO_2$ in the atmosphere; natural plants—trees and forests—will.

Start using "ice-minus," the new genetically engineered bacteria that supposedly lowers the freezing point of crops but hasn't even been approved yet? It is purported to reduce the freezing point by 5 to 7°F, but recent field tests found that it only worked for 2°. Either way, the difference it makes will probably not be worth much as the climatic deterioration accelerates. And the possible side effects could be horrendous. It is known to sometimes cause pseudomonas disease, which affects 40 different crop plants and is dangerous if not fatal to some susceptible humans. Impulsively releasing new genetically engineered organisms into the environment may compound our problems. There are simpler, proven ways to protect crops to the same degree.

But let's brainstorm for more ideas. (First rule of group brainstorming: no criticizing during the idea period.)

## We must store food now

Even if we were to begin massive tree-planting and soil remineralizing tomorrow, and stop using all fossil fuels immediately, the dying of the earth's forests could not be stopped in less than a year or two. And of course nothing on this scale is going to be done for many months, perhaps years (though that will probably be too late), perhaps never. So the $CO_2$ in our atmosphere is going to keep rising exponentially for some time to come.

With it, we are going to see a continuing acceleration of all these things that are already destroying our food crops: spring and summer crop freezes, crop-killing summer heat and drought, floods, high winds, hurricanes, tornados, and so on. The drought that destroyed 90% of all the crops in the southeastern states of the U.S. in the summer of 1986 is only a taste of what's coming. So are the late-June freezes in areas like Canada and the northern U.S. agricultural states.

That is why Hamaker thinks that even if we were to start tomorrow, and even if we are ultimately successful in bringing down the $CO_2$ and stopping the ice age, as many as half the people on this planet may die of starvation in the next five to ten years before the climate can be brought under control.

So another thing we have to start doing *immediately* if not sooner, along with all the others, is stockpile as much food as we can to get us all through the crisis. Grains and legumes, primarily— wheat, rice, oats, rye, dried corn, millet, beans, peas, lentils, etc. These things will keep us alive most effectively, store well without refrigeration, and can be grown quickly, especially on remineralized land without soil-killing chemicals.

To stockpile grains quickly, we also need to stop feeding them to animals to fatten them for slaughter. In the U.S., 80% of all the grain grown is fed to animals! Using grains to produce meat has never made much sense, for a lot of reasons: The amount of grains needed to produce your 8-ounce steak could feed each of 40 to 50 hungry people a cup of cooked grains (this is not to make you feel guilty, just more aware). We need much less protein than we think, and all of it comes best from grains and legumes (protein is not "energy food," carbohydrate is—wheat, brown rice, potatoes, whole-grain pancakes, bread, spaghetti, etc.—as runners have finally learned. Read Pritikin's eye-opening book, *Diet for Runners*).

Carbohydrates are *much* better than protein foods for losing weight safely, comfortably, and permanently. The excess protein most of us still eat (meat, cheese, eggs, etc.), along with the fat and cholesterol it almost always contains, is a primary cause of cancer, heart disease, and all the other degenerative illnesses of our time (early senility, kidney disease, Parkinson's, and so forth). The Gerson Therapy has successfully reversed all of the degenerative diseases (including arthritis, heart disease, kidney disease, multiple sclerosis and cancer) most of the time, with a low-protein, high-carbohydrate, fresh food diet including lots of freshly-made organic juices (see Appendix: *Access*).

Many of us have been gorging ourselves on meat—every day, even two, three times a day. Some of this is doing what's familiar, what our parents did and our friends probably do. But much of it, in the face of all the terrible evidence these days, is probably a need to fill oneself in a society that keeps us empty and powerless. We eat meat like we consume new clothes, cars, and many other things—to make us feel like we're okay, that we belong, that we have substance, when our jobs tell most of us every day that we're quite readily replaceable—and we don't feel we have any power, political or otherwise, to change anything. No wonder so many of us say to ourselves, "I'm going to enjoy myself now, and to hell with the consequences."

But now the consequences are here. Our careless pleasures have come home to roost. We face not meatlessness but starvation in the next few years if we do not make some radical changes, and quickly. Not eating meat and chicken for a few years would seem to be a small price to pay for survival (though some of us, more oppressed than most, perhaps, will feel that life is not worth living without them). Most of us have at least thought about trying vegetarianism at some point, to feel better, to stop having animals killed in our name, and so on. This would be a good time. If you feel you still need some flesh to get you through the week, fish makes more sense now, preferably from deep waters that have not yet become too toxic. One of the nicest things about a low-fat vegetarian diet is that you can eat more food—as much as you want, really—without gaining weight.)

Pritikin and many others have shown that eating no animal flesh provides more energy and optimum health, and that more than a few ounces a week becomes harmful. Just eat all you want of cooked whole grain foods, legumes, and fresh fruits and vegetables, all preferably grown organically without toxic chemicals—and soon, hopefully, on remineralized soil as well. Organically grown foods are also higher in protein, remineralized foods higher still. (Some nonfat dairy products can be eaten on an optimum diet, but you don't need any. Frances Moore Lappé, author of *Diet for a Small Planet*, has recently discovered that it is not necessary to be concerned about combining certain foods to get enough protein: it is sufficient simply to eat whole, unrefined grains and some legumes. The best sources of calcium and other minerals are dark leafy green vegetables like collard greens, kale, broccoli, spinach, and chard, carrots and freshly made carrot juice. Even beans, blackberries, oatmeal, and oranges contain significant amounts of calcium.)

If we quickly remineralize much of our farmland, we will increase yields dramatically and be able to grow enough extra food to provide us with real security for the coming crisis.

The food should be grown in every region of every country, and stockpiled by local community groups and every level of government from towns and cities to states and nations. Vacant lots, rooftops, front and back yards, even one side of some of our neighborhood streets can be taken up and planted with food gardens. If food-growing is decentralized, it will be less likely to be used as a political weapon, a chance to wipe out those enemies someone has always hated.

# How is it going to happen quickly enough?

We have to put tremendous pressure on our local and national governments—an irresistible tidal wave of letters, phone calls, petitions, personal lobbying and demonstrations—which should quickly convince them that we are indeed in an emergency of unprecedented proportions, and that they have to begin immediately to do everything in their power to bring down the $CO_2$ fast. And if we don't get a quick response, we have to raise the ante.

It took a mass movement involving millions of Americans to

finally stop the Vietnam war—and that was threatening the survival of only a small fraction of the people of America; this threatens all of us with annihilation. As Nixon and Kissinger have admitted in their memoirs, American troops were finally withdrawn from Vietnam because the government was afraid of the widespread and escalating violence of the most radical segment of the anti-war movement, and the cost of continuing the war simply became too high. Business districts were trashed, banks firebombed, highways blockaded by thousands of university students. In Austin, Texas, over 8,000 people occupied the state capitol. Million dollar computers were captured and held for ransom, or destroyed.

More than four million students and 170,000 faculty at more than 900 American colleges went on strike, including many jocks, cheerleaders, and fraternity and sorority members. Similar revolts took place in France (including a general strike of ten million workers), Czechoslovakia, Mexico and many other countries in the late '60s. A blue-ribbon commission appointed by Nixon reported that 75% of all American college students favored the goals of the strike! One hundred U.S. art galleries and several museums closed down to protest the war. (When New York's Metropolitan Museum refused to close, 500 artists sat-in there.) An ammunition ship was hijacked by some of its crew. A destroyer was sabotaged before it could sail for Vietnam. GIs burned down reenlistment centers.

And it wasn't all protest. On some campuses alternative schools, "free universities" were set up, to teach and learn about many things—like the economic and political pressures that lead to war, and to other misfortunes such as environmental destruction. Instead of preparing themselves to fit into an existing system which had come to seem dehumanizing, tens of thousands of students and nonstudents began asking what kind of society we could create ourselves which would develop us more fully as human beings, and would be more enjoyable. Unlike most contemporary schooling and work, it was a very involving, democratic, and empowering process, and gave rise to much of what is meaningful in our societies twenty years later.

In a way, the imminent ice age is an opportunity—a much needed one—for us once again to let go of all that is dead in our lives, and to allow ourselves once more to believe that things can be better, and more fun—and to make it happen. We can revitalize ourselves and our environment at the same time. In fact we probably can't save our environment unless we save ourselves in the process.

Are you willing to see yourself as powerful?

There is another resource we may be able to use in the struggle for our survival—an enormous pool of money, the largest pool of capital in the world, and one that is already *owned* by the working people of this country: the employee pension funds. A quarter of a *trillion* dollars. Pension funds own close to half of all U.S. corporate stocks and bonds, and account for 90% of the business of the New York Stock Exchange!

It's not necessarily a question of simply spending this money to ensure our common survival, though a pretty good case could be made for that: pensions are not going to be worth much to any of us if we're dead before we can retire. But these funds can be *invested* in projects that are both essential to our survival *and* can bring a profitable return.

Things like remineralizing forests and agricultural lands and sharing in the increased profitability that results. Like huge tree-planting projects, which will both maximize our chances for survival and bring in profits as the trees mature and are converted to methane and methanol. Like building solar greenhouses and establishing remineralized organic farms in and around cities in every locality, so that we can quickly begin stockpiling food for the next few years to ensure that as few of us as possible will starve, and for regional economic security and our optimal health. Like building solar systems, windmills, and other technology that produces nonpolluting energy to speed the phase-out of all the $CO_2$-spewing fossil fuels. All these things can make money at the same time as they help ensure our survival. They will also create many new jobs, some temporary, some permanent.

Unfortunately, most of this money, though legally *owned* by the people who have worked for it, is *controlled* solely or partly by management (or in the case of public employees' funds, by boards).

The regressive Taft-Hartley Act of 1947 expressly forbade employees of private companies to control their own pension funds. Even if the working people who own it decide they want to use some of it in this way, Congress and the president will have to pass new legislation. It will take a big fight. But we are talking about our survival.

Any elections that come up in the next year or two, in any country, will be among the most important decisions we ever make. Progressive candidates must be supported, those who are most free from connections to big business, most supportive of environmental protection. In the U.S. the Democrats, for all their faults, are clearly more committed to preserving what's left of our environment and controlling pollution and toxics.

## *What if we don't act in time . . . or at all?*

*"I heard the sound of thunder,
it roared out a warnin',
Heard the roar of a wave that could
drown the whole world . . .
And it's a hard, it's a hard,
it's a hard, it's a hard,
It's a hard rain's a gonna fall."*

—BOB DYLAN

*"Most people would rather die than
change their habits."*

—DAVID BROWER

It may be too late already to stop the coming ice age, but we have to act as if it's not. (Or you may prefer to die.) Anyway, I believe in miracles, if your heart is open and you do everything you're supposed to be doing. But what if we take our time now, skeptical, hesitant, lazy, detached, a thousand ways of sticking our heads in the sand? (You'll look at warm sunny days and say, "Ice age? C'mon!") What if we simply laugh at all this silliness and go about our business?

Certainly there are powerful vested interests that want to keep doing business as usual. The oil companies may feel they have the most to lose, not only from selling everyone gas and oil but from their agricultural chemicals as well, many of which are made from oil, if we opt for a remineralized organic agriculture. They *could* gracefully concede that the survival of the human race may be a little more important than their profits, and put their enormous assets to work planting trees and selling alcohol and methane fuels. They might even think of their kids, or anyone else they really love (do oil company executives love anyone? —just asking.)

Unfortunately, they'll probably make a lot more big contributions to members of Congress, suggesting sensibly that the issue needs at least a few years more study before we take any expensive, radical actions. And as Ralph Nader points out, "Eighty percent of the time, Congress comes down on the corporate side of an issue."

John Hamaker is not very optimistic about our chances:

> The establishment is going to do nothing until the weather convinces them that the alternative is death. They will finally mount an ineffective program. When they have the program functioning as well as possible, they will find that the $CO_2$ is still increasing in the atmosphere and there is no way to stop the glaciation. The scientists simply do not understand that we are working against a point of no return. . . .
>
> We are already in a crisis situation. The people who set up the new worldwide program to "study the problem" are obviously unaware of the danger. I have already stated my opinion that we have delayed action so long that we now have a rendezvous with the point of no return—and with death—between 1990 and 1995. Only an immediate, total, and massive commitment to the entire problem of reducing the release of $CO_2$ and related greenhouse gases has any chance at all of proving that prediction wrong.
>
> Maybe it's time to take a decision maker to lunch and explain "the facts of life"—and death.

At the top are the financial tycoons who have been making all the major decisions for the rest of us. They are very well insulated from we plebeians and we couldn't afford to take them to lunch anyway.

The major news media are owned by the tycoons. They know what they can say and what they can not say ... Save your lunch money.

The scientists as a group have bent over backward to support the interests of the tycoons whose minions pass out the grant money. However there is a growing body of scientists who have come to understand that what is profitable for the tycoons is not necessarily good for them and their families. It might pay to take a scientist to lunch. ...

Finally there are the politicians in the legislative bodies. They have the power to change the laws and thus the nation and to provide leadership for the world. Unfortunately they have the herd instinct of sheep.... Just because I haven't found one with both intelligence and political courage doesn't mean there isn't one around. If you can spot a legislator who might prove an exception to the rule, give it a try. ...

I am more convinced than ever that only the fear of death will move nations to make the changes necessary to effect our survival. Any rational person who understands the point of no return must know that death is only a few years ahead. Hamaker has failed to impress that fact on the decision-makers. I'm hoping there is someone out there who can get the job done. ...

Doesn't seem too likely though. F. Raymond Fosberg of the Smithsonian Institution writes:

Lip-service in unlimited amounts, ill-conceived manipulation or exploitation of the environment for short-term advantages, and frantic activity to convert as much as possible of the resource-base into money in the shortest possible time: these are the patterns which I have seen almost everywhere. Exponentially increasing degradation is the rule. And these nations and their leaders are not at all content with devouring their own entrails. The more successful ones among them are shipping their destructive agents, their 'know-how,' their machines, their pesticides, and their bad habits, abroad to gain as much of their neighbors' resources and wealth as possible. ...

As though these processes were not efficiently destructive enough, depending on the initiatives and ingenuities of individuals and ordinary corporations, supra-national or trans-national organisms—cartels and multinational corporations—have come into being. These are organized by those who have a great deal of the money in the world and are out to get the rest of it ... while evading any restraints that may be put on their activities by national laws and tax and tariff barriers....

If as individuals we each go on as usual and leave it to others to change their life-styles ... we will follow the dinosaurs into extinction![14]

Think of it this way: *You* represent all of humanity now. What *you* do now determines whether we make it. You are *infinitely* important.

# Trying to survive if we don't stop the ice age, I: Food

If we were only to go by humanity's past history—the masses of people who prefer their entertainment and sociableness and have no idea what's going on in the world (or feel powerless or don't care), the powerful big businesses who essentially run the world and whose only motive seems to be more profits regardless of the consequences, the politicians who almost always side with big business because that's where their campaign funds come from, the less-developed countries who seem determined to become as polluted and frantic as others have—it doesn't seem like we have much hope of acting in time to stop the deterioration of our climate. So where does that leave us?

In worse shape, clearly. But we don't necessarily have to starve, though it will be much harder to survive than if we had acted in time. Most of us can go on eating, however, if we *quickly* recognize that we are indeed in a crisis situation and start building the life-support system we need. And we don't have much time to waste in starting that either.

The first thing is to stockpile thousands of tons of food, more than we have ever stockpiled before. And the key to growing enough food to stockpile fast is remineralization. If we remineralize our farmlands very soon, yields will increase dramatically within a year or two—double, soon triple, then even more after a few years, up to four or five times present crop yields, as long as the climate holds out. Without remineralization we are lost.

In the U.S., the billions of dollars the government is paying agribusiness *not* to grow food, in order to keep prices up, can immediately be spent to remineralize every farm in the country, in exchange for most of the *extra* crops produced through remineralization, which would go into storage against coming emergencies.

What kinds of crops should we concentrate on? Staple foods primarily, carbohydrates, like grains, beans, and potatoes. Foods that provide energy, have sufficient protein when grown correctly, and will keep for long periods of time without a lot of processing. Fruits and vegetables are important, for their vitamins and minerals. But eating grains, legumes, and potatoes grown organically on remineralized soil will probably provide most of us with more vitamins and minerals than we've been getting for years with our chemically-grown foods, soggy canned or frozen vegetables, and processed fruit juices.

It takes about 2000 square feet of land (40 by 50 feet, for example) to feed each person, using the most efficient gardening methods. This can be reduced by remineralizing, however, perhaps to around 600 square feet (20 by 30 feet). (See various books and other media in the *Access* section for food growing how-to-do-it.) The focus in intensive gardening is on potatoes, legumes, vegetables, and some fruit. Plants are planted in loosely compacted raised beds, well composted with lots of rich organic matter. They are set close to one another so that as they become mature, their leaves touch and create a shady "microclimate" beneath them, which conserves moisture and suppresses competing weeds. Well-composted and remineralized, the plants are strong and highly resistant to insects and disease, so no chemicals are needed. (In fact, any chemicals would destroy beneficial soil organisms like bacteria and earthworms, which are keeping the plants healthy).

The main problems are going to be temperature and water. Simple technology like cold frames, plastic tents and solar-heated greenhouses will make some food-growing possible almost anywhere outside the polar regions, and extend the growing season in the spring and fall. But not all food crops will survive below freezing, and we can expect increasing overnight freezes during the growing season in coming years. Grains (wheat, rice, corn, rye) and legumes (beans, peas, lentils) are destroyed by freezing, and they take up so much space for the amount of food produced that it doesn't make sense to grow them in greenhouses, except perhaps for some corn and beans.

Which food crops are likely to survive summer freezes? Broccoli, cauliflower, spinach, cabbage, carrots, kale, chard, and so on—most of the leafy green vegetables will survive down to about 15°F, root crops to about 10°. Fortunately, the dark leafy greens and carrots are precisely the foods that are highest in calcium, iron, and other minerals, and most all their vitamins are available when they are lightly steamed or eaten raw. So if we don't starve, we should be pretty well-nourished. (What's that, you say you hate vegetables?)

Without much grains and beans to count on, however, we're going to have a hard time getting by. Potatoes may be our salvation. They too are destroyed when the temperature gets down to freezing, but they can be grown in greenhouses which are kept above freezing at night by pumping in heat (fossil fuel heat perhaps, but by that time the climatic deterioration will have become unstoppable; we are unlikely to do anything so expensive before we have to anyway). Greenhouses might also be kept above freezing overnight by lining the sides with black-painted drums, sealed and filled with water or oil, that will retain heat from the day if the sun is bright, and give it off at night. Laying black plastic sheets on the ground around the plants will help keep the soil warm.

There is a simple and inexpensive way to prevent potatoes from freezing during the growing season. The "Wallo'Water" is a little fluted plastic container that is filled with water and surrounds growing plants, expanding as they grow. By keeping frost off and retaining some heat it can keep a potato plant alive from the freezing point (32°F) down to 10°, which may be sufficient to grow lots of potatoes in many cooling regions (potatoes take three months to mature). Cabbage plants have been kept alive with it to 30° below 0, and the other low-temperature plants mentioned above will probably respond almost as well. "Wallo'Waters" can also be used inside cheap plastic greenhouses, for still more protection against freezing. By allowing plants to develop more fully earlier in the season, the "Wallo'Water" also produces plants which withstand summer insect damage and diseases better, without any need for chemicals.

*Tomatoes can't be planted until July 15 in Saskatoon; picture was taken May 9.*

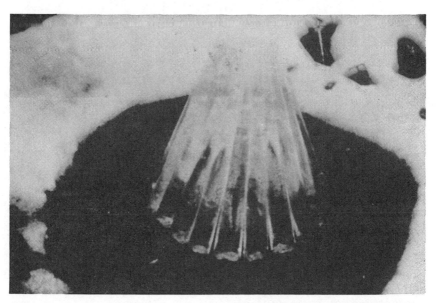

*This picture, taken in February, shows the heat provided by the Wallo'Water. The snow has been melted out three feet.*

*Minot, ND—Normal planting time is June 10. This plant was set out early in April. Their worst storm in 65 years occurred April 27.*

*12,000 Wallo'Waters. Only five fell over. They were putting up between 750 and 1000 per day with a crew of four.*

Fruit will be destroyed at the freezing point, and much lower temperatures will kill the trees as well. Some people will grow a dwarf fruit tree or two in a heated greenhouse, but fruit is likely to become an expensive luxury at best if we fail to stop this thing. The devastating experience of citrus growers in Florida in the last decade (crop-destroying freezes five years out of ten, and increasing) suggests that, if we do not turn the climate around, any fruit growing will soon be confined to the tropics.

There the problem will be excess heat and drought. Rain will decrease, and agriculture will become possible only with expensive irrigation, if then. Many areas will become so hot and dry that almost no food can be grown. (South China, Southeast Asia, and parts of India may do fairly well during the coming ice age, however: they have year-round rivers which will continue to flow from the Himalayas—rivers, moreover, which are rich in finely ground glacial gravel from the mountain peaks, which will continue to renew the soils' fertility each year during spring floods. And agriculture in these regions has relied on human labor for millenia, so there will be no need for new technology, no energy shortage. How ironic that Vietnam will be so much better off than America and France if we do not stop the coming holocaust.)

In the temperate regions water will also be an urgent problem if we don't stop the ice age progression, is becoming one already. Drought will increase during the growing season as the sub-tropical zone extends further into the middle latitudes during the summer. Not only will rainfall be inadequate to grow crops, there will soon not even be enough water for irrigation from underground aquifers, as they get used up. Yet in spring there will be more and more likelihood of flooding, as increased winter snowfall leads to record snowmelts.

So if it becomes clear that we will be unable to stop the climatic holocaust, says John Hamaker, we must quickly build every conceivable lake and dam and catchment area to catch and hold as much as possible of the spring floodwaters, so they can be used for irrigation all summer long. Projects of every size must be built as quickly as our technology, resources, and ingenuity allow. Remember, this is only if we see that we have failed. Dams, for the most part, have

too many environmentally harmful consequences to build any more
unless our survival absolutely depends on it.[15]


# Trying to survive if we don't stop the ice age, II: Money and organization


Where are you going to get your food if the ice age cycle continues?
Are you going to hope that distant agribusiness corporations keep
the supermarket stocked for you? Are you going to grow food
intensively in your back or front yard—and stay up all day and night
to defend it?

To have any food security at all, food production has to be
decentralized as much as possible—so that you or people you know
can make sure it gets grown and distributed fairly, to minimize the
costs and hazards of distribution (people will be holding up refrig-
erated tractor-trailers instead of Brink's armored cars). But if it's
everyone for themselves, there's going to be constant war on
every block.

The only solution, as I see it, is for food production and distribution to be organized within counties and fairly small districts.
Resources and expertise can be pooled on a scale that allows
face-to-face meetings between representatives of different cities and
towns, land will be available in and around cities to adapt for agriculture of various kinds, and most importantly, everyone in the
county can be fed so the violence of desperation is kept to a
minimum. If food and resources are scarce, of course, everyone can
be required to put in a certain amount of time doing some agricultural
work from time to time in order to be entitled to food, and foolproof
identification cards and record keeping will be important.

This may provide at least enough food for everyone in the area so nobody will starve. Then individuals, neighborhoods, and groups can do whatever they want to provide more and better food for themselves or for sale. And jobs will be created in local food processing (glass canning, solar drying, preparation, and so on) and distribution as we necessarily wean ourselves from unaccountable distant entities.

Where is all the money going to come from to create large-scale independent agricultural and distribution systems in every locality? In some areas, hard work will be the primary commodity, but a certain amount of equipment and supplies will be needed most places (perhaps more so in the more developed countries, where people are used to having things done for them on a huge scale, with gigantic equipment, far away). Lots of land will be needed, and lots of new greenhouses, cold frames, and "Wallo'Water"s.

The giant pension funds can help greatly. Wealthy folks may recognize that their own survival and self-worth will be maximized more by helping to build new community life than by holing up somewhere and trying to make it alone. But this may also be a golden opportunity for cooperative enterprises of all kinds, from small communal arrangements to block and neighborhood associations which organize food production and even preparation. It may be the opportunity we have needed to get back our long-lost sense of community and belonging.

## The ancient prophecies

A number of very old cultures produced prophecies about the time we are living in now. Hundreds or thousands of years ago, sometimes a gifted individual or the spiritual leaders of a nation were somehow able to envision what was coming, usually in broad outline and sometimes with uncanny exactness. (Perhaps some of their powers came from eating more complete food, grown on soil which had not been so depleted since the last ice age; and not having television, magazines, and shopping centers to be mesmerized by.)

Quatzalcoatl II was a Mayan spiritual leader who was born in 947 in what is now Mexico/Central America. The Mayan people had divided all of recorded history into five ages. The first four had ended by hunger, winds, fire, and water. The final age was to be divided into thirteen 52-year cycles of light and choice, called "the heavens," followed by nine 52-year cycles of increasing darkness, "the hells."

Quatzalcoatl II added several specific predictions of his own. He said that a man like him in appearance but not in spirit, light-complexioned and bearded, would come from the direction of the rising sun, on huge canoes with wings. Like himself, this man would wear a feathered plume on his head, and his clothes would shine like the sun.

More than 500 years later as predicted, in 1519 (on Good Friday), the Spaniard Hernando Cortez arrived with his armies in huge sailing vessels from the east. Light-skinned and bearded, he was dressed in shining armor, and wore a feather plume in his helmet. He attacked the Indian nation, which fought back courageously for almost two years but was finally defeated and destroyed. The nine hells had begun ("Cortez conquered Mexico," we were forced to memorize in school. Certainly one of the hells.)

In recent times, the eighth hell began in 1883, as the forces of nationalism started their inexorable drive toward the unprecedented horrors of World War I. The ninth and final hell began in 1935—the year Adolph Hitler broke the Versailles Peace Treaty and the world moved toward the even greater horrors of World War II, including the genocide of both the concentration camps and the first atomic bombs.

The ninth hell ended in 1987, presumably on August 16. Sometime after that, earthquakes, fire, and explosions are prophesied to reduce much of civilization to rubble, "melting the very elements with fervent heat." The intensity of humanity's suffering, however, is to depend on the choices it makes. This will be a time of supreme cleansing and purification, which can either be resisted or welcomed. Whatever the outcome, a new age of cooperation and peace will be born among those who survive.

The Tibetans have also long believed that history occurs in enormous cycles. They say we are now nearing the end of the 26,000-year cycle known as the Kali Yuga, the Dark Age. A great purification is coming, marked by cataclysm—but again, its severity will depend on how well people are able to overcome their ignorance and selfishness. Padmasambhava, the founder of Buddhism in Tibet more than a thousand years ago, specifically prophesied, "When the iron birds fly and the horses run on wheels, the Tibetan people will be scattered over the earth. . . ." In 1960 China attacked Tibet, and many people, including the Dalai Lama and other spiritual leaders, were forced to leave the country.

The word *Hopi* means "people of peace." The Hopi pueblos are thought to be the oldest continually inhabited villages on the North American continent. The sacred symbols of the Hopi culture are the sun and the swastika, the latter representing the spirals of energy sprouting from a seed in the four directions.

The ancient "gourd of ashes" prophecy stated that when humans misused material power, the peaceful symbols would be perverted and used to destroy. In the Second World War the sun was imperial Japan's symbol, the swastika Nazi Germany's. A "gourd full of ashes" would be invented which, if dropped from the sky, would boil the oceans and burn the land.

Ancient Hopi legends speak of "horseless chariots" that would roll along "black snakes" across the land, "cobwebs" through which people would speak over great distances, and "man-made houses" in the sky. When these things came to pass, and if the sacred symbols were misused, it was predicted that the Hopi ceremonial ground would be defiled. Now in the Four Corners area where the Hopi live, strip-mining of coal at Black Mesa, by powerful outside interests, goes on day and night. Hopi water is no longer pure, and a power plant fills the skies with black smoke. And the U.S. government, assisted by a young, naive Hopi tribal council it helped install in power against the wishes of the elders, is now removing many Navajos from lands they have been sharing with Hopis for centuries, with much resistance (the old Navajo women are leading the resistance), in order to more quickly get access to all the coal that lies beneath the Indians' feet. The law to relocate the Navajos against their wishes was explicitly passed by the U.S. Congress.

The next phase of the Hopi prophecies, 1980 to 2000, foresees great confusion, famines, and natural catastrophes such as earthquakes and tidal waves—all as part of the necessary purification. Again, how severe this purification will be depends on whether humanity chooses to resist or to be transformed.

Many other Indian tribes have long predicted the coming of a Great Purification. A hundred years ago the Mesquakie nation prophesized a box that would sit in a corner, in which people would see things happening far away. They said that when that happened the animals would be dying. And when many species were becoming extinct, the earth would revolt against its inhumane treatment and create great earthquakes and floods.

This is the message sent by Chief Seattle, of the region which is now the state of Washington, to President Pierce in 1854, reluctantly agreeing to sell his people's ancestral lands:

> How can you buy or sell the sky, the warmth of the land? ... If we do not own the freshness of the air and the sparkle of the water, how can you buy them?
>
> Every part of the earth is sacred to my people. Every shining pine needle, every sandy shore, every mist in the dark woods, every clearing and humming insect is holy in the memory and experience of my people.... We are part of the earth and it is part of us....
>
> We know that the white man does not understand our ways ... he is a stranger who comes in the night and takes from the land whatever he needs ... and when he has conquered it, he moves on.... I do not know. Our ways are different from your ways. The sight of your cities pains the eyes of a red man. But perhaps it is because the red man is a savage and does not understand.
>
> There is no quiet place in the white man's cities. No place to hear the unfurling leaves in spring, or the rustle of an insect's wings.... The white man does not seem to notice the air he breathes. Like a man dying for many days, he is numb to the stench....
>
> I have seen a thousand buffaloes on the prairie, left by the white man who shot them from a passing train.... Whatever befell the earth befalls the sons of the earth....

This we know: The earth does not belong to man; man belongs to the earth. This we know. All things are connected like the blood which unites one family. All things are connected.... Man did not weave the web of life: he is merely a strand in it. Whatever he does to the web, he does to himself....

One thing we know, which the white man may one day discover—our God is the same God. You may think that you own Him as you wish to own your land; but you cannot.... This earth is precious to Him, and to harm the earth is to heap contempt on its Creator....

And now this message comes from the Native American community, via the newspaper of the Mohawk nation, *Akwesasne Notes:*

The prophecies and vision of our grandfathers are upon us. The The Chief of Trees, the Maple, is dying from the top down as we were told would happen ... tornadoes have multiplied and visited the four directions.... Etenohah, the Earth we call Mother, has tears running down her face; great floods and rains are everywhere and people are running about in fear and confusion. The Earth has shaken herself ... and mountains are stirring, smoking, sailing their powers over the lands.... These are the powers the Great Spirit has put here to work in harmony with people through prayer, ceremony, and respect.... We have failed, and we are being warned.

We must heed the warnings being visited upon the earth. The drumbeats of our hearts will cease and we shall have destroyed what we are sworn to protect, and there will be no life or future for our children.

# *A new beginning, or The End?*

*"El pueblo, unido*
*Jamas sera vencido."*
*(The people, united,*
*Will never be defeated.)*

—Chilean Revolutionary Slogan

> *"Standing apart from the slagheap of*
> *gutless conformity."*
>
> —AD FOR NONESUCH RECORDS

We are always surprised when the garbage we forgot to take out begins to stink.

This crisis has been coming for a long time. Chief Seattle and many others who lived close to the land saw it more than a hundred years ago, but it has been building ever since the expansion of our numbers began using up the forests and our thoughtless practices began polluting the streams. Long before these climatic changes began to move toward crisis and irreversibility, thousands of conservationists and ecologists were trying to show us what we were doing to our home, usually with little success.

Infinite greed and lust for power were inexorable—and all of us have been implicated to some degree. Which of us has not craved More, and gotten as much as we could? How many of us have become involved in the struggle to stop the destruction, the pollution, the desecration of all that has been entrusted to us? This life or death crisis is shocking, but it should not have been unexpected. Things are just catching up with us sooner than we thought they would.

Biospheric chemist James Lovelock has developed a theory he called the "Gaia hypothesis" (Gaia rhymes with papaya): that the planet Earth is a living organism—Gaia—which maintains itself between certain narrow limits of temperature and other variables to provide an optimum environment for life. More than 20 such variables (the temperature of the air, the salinity of the oceans, the presence of certain gases in the atmosphere, etc., have already been identified. The composition of the atmosphere is among the most crucial of these—Lovelock calls it "the circulatory system of the biosphere" (all life on earth), and has attempted to show that life can regulate the atmosphere to keep it hospitable to life.

The way our species has not only massively destroyed so many other forms of life on this planet, but has finally learned how to begin destroying the very atmosphere itself, suggests that our kind may have become a kind of cancer in Gaia, a threat to the stability of the whole Earth-organism. And that the Earth may be about to rid itself of us.

The ice age alone wouldn't do it, of course. A small percentage of us would survive, perhaps millions, and if past history is any example, these and their descendants would most likely go on to destroy us again, limited only by the power of their technology.

What may well get rid of us, however, is the worldwide nuclear war which may come in the next few years from the most unimaginable competition for rapidly dwindling food supplies. The USSR, one of the two nuclear giants, has been unable to produce all its own grain for the past decade because it sits so far north and has little agricultural land in the warmer temperate regions. As this is being written, a television commentator has announced this evening that Moscow and Scandinavia are experiencing the coldest winter in all their recorded history. Is Gorbachev going to sit quietly by and let his people starve to death while the U.S. and other countries are still eating, or is he going to demand sharing of whatever is left? Are France, or Britain, or the U.S., or any of the other nuclear powers whose farmlands become unable to grow food going to allow others to keep on eating?

If we manage to depart the scene, Gaia will survive very well without us—she did for billions of years before we showed up. And she may very well produce other species as complex and elegant as we are, but with more respect for this home, for the rules of the game. The cockroaches will survive us, in any event. Nuclear radiation doesn't seem to affect them.

Are you ready to give up your body, and in a most painful way? Can you picture the earth without us?

> *"If you don't like the news,*
> *go out and make some of your own."*
>
> —Radio Commentator "Scoop" Nisker

If we want to survive we are going to have to quickly become an asset to Gaia. We have a lot of work to do. Even without this immediate crisis, our rape of the world in which we live probably

could not have gone on many more decades without our whole way
of life crashing to the ground. Daniel Arap Moi, president of Kenya:

> Because of thoughtless development, over-exploitation, mass pov-
> erty and infinite malpractices, havoc has spread across the natural
> environment. There is no doubt whatsoever that continuation of
> the current trends will lead to total collapse....
>   ... the key factors in human salvation can only be political
> will.... The needs are immense, and beyond talking in comfortable
> arenas, will require taking coats off and getting honorably dirty.

"Let the punishment fit the crime" is an old idea. An ice age
might be thought to be a fitting end for a species that has abused
and wasted energy in every conceivable way, from clearcutting
forests, from burning trees without even replacing them, from
gas-guzzling cars to that unspeakable obscenity, the endless black
hole of the nuclear arms race. It seems entirely appropriate that we
don't have any other planet to go to, now that we've almost ruined
this one. It's a tough way to learn that everything and all of us are
connected, but it seems to be the only way most of us learn.

The imminent ice age can be looked at as a much-needed kick in
the pants from Mother Nature. A very swift kick if we don't feel it
now and get off our asses pretty fast. If we're not here to learn, to
grow, to evolve, we're nothing, and we might as well get out of the way.

This ultimate crisis, plus the increasing threat of a nuclear holocaust, also seems to be pretty powerful evidence that we need a
stronger United Nations. Not a world government, which could turn
out to be oppressive, but a UN with sufficient power to regulate
activities that truly threaten our survival on this planet—activities
like polluting our common environment and building weapons that
have the power to blow all of us away.

> *"When you look into an abyss,*
> *The abyss looks into you."*
>
> —FRIEDRICH NIETZSCHE

Some will say, "We've already manipulated and interfered with nature
too much. If the ice age is due, we shouldn't try to stop it. Let it

take its course. If most of the human race dies in the process, that is what nature intends. It will be a necessary cleansing." Some who call themselves Christians even welcome such an apocalypse, speaking of Armageddon.

Much could be said in response to that point of view. One answer is the words of a poster at High Hopes School in Burlingame, California, obviously written against the nuclear arms race: "A child is God's opinion the the world should go on."

Christians who look forward to mass death may wish to remember these words: "I have set before you life and death, blessing and curse; therefore choose life, that you and your descendants may live."

My answer (I've only recently begun to live—that is, live without pervasive fear) is that simply in order to do what we have to do to stop the ice ages—feed the earth, plant billions of life-giving trees, learn to live without polluting life's common environment so badly— we will have evolved to a higher level of consciousness, and we will have earned the right to be here.

Many people wonder *why* we're here, what the meaning of life is. I can't tell you. But I'll betcha that throwing yourself into this struggle with your heart and soul will help you find out a lot about that. And will transform you into a new person—more who you really are.

I would not even be surprised if the process of coming to grips with this threat to our common survival were to be the key to ending the nuclear arms race insanity. Or if the institutions that help us make the transition from a fossil-fuel-guzzling species to one that learns how to make do with renewable energy were the prototypes of the institutions that will allow us finally to convert the factories of death into factories for life.

The great agriculturalist and philosopher Rudolph Steiner came to believe that humanity is unable to rise to a higher spiritual level because it does not have the necessary physical sustenance. Writing as early as 1924, he said:

> Nutrition as it is today does not supply the strength necessary for manifesting the spirit in physical life.... Food plants no longer

contain the forces people need for this.... The time will come when the people of the Earth will starve in the midst of plenty.

So we come full circle. Starving for minerals and other nutrients in our food, perhaps our normal cravings thus become insatiable: for meat, for energy, for all the world's resources, for power and control over everything.

Maybe then there *is* a way out of this labyrinth: minerals, truly nourishing food, sharing ideas, building working/caring communities, developing our bodies and our minds, finding our strength, and taking back our power. Creating truly democratic, decentralized societies that will sustain us the same way they sustain the world.

## *Taking back our power*

> *"One's real life is often the life that one does not lead."*
>
> —OSCAR WILDE

> *"We are stardust, we are golden,*
> *And we've got to get ourselves*
> *Back to the Garden."*
>
> —JONI MITCHELL

We have been programmed to accept things as they are. To do our jobs, get our little piece of the action, and keep our mouths shut.

We're taught to behave ourselves. To go along, not make trouble, not ask too many questions. As Ralph Nader says, "We are told that freedom is if you don't like the program you can turn it off." We've been "bought off," as Marian Kester puts it, "by a few miserable gadgets we call our 'Standard of Living'."

And so we retreat, into many escapes. Into egotism, and the

macho illusion of invulnerability which leads so many young men to their tragic deaths, and the world to the brink of nuclear holocaust.

We escape into work, into success, status, being somehow better than the next guy, the other race, the other country. Into passivity, like alcohol and constant entertainment. And into isolation, masks, keeping up a good front. Richard Pryor says, "People don't talk to each other at all, no matter what color they are."

And into cynicism. It's almost necessary to be cynical in modern societies, to try to get some perspective on all the lies and threats we sense around us. As Harry Frankfurt, chairman of the department of philosophy at Yale University, points out, "One of the most salient features of our culture is that there is so much bullshit. Everyone knows this." But Lily Tomlin reminds us that "No matter how cynical you become, it's never enough to keep up."

And yet we keep going along with the system that keeps us down, that dehumanizes us, that threatens us with death every day. Are we simply afraid to speak up? Or was Dostoyevsky right when he said, "There is only one thing people love more than freedom, and that is slavery."

> *"Still—in a way—nobody sees
> a flower—really—it is so
> small—we haven't time...."*
> —Georgia O'Keeffe

> *"Extinction howls outside the door."*
> —John Seed

To be or not to be, that's the question. Not what do you want to be, but how much do you want to be? And how alive do you want to be? The state motto of New Hampshire is "Live free or die." It's on all the license plates.

That is what it's coming down to. We have to step outside our accustomed roles, our comfortable routines, our predictable days, or we're just not going to be here much longer.

It's not as hard as it may look. We were free once, maybe only for a short time, but really free: when we were little kids. In fact the kid in each of us may be the only part that is really alive. The great sculptor Brancusi said, "When we are no longer children, we are already dead." Is your kid still there? Hi, kid.

How do we become alive, free little kids again? Just by *letting go,* taking off the brakes—our bodies are *screaming* to break free. All we have to do is *allow* ourselves the freedom, by seeing things a little differently than we've been taught. Stephen Levine: "... there is nowhere to go and nothing to have and nothing to be—and that's freedom." (And *with* that awareness, are there any changes you've been wanting to make in your life? About the job you're no longer getting satisfaction from, the relationship that's no longer meaningful enough, what you want to do with your money, and so on. This would be a good time, here on the edge of the abyss.)

Thomas Paine, American revolutionary, 1776: "We have it in our power to begin the world again." Thomas Jefferson, third president of the United States, speaking of the success of the American War of Independence which we celebrate on the 4th of July: *"The revolution began in the minds of the people."*

Neil Young said it well: "Be on my side, I'll be on your side." And "It's gonna take a lot of love to get us through the night.... "

Colin Wilson had a suggestion: "A trick I recommend ... is just to look at everything as if you were seeing it for the last time...."

The key to our survival is how much we can feel now. Feeling the fear, even the despair as it comes, is essential. Feelings are one of the surest signs that you're alive.

Patricia Ellsberg:

> Don't polarize hope and despair.... Just be open, fully aware. That is the scariness of this time. If you let it flow, if you let that flow—those impacted feelings of despair—you'll see that the energy starts coming.

Joanna Macy:

> I believe we're not born into a world and given a situation we can't
> handle.... We're up to it. But it's very scary, because you don't
> know how.

John Steiner:

> It's okay for men to express their feelings and their own emotions
> and outrage and even hysteria about these issues, ways of feeling
> and expression that have been said to be the way women react
> .... And it is the entering of how we *feel* about this stuff, not just
> how we think about it or intuit about it or dream about it, which
> is part, I think, of the solution.

Helen Caldicott:

> Every single one of us can be as powerful as the most powerful
> person on the planet.... We are put here, I believe, by God, to
> save the planet. No other generation has had such a responsibility
> placed on its shoulders....
>
> And you know it's the most joyous thing to work together to
> do this. It unites everybody: rich and poor, black and white,
> Russians and Americans.... And if we don't spiritually evolve now
> ... we're not going to make it.

Power to the people and the trees! Power to the microorganisms
and the rocks! Power to the farmers! Power to the tree planters and
remineralizers, the methanol makers and solar energy developers!
Power to every beautiful form of life, to life itself.

We're got an enormous job to do, and very little time. In
the name of love and music, of rivers and stringbeans, of heartbeats
and breath, of tears and swearing and everything that's holy, let's get
on with it.

## NOTES TO CHAPTER FOUR

1. Responding to the pressure of a nationwide boycott, Burger King recently (July 1987) agreed to stop buying Central American beef. But I don't trust them for a minute, or any of the fast-food restaurants that have always denied they buy it. It is known that 90% of rainforest cattle end up as American hamburgers, mostly in fast-food places. If nobody is buying it now, where is it going? And who's going to repay all those World Bank loans that set the cattlemen up in business? It doesn't make any sense to think that the fast-food places have really stopped.

2. Brazil contains the single largest remaining rainforest in the world in the Amazon river basin, called Amazonia. The Brazilian government has recently launched a vast mining project called Grande Carajas (carajas are a type of howling monkey, and a group of Indian tribes threatened with extinction). It would displace one-sixth of the entire Amazon rainforest with huge mines and dams. Tucurui Dam, already under construction, would flood 800 square miles of forest (*Newsweek,* February 18, 1985).

3. The World Bank was stung by widespread criticism of its environmentally destructive policies recently—like rainforest road building and other development, which led to the relocation of thousands of poor farmers who subsequently found the land would not support them for more than a few years. Critics asserted that its lending programs often destroyed the very natural systems that are essential to sustained development, like forests, watersheds and farmlands. The Environmental Defense Fund says that 17 congressional hearings have documented the World Bank's negligence in the past few years.

    The bank recently announced that environmental concerns would become central, and that the 17 staff people responsible for environmental issues would be increased to 100. I think this is just window dressing. The World Bank and other big development banks are not going to stop funding their hugely profitable ventures, like giant dams, deforestation for lumber and cattle ranching, and the transformation of small family farms into large-scale export-crop farms. That's what they do, that's what brings them the big returns on their money. They lend $20 billion every year, followed by another $40 billion each year from other lending institutions. They're hardly going to stop because a few people have gotten upset.

    We're facing an enormous political battle. A life and death struggle.

4. The U.S. even contains a rainforest, the Tongass National Forest in Alaska, the last great temperate-zone rainforest on the planet. It is being steadily destroyed by two giant logging companies that hold 50-year timber contracts with the U.S. Forest Service and get $50 million in direct government subsidies each year for cutting down the trees. The Forest Service is losing

99¢ on the dollar. The Alaskan fishing industry says that logging in the Tongass is destroying salmon-spawning streams, the local population says it's destroying the wildlife. Senator Proxmire and Congressman Mrazek have proposed a bill to sharply reduce logging in the Tongass.

5. Many other good ideas can be found in Malcolm Margolin's handbook, *The Earth Manual: How to work on wild land without taming it* (1985).

6. The three or four tons per acre is an approximate figure. In areas where the soil has already become extremely acid, five or more tons may be needed (some will go toward buffering the soil, some toward restoring very weakened trees).

7. Robert Schindele is an Austrian manufacturer of wood veneers. In 1980 he built a small logging road through a square mile of woods he owns near Grimsing on the Danube River. He excavated rock from a hillside on his property and had it spread on the road bed. Heavy equipment ground some of it to powder, which high summer winds blew onto parts of the forest next to the road. Schindele, well aware of *waldsterben* (forest-death), noticed about four weeks later that the spruces in the areas covered by the fine rock dust—whose needles, like the trees on all of his property, had been turning increasingly yellow—were turning back to a healthy dark green. Thirteen acres of trees were coming back to life. During the next four years they continued to improve.

Schindele ground up more of the rocks for experiments. He planted 1000 larch trees on a treeless tract of land that he was told had very poor soil, and remineralized 10% with his *gesteinmehl* (stone-meal). The untreated trees were viciously attacked by trunk chafers. The remineralized trees were almost untouched.

Schindele began trying to get government officials to see how the forests of Europe could be saved. He did things like bringing a group of officials and scientists out to the woods. A professional forester said, "Now, Herr Schindele, here you have a fine example of a dying tree. If you can bring it back to life with your method, I'll kneel down and kiss its roots ... and your feet!" The following week Schindele and his associates removed the ground cover around the tree and applied 40 kilos (about 18 pounds) of stone meal to the area over the roots, then replaced the ground cover, and watered the tree well. They brought the forester back within *three weeks*, and he had to admit the tree had darker, fresher needles than the other trees around it. Now, he reneged, however, he said he would only kiss Schindele's feet if the tree survived the winter and was alive the following year.

Giles Petitpierre, a member of the Swiss Federal Parliament, reportedly began experiments with rock dust in November 1985. Other stories of European efforts to get governments interested in remineralization have been going around for some time. So far, however, no government agency seems to have begun remineralizing forest lands in a major way.

For this information from Europe I am indebted to Christopher Bird, who is completing a book that will include this material. He may be contacted at 3414 N Street NW, Washington DC 20007. (202) 338-3839.

8. Hamaker says that remineralizing tropical soils will eventually soften up the shallow rock-hard layer of congealed minerals called laterite which often lies just 4 to 6 inches below the surface and makes many tropical soils difficult to grow any crops on. Soil physicist Rattan Lal said "The only thing you could do with laterite is dynamite it" (*New York Times*, January 18, 1987).

9. The Federal Clean Air Act mandates certain limits on urban pollution. Denver has had a terrible smog problem in recent years, especially in winter. So the Colorado Air Quality Control Commission recently began requiring that "oxygenated fuels" (these include ethanol, methanol, and MTBE, an ether compound made from oil) be added to gasoline during the winter only. There have been some complaints that adding ethanol can sometimes cause some problems in hot weather, like a clogged fuel line or vapor lock. Dan Fong at the California Energy Commission tells me that these are problems peculiar to mixing oxygenated with petroleum fuels—they don't mix that well, in spite of detergents that are being added these days, and air bubbles sometimes form and cause problems. He says that problems do not occur with pure methanol and ethanol fuels, or with mixed fuels in cars which have been slightly modified.

10. Hyman Gesser, a chemist at the University of Manitoba, recently announced the development of what he calls a cheap, one-step process to make methanol from natural gas. Department of Chemistry, University of Manitoba, R3T 2N2, Canada. (204) 474-8880.

It's probably not going to be that easy to phase out gasoline, unfortunately. Diana Johnstone, writing in the newsweekly *In These Times*, suggests that gasoline prices are as high as they are because the U.S. government has arranged a secret deal with the Middle East oil-exporting countries such as Iraq and Iran that we will pay higher prices for this oil if they buy their military weapons from us. The former democratic president of Iran, Abolhassan Bani-Sadr, deduced from budget figures that the huge arms sales had to be barter deals—oil for arms. The Western oil companies have the power to keep oil prices lower, but then the Western arms merchants wouldn't be able to make as much money selling their wares. It costs Iran $5 a barrel to produce oil, and Western oil companies have recently agreed to pay $18 a barrel for the foreseeable future. "Oil specialists were surprised by the announcement," the *New York Times* reported. One said, "I've called several of the companies today, and I found that officials at very high levels were very surprised by the news" (February 4, 1987).

Though Reagan has put American flags on Kuwaiti oil tankers to keep the oil flowing from the Persian Gulf, the United States and other Western countries have a stake in keeping wars going and tensions high in the Middle East—to maintain a lucrative and ongoing market for Western-made weapons of war.

The real nature of international politics is suggested in the following horror story. Christopher Hitchens wonders (*The Nation*, June 20 and July 4/11, 1987) why Reagan shipped a planeload of arms to Iran in July 1981 when there were no longer any hostages being held. Perhaps, he suggests, it was a deal made the previous year, not to release hostages but *to keep them captive longer*—until Jimmy Carter was safely voted out of office, in large part over the unresolved hostage situation. "Keep the hostages until we have won, and we will supply you with weapons when we take power." If Carter had succeeded in getting the hostages released before the election it "would have vindicated Carter's Rose Garden diplomacy and presumably secured him a second term." The hostages were released just a few weeks after Carter was voted out, *on the day Reagan was inaugurated*. Hitchens presents considerable evidence in support of this scenario. He says "Congress should start asking about the original sin in which this whole bloody administration was conceived."

The point here is that enormously powerful interests are at stake in these questions of energy use, interests which may stop at nothing—including the death of most of the people in the world in the coming ice age—to retain their power and profits. (One might think that their profits would be considerably reduced if most of their customers starved to death, but they probably don't think that far ahead. Or perhaps they would simply plan to raise the price of gas to make up for the loss of profits.)

However, there's no reason we can't make it as easy as possible for the oil companies to move into renewable fuels, in order to secure their help and cooperation. Ethanol and methanol have to be refined, and they have refining equipment that can do a lot of it. Their profits might decrease some, but it needn't be a question of putting them out of business or their putting most everyone else out of business. If they put their resources behind the transition, we can accomplish it that much faster, with the greatest likelihood of survival for all of us.

11. Besides reducing the threat of nuclear war in the Persian Gulf, eliminating our dependence on fossil fuels could have other security benefits. Hal Harvey, director of the Rocky Mountain Institute's Security Program, says, "By promoting renewable energy systems in the Third World, we could eliminate many nations' pretexts for acquiring nuclear reactors" and thereby the means for acquiring nuclear weapons.

12. Here is a chart of the past, present, and projected future world oil production. Dozens of economic and geologic variables were fed into a computer at the University of New Hampshire's Complex Systems Research Center to estimate future production. It shows that we're going to run out of oil

anyway in only about three decades, in spite of continued exploration, because we've simply used up the world's oil. It was estimated that the United States would be virtually out of oil by the year 2020, only about 30 years away.

Seems like it would be a shame for us to die for it now, doesn't it?

**FIGURE 15**

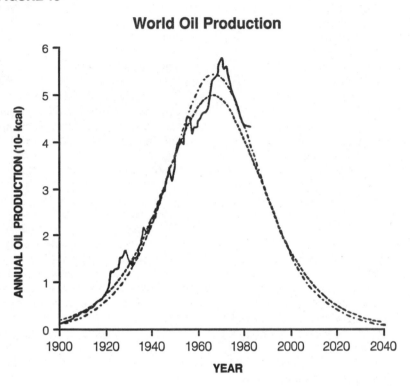

## World Oil Production

Source: *Beyond Oil*, from Carrying Capacity, Inc., 1325 G St. NW, Suite 1003, Washington D. C. 20005.

13. Similar to Philip Abelson's projection, A. Barrie Pittock (1983) of Australia's CSIRO research group recently wrote: "Permanent storage of $CO_2$ in increased biomass, e.g., huge standing forests, could, with a major world reforestation effort, store perhaps 10 or 20 years' worth of global fossil fuel production." With remineralization, the world reforestation effort might produce new forests which would eventually store 60 to 80 years' worth of fossil fuel production, taking us well back from the brink that our unwitting fossil fuel burning has brought us to. Remineralization of existing forests will give us even more security, and the combined effort will stave off the next ice age indefinitely.

14. In 1977 at a meeting in Nairobi, 94 nations agreed to mount a massive campaign to stop the spread of deserts, by changing grazing and irrigation practices, moderating firewood use, and so forth. Ten years later the UN reported that there was "not a single success story to be found." A program which would cost $90 billion was outlined, with expected economic benefits of more than $500 billion. Yet only $6 billion was actually spent, and deserts continued to encroach on millions of acres of arable land a year. The intimate knowledge of local people about varieties of plants was ignored. The director of the UN's Environment Program said, "Our problem is we have been working too much with governments. Bureaucrats don't go out into the field." An advisor to the program said "an overwhelming majority of antidesertification projects actually promote desertification" (*San Francisco Chronicle,* February 18, 1987, p. 4).

And on another ominous note, industry opponents of acid rain legislation were the largest spenders among all U.S. Capitol Hill lobbyists in 1986. They are financed largely by electricity and coal companies. A House bill to control acid rain that began with 160 sponsors eventually died in committee. A Senate bill never even came up for a committee vote (*New York Times,* June 1, 1987).

These are the kinds of things we're up against.

15. Reagan's Interior Secretary Donald Hodel has proposed tearing down the dam that created California's Hetch Hetchy reservoir many years ago which supplies water to San Francisco, in order to restore the beautiful valley near Yosemite that it filled. Whatever the merits of such a proposal might be in a more secure and stable world (and I'm very suspicious of anything that environment-wrecker Reagan's interior secretary would propose), it clearly makes no sense in the context of the potentially imminent climatic devastation to come.

# Appendix: Access

Larry Ephron (E-fron), director of the Institute for a Future, a tax-exempt, nonprofit educational corporation. I have also produced and directed a documentary film on this material, *Stopping the Coming Ice Age*, which presents the story in a very condensed, easy-to-understand form, suitable for fourth-graders to adults; and a great deal of exciting, visible evidence of remineralization and the people involved in it on several continents.

*Stopping the Coming Ice Age*, an hour-long film, is available in the following formats: VHS and Beta ($20 to individuals, $65 to organizations); ¾" tape ($145); and on 16mm film ($625). It is also available in 1" for broadcast, and minus the narration for foreign language dubbing.

Quantity discounts on this book are also available through the Institute:

      1 to 10 copies at $7.50 each
      11 to 25 copies at $7.00 each
      26 to 50 copies at $6.75 each
      51 or more copies at $6.50 each

All prices are plus any applicable taxes. Please add $2.00 to each complete order for postage and handling. Mail or phone orders. Major credit cards, institutional purchase orders accepted. (Credit cards please include correct name, and expiration date.)

You can also become a member of the Institute and receive periodic updates of new information, ideas and resources that maximize our chances of survival. Membership is tax-deductible, $20/year.

Tax-deductible contributions of any amount to further the work of the Institute for a Future are warmly welcomed. They will be used to publicize the film and this book worldwide, to help organize the worldwide effort to stop the coming ice age, and for other health-related and environmental projects including a nutritional approach to healing AIDS.

Institute for a Future, 2000 Center Street, Berkeley, CA 94704, USA. 1-800-441-7707. In California, (415) 524-2700.

John Hamaker, Route 1, Box 158, Seymour, MO USA. (417) 935-2116. He should get the Nobel Prize. Copies of his and Don Weaver's book, *The Survival of Civilization,* may be ordered from him at $12 (quantity discounts start at three books). It contains some important material not covered in this book, especially some of John's writings on the tectonic system (including a geological explanation for the Bermuda Triangle anomalies) and on economics, plus rich observations and additional evidence on soil demineralization and the deterioration of our environment.

John is a poor farmer now, and not in the best of health after many years working in the oil and chemical industries. He's too proud and self-sufficient to want any help, but I feel he deserves enormous gratitude from all of us, and think we should give him some help he can't refuse. If thousands of us were each to put a $5 or $10 bill in an envelope and send it to him—with no return address, or he'll simply mail it back—I think he might figure out a way to use it to become a little more comfortable in his old age, maybe even do a little more research. (But don't tell him I suggested it.)


Don Weaver, coauthor of the Hamaker book. Also publisher of the "Solar Age or Ice Age? Bulletin," which has been updating the evidence for the past few years and contains more of John's writings on the tectonic system and so on, and the contributions of people all over the world. Copies of the Hamaker-Weaver book may also be ordered from Don at the same price and discounts. Box 1961, Burlingame, CA 94010, USA. (415) 342-0329. As of this writing he's looking for land in northern California and the funds to create a demonstration farm and do controlled studies to show the dramatic differences that adding gravel dust makes in both quantity and quality of crops.


John Hamaker has designed simple gravel grinders which grind rock against rock. He says that his 'rocker box' design, which is sketched below, can be built cheaply and easily by any machine shop. His rotary grinder, which is more efficient but somewhat more difficult to build, was patented many years ago but is now in the public domain. Plans can be obtained from the U.S. Patent Office (Patent No. 3,552,660).

Here is his rocker box grinder:

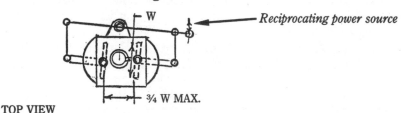

TOP VIEW

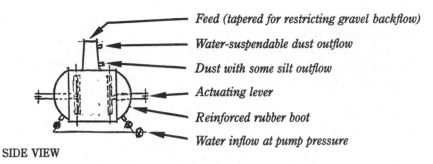

Feed (tapered for restricting gravel backflow)

Water-suspendable dust outflow

Dust with some silt outflow

Actuating lever

Reinforced rubber boot

Water inflow at pump pressure

SIDE VIEW

The actuating levers can be connected to synchronizing cylinders or tied together with the linkage shown. The box can be rectangular or cylindrical. A useful small grinder might have 18″ square plates with 12″ between them, though they can be made quite large. The box should allow for a minimum of 2″ inactive compacted gravel around the sides of the chamber. Adjustable flanges at the corners of the chamber are set at a distance of 0.005 from the moving edge of the plates. The water outflow goes to a 2-compartment settling pit, and is recirculated.

Flange

.005

TOP VIEW
(DETAIL)

## HAMAKER RESOURCE PEOPLE

These are people throughout the world who are knowledgeable about the work of John Hamaker and qualified to speak on various aspects of it.

Joanna Campe, publisher of "Soil Remineralization: A network newsletter." She helped facilitate the filming in Europe. The newsletter often has information on where to find gravel, grinding and gravel dust, and coordinates a loose network of people involved in soil remineralization worldwide. 152 South Street, Northampton, MA 01060, USA. (413) 586-4429.

Betsan Coats, 8 Kate Street, Alexandra Headland, Queensland 4527, Australia. Betsan has probably talked about remineralization to more people on more continents than anyone else. A friend of the late Richard St.Barbe Baker, founder of Men of the Trees.

Through Betsan you can contact Charles Peaty, a founder of Men of the Trees in western Australia, who has invented a mechanical tree planter with which two people can plant 500 trees an hour.

Maria Felsenreich, Hochwaldstrasse 37, A-2230 Ganserndorf-Sud, Austria. Telephone (0043) (022) 82 72 60. The main crusader for remineralization in Europe.

Renate Meier, 71 avenue Bois-Chappelle, CH-1214 ONEX (Geneva), Switzerland.

David Miller, Department of Biology, Oberlin College, Oberlin OH 44074, USA.

Dick Hogan, The Woolman Institute, Wilmington College, Wilmington, OH 45177, USA. (513) 382-2036.

Alden Bryant, Earth Regeneration Society, 470 Vassar Avenue, Berkeley, CA 94708, USA. (415) 525-4877.

Fred Wood, Earth Regeneration Society, 2346 Lansford, San Jose, CA 95125, USA. (408) 269-9327.

Vivian Menaker, Box 118, Haines, Alaska 99827, USA.

Ian Phillips, Little Meadow, Droride Land, Dartington, Totnes, Devon, England.

Mark Fielden, 182 Holland Road, London W14 8AH, England.

Kay Hubble, 10 Embankment Gardens, London SW3 4LJ, England.

Eileen Noakes, Three Ways, Ringmore, Nr. Knightsbridge, Devon PQ7 4HL, England.

Harold Lane, 20 Fresherin Point, Isle of Lewis, PA86 OHE, Western Isles, Scotland.

Haydn Jones, Glasfryn, Valley Road, Llanfairfechan, Gwynedd, Wales, UK.

Edmundo Kandler, Apto 2569, 1000 San Jose, Costa Rica.

Carlos Avclinc, Rua Thomaz 133, apto 202, 93000 Sao Leopoldo RS, Brazil.

Maria Noemi Molina, Las Heras 1133, 5600 San Rafael, Argentina.

Nilam Pandey, Box 3485, Links, Khatmandu, Nepal.

Sri S. Krishnamurthy, Shanti Kuntgo, VI Main-V Block, Jayanagar, Bangalore, India 560041.

Geshe Achok Rinpoche, The Tibetan Library, Dharamsala, Kangra Drive, HP 176215, India. (For Tibet)

Vernon Lawrence, Environs Management Systems, GPO Box 473D, Melbourne 3001, Victoria, Australia.

Jeannie Stevens, RMB 1105, Wodonga 3961, Victoria, Australia.

Chris Farmer, 14 Silica Street, Lightning Ridge, NSW 2830, Australia.

Cheri Foale, c/o Post Office, Aldinga Beach, SA 5173, Australia.

Keith Gray, Nagakuru, R.D.I., Rotorua, New Zealand.

C.A. Bunton, Box 22023 N3, Kloofsig 0034, Pretoria, South Africa.

Stuart Johnstone, 13 Lincoln Way, Meadow Ridge, Capetown 7800, South Africa.

## CLIMATOLOGISTS WHO CAN BE ASKED TO EVALUATE THIS MATERIAL

These are mainstream scientists, some of whom have expressed strong support for this theory and grave concern about its implications; the others have published research which seems to support the theory, and appear to be fair-minded, objective, and not completely locked into a competing approach such as the Milankovitch orbital theory or computer modeling.

Wibjörn Karlén, University of Stockholm, Stockholm, Sweden.

Pierre Lehman, Société de l'étude de l'environment, Rue du Midi 33, 1800 Vevey, Switzerland. Tel. 021/51 05 15.

Kenneth Watt, University of California, Davis, California 95616, USA. (916) 752-1558.

Sir H. H. Lamb, University of East Anglia, Norwich NR4 7TJ, England. Tel. Norwich 56161.

Svend Th. Andersen, Geobotanical Department, Geological Survey of Denmark, Thoravej 31, DK-2400, Copenhagen NV, Denmark.

Victor Kovda, Institute of Soil Science and Photosynthesis, USSR Academy of Sciences, Puschino, Moscow Region 142292, USSR.

Paul Gersper, Department of Plant and Soil Biology, University of California, Berkeley, CA 94704, USA. (415) 642-6000.

Margaret Davis, Department of Ecology and Behavioral Biology, University of Minnesota, 318 Church Street, Minneapolis, MN 55455, USA.

Ian Whillans, Ohio State University, 125 S. Oval Mall, Columbus, OH 43210, USA. (614) 292-6446.

E. Roeckner, Meteorologisches Institut der Universitat Hamburg, D-2000 Hamburg 13, Federal Republic of Germany.

J. Biercamp, Max-Planck Institut fur Meteorologie, D-2000 Hamburg 13, Federal Republic of Germany.

C. Bertrand Schultz, Nebraska Academy of Sciences, Lincoln, Nebraska, USA.

Gregg Marland, Oak Ridge Associated Universities, Box 117, Oak Ridge, TN 37830, USA.

Ralph Rotty, Institute for Energy Analysis, Oregon State University, Corvallis, OR 97323, USA.

Charles Bentley, Geophysical and Polar Research Center, University of Wisconsin, 1215 Dayton Street, Madison, WI 53706, USA. (608) 262-1234.

Reginald Newell, Massachusetts Institute of Technology, 77 Massachusetts Avenue, Cambridge, MA 02139, USA.

Ray Bradley, Department of Geology and Geography, University of Massachusetts, Amherst, MA 01103, USA.

George Woodwell, Woods Hole Research Center, Box 296, Woods Hole, MA 02543, USA.

James Lovelock, Coombe Mill, St Giles on the Heath, Launceston, Cornwall PL15 9RY, England.

## SOURCES OF GLACIAL GRAVEL, GRINDERS AND DUST

Check with local gravel pits. Ask if they have glacial or mixed gravel dust, or crusher screenings from mixed gravel, and how fine it is (how much will go through 200 mesh), and can they grind it finer. If it's only one-sixth dust, for example, add six times as much. Cement kiln dust is another possibility; check with cement manufacturers.

To check a sample of dust for fineness, fill a glass about half full of dust and cover with about 2 inches of water. Shake vigorously and let it settle overnight. You can see the relative proportions of fine dust and coarser sand.

Plans for Hamaker's very efficient rotary grinder that grinds rock against rock can be obtained from the US Patent Copy Exchange Service, 519 Congress St., Portland, ME 04101, USA. (207) 773-8463. $5.00 should be enough. The patent number is 3,552,660. Unfortunately his patent expired just a few months ago. Manufacturers who profit from his design might feel like sending him a contribution anyway (unmarked bills, no return address or he'll probably return it).

A new rock crusher which uses sound waves is being developed in Australia. It uses less energy and minimizes wear on machine parts. Interested manufacturers, distributors, and customers can contact P.J. McDougall, Sonic Technology Australia Ltd., Unit 3, 97 Lewis Road, Wantirna South 3152, Victoria, Australia. Phone (3) 222-2974.

*On forests:* About 3 tons of finely ground dust per acre (1,900 tons per square mile). Where the soil is already very acid, add more dust, and 1 part limestone to every 3 parts dust.

*On farmland:* About 10 tons per acre of finely ground dust every ten years (or 5 tons every five years) or more, up to perhaps 50 tons every ten years. Adding organic matter will speed up growth tremendously.

John Hamaker has plans for an efficient rock grinder that can be built in small or very large sizes for various needs. Mark Williams may have improved on its design, and has also designed a grinding/spreading machine and a solar-powered grinder.

The most efficient way to remineralize agricultural and many forest lands will be through local efforts with a lot of small and medium-sized grinders, since transporting gravel long distances is expensive and produces additional $CO_2$. On the other hand, we may only be able to cover large areas of many forests quickly by using planes. Hamaker has suggested that an existing organization such as NASA be commissioned to organize a world-wide effort in the shortest possible time.

Since transportation can be the largest cost in obtaining gravel dust, local sources are best if they can be found. Additional sources are listed in Joanna Campe's "Soil Remineralization" newsletter. Unscreened crushed gravel the consistency of sand (which contains dust) from a local gravel pit is much more economical than shipping dust significantly longer distances. But higher yields will be obtained more quickly with dust.

### United States
Check your local Yellow Pages under "Sand and Gravel" or "Gravel" or look in the index at the back under "Gravel."

Mark Williams is currently offering finely ground river gravel for $6 per 70-pound bag, or about $290–$370 per ton delivered in the United States. Locally (he's in Arkansas) he can sell it for $14/ton for 10 tons or more. He is also offering franchises, which will provide a leased grinder, bags, and labels. He estimates franchisees can make about $25 per hour and up to $50,000 a year with very minimal investment. He is also looking for investors to produce his grinder/spreader and solar-powered grinder and to expand the operation. Route 1, Box 199B, Horatio, AR 71842. (501) 832-2444.

Rollin Anderson, Azome Utah Mining Company, Sterling, UT 84665. (801) 835-4821. A large rock-dust deposit.

Vulcan Materials, Drawer 8834, Greenville, SC 29604. (1-800) 433-8663. A number of gravel sites, mostly in the South.

Jon Biloon, Dr. Soils Glacial. Box 891, Captain Cook, HI 96704. Glacial gravel imported from British Columbia to Hawaii. A commercial farmer getting outstanding results with gravel dust.

### United Kingdom
David Langley, Redland Aggregates, Bradgate House, Groby, Leics. LE60FA. Tel. (0530) 242151. A list of 80 quarries in the U.K.

### France
Société des Carrieros de St. Nabor, 67530 Ottrott, St. Nabor. Tel. 8895 8814.

*West Germany*
Lava Union, D-5485 Sinzig.

*Austria*
Georg Abermann, Sanvita, Postfach 44, A-6370 Kitzbuhl. Tel. 05356 4333.

Alfred Winter, Stocklstr. 8, A-5020 Salzburg. Tel. 0662 8042 2633.

*Switzerland*
Firma Zimmerli, Mineralwerke AG, Hohlstr. 500, 8048 Zurich. Tel. 641040. Hans Rutz, Director. Like Australian Mineral Fertilizers, below, they do analyses of soil and rock and provide many types of rock mixture to suit various conditions. For larger-scale remineralization of forest land, their plant could be made available to grind mixed gravel quickly.

*Australia*
Australian Mineral Fertilizers, Hendon Industrial Park, 113 Tapleys Hill Road, Hendon 5014. Tel. 08 268 9222. They have a large capacity and are prepared to expand to serve other continents. They also lean toward mineral analyses of soil and rock, which is fine as long as the analysis is complete enough and doesn't slow people down. They are certainly available to grind mixed gravel for Australia.

Bill Trollope, 229 Bobbinhead Road, Turramurra, NSW 2094. He has developed a prototype of Hamaker's grinder and is looking for investors.

## SOME PEOPLE WHO HAVE BEEN FARMING ON REMINERALIZED LAND AND/OR DOING EXPERIMENTS

Dan Hemenway, TERRA: The Earth Regeneration and Reforestation Association (with Joanna Campe), 40A Brooks, Worcester, MA 01606, USA. (617) 853-7041. He's also publisher of the *International Permaculture Yearbook*, on sustainable agriculture.

Perry Spiller, The Soil Association of New Zealand, Fernhill Post Office, Hawke's Bay, NZ. Tel 64 70 799-429. They also publish a magazine on organic agriculture, "Soil and Health."

Alan LePage, LePage Road, Barre, VT 05641, USA.

Oliver D'Hotman de Villiers, Westage, Natal, South Africa.

Helmut Snoek, Hochgratstr. 6, D-8991, Opfenback, West Germany. Tel. 0831 85636. Author, many years of controlled research.

Dennis Eberl has been doing controlled studies of phosphate rock dust mixed with zeolites in agriculture. Mail Stop 513, Denver Federal Center, Denver, CO 80225. (303) 236-5042.

Ward Chesworth has been studying rock decomposition as it relates to agriculture. Dept. of Land Resource Sciences, University of Guelph, NIG 2W1, Ontario, Canada.

William Fyfe has studied population and soil fertility with respect to the availability of nutrients from the weathering of rocks. University of Western Ontario, Canada.

Hans Steiner, Mayor of Stuhlfelden, Austria. He reports that some farmers in his region have remineralized their fields, and are consequently producing crops that taste better, so they are getting a higher price. He wants to interest the Austrian government in using a large quantity of rock dust near Stuhlfelden that has been brought up from a mining operation, to remineralize the dying forests. Alfred Winter, director of the Austrian National Parks in the state, is working with him on this. Winter: Stocklstrasse 8, A-5202 Salzburg, Austria. Tel. 0662 8042/2633.

Alvin Filsinger, Box 130, Ayton, Ontario NO6 1CO, Canada.

Vivian Menaker, Box 118, Haines, AK 99827, USA.

Rod Sjoberg, K-Ridge Farms, Box 60, Speers, Saskatchewan, Canada SOM 2VO. (306) 246-4936.

A. Whyte, Box 48146, Roosevelt Park 21129, South Africa.


## SOME PEOPLE WHO HAVE BEEN REMINERALIZING FOREST LANDS

Georg Abermann, Sanvita, Postfach 44, A-6370 Kitzbuhl, Austria. Tel. 05356 4333.

Robert Schindele, A-3122 Gansbach-Kicking, Austria. Also a source of gravel dust.

Pierre Lehman, Société de l'étude de l'environment, Rue du Midi 33, Vevey, Switzerland. Tel. 021/51 05 15.

Gernot Graefe, Bergstr. 6A, 7088 Donnerskirchen, Austria. Tel. 02683-8543. He is a member of the Austrian Academy of Sciences, and did a government-sponsored study of remineralization plus composting.

Freda Meissner-Blau, a member of the Austrian Parliament and some of her fellow Greens remineralized some forest land and are very interested in the government remineralizing all of Austria's dying forests.

Jeannie Stevens, c/o P.O. Pioneer, 7254 Tasmania, Australia.

Sri Aurobindo Ashram, Auroville, Pondicherry, India.

Joanna Campe's newsletter has names and addresses of many others involved in remineralization. Back issues are available.

Jan Brewer has designed "clay bombs" carrying tree seedlings and gravel dust for reforesting remote areas from aircraft. Jan D. Brewer, D-06498, 8336, Bo-8101, San Juis Obispo, CA 93401-0001, USA.

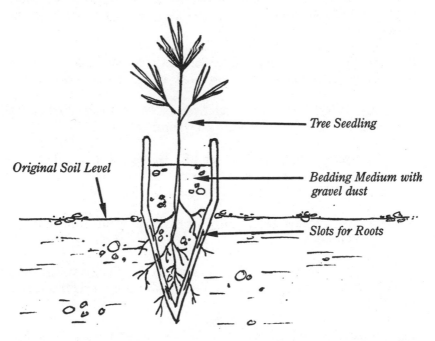

*Tree Seedling*

*Original Soil Level*

*Bedding Medium with gravel dust*

*Slots for Roots*

A CLAY TREE-PLANTING "BOMB"

## ENVIRONMENTAL ORGANIZATIONS
## TO HELP ORGANIZE THE FIGHT
(with your participation and large contributions)

New Forests Project, 731 Eighth St. SE, Washington DC 20003. They are already working in dozens of countries, helping people plant trees. They have a lot of knowledge about what to plant where to maximize growth and benefits. Local university departments of forestry and botany may also be able to provide information specific to each region on fast-growing and drought-resistant trees.

Rainforest Action Network, 300 Broadway, Suite 28, San Francisco, CA 94133. (415) 398-4404. Trying to stop the clearcutting, using media and lobbying.

Sierra Club, 530 Bush Street, San Francisco, CA 94108. (415) 776-2211. One of the largest environmental public education and lobbying organizations.

World Wildlife Fund, 1250–24 St. NW, Washington DC 20037. (212) 293-4800. They are already involved in saving rainforests and seem to have a good overview of what needs to be done.

National Audubon Society, 950 Third Avenue, New York, NY 10022. (212) 546-9100. Another large organization dedicated to environmental preservation.

Rainforest Information Centre, Box 368, Lismore NSW 2480, Australia. Also Sahabat Alam Malaysia, 37 Lorong Birch, 10250 Pulau Penang, Malaysia.

Greenpeace USA, 1611 Connecticut Avenue NW, Washington DC 20009. (202) 462-1177. They do some work on stopping acid rain.

Friends of the Earth, 530–7 Street SE, Washington DC 20003. (202) 543-4312. A smaller, quite progressive education and lobbying organization. Friends of the Earth—U.K., 377 City Road, London ECV 1NA, England.

Environmental Defense Fund, 257 Park Avenue South, New York, NY 10010. (212) 686-4191. Lawsuits!

Earth Island Institute, 300 Broadway, Suite 28, San Francisco, CA 94133, (415) 788-3666. Founded by David Brower, who also founded Friends of the Earth.

Earth First!, Box 5871, Tucson, AZ 85703. (602) 622-1371. One of the most radical environmental groups. As Greenpeace people put themselves in front of whaling ships, and Sea Shepherd people *sink* whaling ships, Earth First!ers do similar things to save trees.

Other U.S. organizations can be found in the book *Green Politics* by Fritjof Capra and Charlene Spretnak (New York: Dutton, 1984). See also Brian Tokar's *The Green Alternative: Creating an ecological future,* available for $7.95 from R. & E. Miles, Box 1916, San Pedro, CA 90733. (213) 833-8856.

In the United States, you can contact your congressional representatives at their local offices (white pages of the phone book if you know their names), or by writing: Senator or Representative _____, Washington DC. The zip code for Senators is 20510, for Representatives 20515. If you don't know their names ask Information, 411, or call your City Hall.

London Centre for International Peacebuilding, Mrs. Eirwen Harbottle, Wickham House, 10 Cleveland Way, London E1 4TR, England. Phone: (01) 790 2424. Telex: 932011 GEN FIN G.

Klaus Steinbeck and his colleagues at the School of Forest Resources, University of Georgia, Athens, GA 30602, USA, have been doing research on fast-growing trees, especially those that re-sprout by themselves after cutting. (404) 542-1376 or 542-4744.

There are now Green parties in most of the countries of the Northern Hemisphere, and environmental organizations operating in most of the countries of the world. Seems like we've got a shot at it.

## SOME ENVIRONMENTAL MAGAZINES AND NEWSPAPERS

*Whole Earth Review,* 27 Gate Five Road, Sausalito, CA 94965, USA. They also publish the Whole Earth Catalogs, which are an invaluable source of information on living lightly on the earth.

*TRANET,* the Transnational Network for Alternative/Appropriate Technology, Box 567, Rangely, ME 04970, USA. (207) 864-2252. Human scale technology that protects the environment as much as possible and puts power back in people's hands.

*Raise the Stakes,* published by Planet Drum Foundation, Box 31251, San Francisco, CA 94131, USA. (415) 285-6556. Revitalizing the earth within bioregions, areas that share a landscape and culture.

*Green Letter,* Box 9242, Berkeley, CA 94709. A connection to the green movement throughout the U.S. Another is the Committees of Correspondence, Box 30208, Kansas City, MO 64112, USA. (816) 931-9366.

*New Age Journal,* 342 Western Avenue, Brighton, MA 02135, USA. Holistic health and environmental issues.

*New Options,* Box 19324, Washington DC 20036. Not too environmental, and a little confused sometimes, but good information on what's going on in many other organizations.

Many of the environmental organizations listed above also publish regular newsletters or magazines for their members.

## BOOKS AND OTHER MEDIA ON ORGANIC FARMING AND GARDENING AND OTHER INFORMATION WE'RE GOING TO NEED TO SURVIVE

*How to Grow More Vegetables Than You Ever Thought Possible on Less Land Than You Can Imagine,* by John Jeavons. The bible on biointensive gardening and farming, for self-sufficiency and income. $6.50 postpaid from Ecology Action, 2225 El Camino Real, Palo Alto, CA 94306, USA. (415) 328-6752. ($6.90 in California.) Slide show and script on same: $12.50 rental. Also the book, *How to Start Your Own Income-producing Mini-farm* for larger-scale projects.

*Intensive Gardening Round the Year.* Food self-sufficiency for colder regions and colder times—all the latest technology and ideas. $15 postpaid from The Stephen Greene Press, Box 1000, Fessenden Road, Brattleboro, VT 05301, USA.

The "Wallo'Water," is a small fluted plastic tepee that stores heat and lowers the temperature at which plants freeze. Extends the growing season, can greatly increase yields (triple or more in some studies). In extreme conditions can be used in conjunction with black plastic ground covers and solar greenhouses. $2.50 each, 100 at $1.50 each, 5,000 at $1.25 each. From TerraCopia, 2365 S. Maine, Salt Lake City, UT 84115, USA. (801) 466-0610.

*An Attached Solar Greenhouse,* by Bill Yanda. Heats your house while you grow some of your food in it, all year long. Step-by-step instructions. $2 from The Lightning Tree, Box 1837, Santa Fe, NM 87501, USA.

*The Food- and Heat-Producing Solar Greenhouse: Design, Construction and Operation,* by Bill Yanda and Rick Fisher. $5.75 from John Muir Publications, Box 613, Santa Fe, NM 87504, USA. (515) 982-4078.

Solar greenhouses for the coming times: Use triple-glazed polycarbonate plastic with an acrylic coating (200 times stronger than glass, should withstand most hail and winds to 100 mph or more); a clear wall facing south at a 45° angle so snow falls off; the solar heat is stored in 55 gallon drums of water or fiberglass tubes, painted black. Needs no fossil fuel heating at all. Produces food all year long. If skies are cloudy, yields will drop somewhat; compensate with more composted organic matter, which will both enrich the soil and produce more $CO_2$ that will speed up growth. They're growing bananas and oranges in Cheyenne, Wyoming (lots of wind and long, cold winters) in a community solar greenhouse now. Cheyenne Botanic Gardens, 710 S. Lions Park Drive, Cheyenne, WY 82001, USA. (307) 637-6458.

*Rainbook: Resources for appropriate technology.* A look at almost everything that's going on in the field of human-scale, self-reliant, nonpolluting technology. Hundreds of illustrations. From Schocken Books, 200 Madison Avenue, New York, NY 10016. (Send $12 and ask for change.)

*The Mother Earth News Guide to Self-reliant City Living,* $4.25 from Mother Earth News, Box 70, Hendersonville, NC 28791, USA. (704) 693-0211.

"Self-reliance." Neighborhood-scale technology and skills, published by the Institute for Local Self-reliance, 2425-18 St. NW, Washington, DC 20009. (202) 232-4108. Send $1 for sample copy. Send a large stamped envelope for their list of books.

"The Cornucopia Project Newsletter," from Rodale Press, 33 E. Minor St., Emmaus, PA 18048, USA. Organic farming and gardening. Ask for a sample copy. They also have a list of 100 places around the United States to live and learn organic methods and a directory of organic farms, wholesalers, and natural food stores in the United States.

Other internships to live and learn organic farming: Greenpeace Experimental Farm, RR1, Denman Island, British Columbia, Canada V0R 1TO; The Farallones Institute, 15920 Valley Road, Occidental, CA 95465, USA, which also has classes; and the Natural Organic Farmers Association, Craftsbury Commons, VT 05827, USA.

"Acres U.S.A.: A voice for eco-agriculture," a monthly newspaper on organic farming without pesticides or chemicals. They published John Hamaker's original articles, first on remineralizing farmlands and then on climate. 10008 E. 60th Terrace, Kansas City, MO 64133, USA. (816) 737-0064.

*The One-Straw Revolution,* by Masanobu Fukuoka. No-plow, minimal-technology, minimal-work farming by a microbiologist and very special man. $6 postpaid from Sun Mountain Center, 35751 Oak Springs Drive, Tollhouse, CA 93667, USA. (209) 855-3710. Also see his more detailed workbook, *The Natural Way of Farming,* $18.50 postpaid from the same source. Sun Mountain also offers guided weekend tours of California farms, comparing big agrochemical corporations with organic alternatives.

"A Solar Food Dryer." Information from Solar Survival, Box 119, Harrisville, NH 03450. Enclose a donation for postage and handling.

For ideas on how to free much more land in and around cities to grow food on (short of armed conflict), contact: The Trust for Public Land, 116 New Montgomery Street, 4th floor, San Francisco, CA 94105. (415) 495-4014; regional offices in Cleveland, Tallahassee, Santa Fe, and Burton, WA. Or the Institute for Community Economics, 151 Montague City Road, Greenfield, MA 01301, USA. (413) 774-7956; speakers are available for community meetings, conferences, and workshops, and they help fund cooperative ventures. Also, "Citizens Action Manual: A guide to recycling vacant property in your neighborhood," free from National Park Service, Attention PARTS, 440 G St. NW, Washington DC 20243.

Community food gardening is already going on in many cities of the United States, with land and water usually provided free by the city and people tending small plots side by side. Call City Hall; The National Gardening Association, 180 Flynn Ave., Burlington, VT 05401, USA. (802) 863-1308; or American Community Gardening, Association, 909 York, Denver, CO 80206, USA. (303) 575-2547.

*DNA for Beginners,* a cartoon book that shows why we can't rely on genetic engineering to solve our food or health problems, and why we'd better not try. Writers and Readers Publishers. Ask your local bookstore.

*The North Will Rise Again: Pensions, Politics and Power in the 1980s,* by Jeremy Rifkin and Randy Barber, from Beacon Press, 25 Beacon Street, Boston, MA 02108, USA. Send $12 and ask for change. *The* book on pension fund capital, how it's being used against us, and all the great things we could do if we got control of it back.

If you still need more inspiration, call your local video store and see if you can rent the feature film *Amazing Grace and Chuck* (Tri-Star Pictures,

1987), starring the Denver Nuggets' forward Alex English. It's a funny, heart-stirring fantasy about how one young little leaguer finally stopped the arms race. (But I hear the film has been suppressed, because its message is so subversive. If your local video dealer doesn't have it, ask them to see if they can get it.)

We also have to create more of our own media of communication if we're going to get through this crisis. The mass media are controlled by the same corporate interests that would like to retain the status quo as long as possible. (Public television in the U.S. even gets much of its funding from the oil companies!) My first article on this material, for example, was sent out by Words by Wire in July 1986, to some 50 newspapers in the U.S. and Canada. Only two printed it, with little public notice. A precious year and a half was lost. This book was also turned down by five or six major publishers in the past year. I have to say, however, that only one progressive or alternative paper or magazine has printed it, while several have turned it down. That kind of thing makes me think our chances are kind of slim.

In terms of the scale at which the great nurturing of the earth must be done, both highly centralized high-tech activities and decentralized, low-tech actions are essential. In other words, we have to do everything we can as quickly as we can, or we are probably lost.

We have to put every conceivable kind of pressure on our local, state, and federal governmental bodies, comparable perhaps to what it took to stop the Vietnam war, or the Paris strike of 1968, maybe a lot more. And then go out and do everything we can ourselves, individually and with our families, friends, and neighbors, to plant trees, remineralize the forests and farms, share rides and every possible thing instead of buying things that require energy, and do everything we can to stop using all the fossil fuels for the next two to three or four years.

The work we have to do can help make us whole. It is nurturing and physically challenging at the same time, and should help us integrate our masculine and feminine sides, which is also long overdue for many of us.

It might be useful here to try to sketch what I think will happen if we don't act in time.

Those who can will try to secure land for themselves, and build as many greenhouses as they can afford. They will also have to find a reliable source of irrigation water, as summers become increasingly and unbearably hot and dry and drought becomes more and more widespread. Most rivers and streams will not be reliable in the severe drought to come if we do not act to stop the ice age in time, as they are likely to dry up during the growing season. This may be an insurmountable problem in most of the agricultural regions of the world. (In the U.S., even the underground aquifers are drying up.)

Then there are the hurricanes, tornados, high winds, hail, floods, and summer freezes that will destroy increasing amounts of any crops planted if the ice age progression is allowed to continue.

The skies will become increasingly overcast, and even solar greenhouses and other devices may eventually not be sufficient to keep many crops from freezing some nights during the growing season. So some additional source of heat would have to be provided to greenhouses, meaning some reliable long-term source of fuel would have to be secured, not to mention all the fuel for cooking, heating, and so on. (Though as far as cooking is concerned, some people are able to live quite well on raw foods, sprouting beans and seeds, etc., and may well be healthier than those who eat primarily cooked food.)

Obtaining the land and building the necessary agricultural technology would be expensive. If we do not do it together, relatively few people will be able to afford it in any country. Those that realize they have no access to land and equipment and thus to survival are likely to become a threat to those that do. A police state would most likely develop if it became clear that the necessary actions would not be taken in time, and mass starvation was expected.

It would become a war of all against all. Snipers and terrorists would be everywhere. No one who had even a piece of land would be able to venture out of their compounds without armored cars, perhaps not even then. Hired guns in the form of police and militia would be everywhere, and like all hired guns they would terrorize whomever they chose. There might even be cannibalism as people's stores of food ran out.

There would not likely be any "entertainment" (the worst thing, right?). Television and radio stations might well be blown up by competing factions, and there might not even be any lasting source of electricity if the power lines were similarly destroyed. Gasoline tanker trucks would be commandeered or hijacked, natural gas lines sabotaged. So now probably no fuel but wood, and only while nearby trees last. So no reliable fuel to heat the greenhouses, or pump water for irrigation. So the vast majority of people would starve to death, in spite of their wealth or influence, if they were not killed first.

This message may scare you, which would be fine, especially if it helps you wake up quickly and get working on stopping the ice age. But it is a message primarily for the power brokers of the world, whose decisions will be crucial if we all are to survive. Think of your beautiful kids, power brokers! Their lives are going to be cut much shorter than yours if we don't succeed. Think of everybody you care about. (Do you really care about anybody? How $ much?)

The likely outcome if we do not try quickly or hard enough is a message that needs to be heard by everyone whose first impulse will be to try to save their own ass, instead of turning immediately to the much more urgent and solvable problem of stablizing our common climate. Please do not think, rich and powerful person, that you can turn your back on the rest of us and go it alone. There are too many people who are already armed and angry, especially in the U.S., thousands of Vietnam veterans who have have not forgotten what was done to them, blacks who have been excluded and despised for centuries, right-wingers who think they are better than everybody else, etc., who are not likely to let you happily go on eating, no matter how carefully hidden your compound, while they starve to death. If we do not come together around this common threat, this will be a time of retribution and of cataclysm.

We are all in this together, like it or not. We can all live, if we get the message the first time we hear it and start moving. We are all very creative people. If we don't move on this quickly, it seems very likely we will destroy one another.

It seems possible that there could be other scenarios, less bleak than the hell just described, even if we do not succeed in stopping the ice ages. People could cooperate instead of competing, organizing every available resource for the common good, keeping as many people as possible alive. Beautiful things could happen, sacrificing for others, creativity and heroism of all kinds. Undoubtedly these things would take place in some localities. But one wonders how societies so imbued with competitiveness and individualism, prejudice and mistrust, could transform themselves in the face of such a crisis.

As Pogo says, "We have met the enemy and he is us." An enemy who can probably only be subdued with laughter, insight, and kindness.

*This is for Charles, Lynne,*
*and Daniel, my rocks*

# Acknowledgments

My debt, our debt, to John Hamaker is of course limitless.

I am also greatly indebted to Don Weaver, who "discovered" John's articles in *Acres U.S.A.* and collaborated with him in writing the book they published in 1982. Since then, Don has been publishing a newsletter on this material, which provided me with a great deal of additional scientific material and leads. Without him, this book would probably never have been written.

Hamaker and Weaver's book was first sent to me by Charlotte Gerson, president of the Gerson Institute.

My long-time close friend and associate Charles Brusman has been doing a great job running the clinic we share responsibility for, which has given me additional time to work on this book. I am very grateful for both his support and his friendship.

I would like to thank the scientists who had free-wheeling conversations with me, including Gifford Miller, Reid Bryson, Kenneth Watt, John Pastor, David Smith, Steve Porter, Orman Granger, Paul Gersper, and others. And everyone who has talked to me about this material or provided information. All the writers and publishers who supply my reading habit.

I would also like to take this opportunity to thank the many therapists who have helped me grow and let go. They include Gene Sagan, David Schiffman, Harry Sloan, Bill Roller and Vivian Nelson, Art Raisman and especially Daniel Lapin. Rolfers and other bodyworkers, including Owen James, Peter Melchior, Ed Taylor, Cindee McAllister, Kenny Mizono, Connie Call, and Martha Winneker. Rena Katznelson Blauner for dragging me into therapy many years ago, and all the other members who have worked with me in groups. Mitsui Manufacturers Bank for believing in us when no one else would. And Epson for donating the computer this book was written on.

All the other people who have been especially important to me, including but not limited to Mike Potter, Sylvan Zucker, Harry Ratner, Dutch Voll, G.L. Fox, Joyce Himes Fox, Stan Lyman, Vera Haile, Gertrude Selznick, Larry Schonbrun, Lew Sherman, Lynn Adler, and Stan Weisenberg. All my lovers over the years. The many nice people who have been associated with the clinic.

All the musicians whose work/play I've been inspired by, including

among many others Rostropovich, Mozart, Dennis Brain, Neville Marriner
and the Academy of St. Martin in the Fields, Dvorak, Schubert, Beethoven,
Paul Simon, Joni Mitchell, Sting, Keith Jarrett, John Coltrane, Van Morrison
and James Taylor. The discoverers and manufacturers of psychedelics.

And all my friends, who mean so much to me, including my loving sister
Lynne Sarafian, Charles Si Kroll (Redwood), David Glick, Sue Eisenberg,
Flynn Harrison, Janet Levine, Stan Messer, Dmitri Devyatkin, my won-
derful nephew Greg Sarafian, and all my friendly relatives.

*Larry Ephron*
Berkeley, California
January 1988

# Endnotes

## CHAPTER ONE: WILL WE HAVE TO STOP EATING SOON?

*Cover and First Page:* The quote from the *National Geographic* is from an article by Senior Assistant Editor Samuel W. Matthews called "Ice on the World," January 1987. Buckminster Fuller wrote these words to John Hamaker and Don Weaver a few years ago. Kenneth Watt has been writing the "Annual Review of the Environment" for *Encyclopedia Brittanica* since 1976. He wrote the statement quoted to Hamaker and Weaver. Victor Kovda is also head of the Institute of Soil Science of the USSR Academy of Sciences.

*p. 4* The statement about seven such winters consecutively being enough to establish an ice-age ice cover comes from Kukla and Kukla (1974).

Figure 2 is reprinted from Williams (1978).

*pp. 3–11* The information on record cold and snow cover, drought and flooding comes from many U.S. newspaper accounts. Again in November 1986 the entire east coast of the United States was hit with a new cold wave that shattered old records; in January 1987 all of Europe and Scandinavia and parts of the Soviet Union were hit with the coldest weather in all their recorded history.

*p. 6* The decrease in the growing season is reported in Philip W. Suckling, *Physical Geography,* 7:3 (1986); and John A. Brown, *Nature,* 260:420 (1976).

*p. 7* I analyzed hurricane data from U.S. Department of Commerce, National Oceanic and Atmospheric Administration, "Technical Report," 1985.

*p. 12* The Imbrie paper cited is Imbrie and Imbrie (1980).

*pp. 16–17* Lester Machta is quoted in Green (1977). I can't find the reference on Jay Harmon. David P. Adam (U.S. Geological Survey, Menlo Park, California) spoke to Don Weaver; however, he seems to believe that the ice age cycle can occur simply as a result of feedback processes involving heat transfer from the oceans (Adam, 1975); Kenneth Watt and Paul Gersper are quoted on the cover. The buildup of polar ice from heating in the tropics is becoming increasingly recognized by climatologists, such as Roger G. Barry (1985). See also Ruddiman and McIntyre (1979). Dominique Raynaud is a French glaciologist. Ian Whillans is at Ohio State University. For a Russian perspective see Volkov and Zakharov (1977) and Kondrat'ev (1986).

Raynaud and Whillans are quoted in *Newsweek,* October 5, 1981: "We think that by raising temperatures, $CO_2$ makes more snow fall over Antarctica and increases the rate of accumulation on the ice." Even in spite of popular articles like this which are readily available to everyone in Congress (a large box in the *Newsweek* article said "The 'greenhouse effect' could raise sea levels by 20 feet. Then again, it might make the glaciers grow"), Congressional hearings on $CO_2$ and the greenhouse effect *have never even raised this question.*

See Lamb (1982), Schneider and Londer (1984, p. 216), and Ruddiman and McIntyre (1979).

Choudhury and Kukla's (1979) finding that $CO_2$ delays snowmelt is also consistent with the perspective presented here.

*p. 18* The forester in the Black Forest is quoted in *Resurgence,* Nov.-Dec. 1984. Arthur H. Johnson and Robert I. Bruck are quoted in an article in the *New York Times,* Feb. 26, 1984. Hans Enghardt made his "five seconds to midnight" warning in 1983!—*New York Times,* Nov. 6.

*p. 22* W.R. Day's work relating the health of vegetation to the condition of the soil can be found in several articles (1929, 1938, 1950). Other work in this area includes J.S. Boyce (1948), S.A. Graham (1952), R.F. Anderson (1960), and Wood and Bedard (in White 1977).

St.Barbe Baker's observation is described in an article in *Akwesasne Notes,* which was edited from a transcript of the Permaculture Design Course published by Yankee Permaculture, Box 202, Orange, MA 01364, USA. Permaculture is Mollison's name for sustainable agriculture.

*p. 23* The gradual demineralization and acidification of the earth's soils during interglacial periods and its effects on tree life has become well-known over the past few decades. References include Dimbleby (1962, 1964), Turner and West (1968), Godwin (1973), Davis (1976) and Watts (1979) among others. Svend Andersen's work (1966, 1969) is also cited in the Bibliography.

*p. 23* See Likens, et al. (1977).

*p. 27* The long-term connection between ice buildup and volcanism comes from Rampino, Self, and Fairbridge (1979).

*p. 29* John T. Hollin's (1980) paper was also presented in *Nature.*

*p. 31* I haven't been able to verify it, but it has been said that the tropical rainforests produce 80% of the world's oxygen. Some of the statistical references on the rainforest came from Norman Myers (1984). An in-depth look at the rainforest and the threats to its survival can be found in Catherine Caufield (1985). For much of the political information I am indebted to a succinct and comprehensive article by Jonathan Montague (1986).

*p. 34* Jack Walters and George Marek were quoted in an article in *Macleans,* Jan. 14, 1985.

*p. 37* Research on some of the other greenhouse gases that are rapidly rising is presented in articles by Richard A. Kerr (1984), and Hansen, Lacis, Rind, and Russell (1984).

*p. 38* Some of R. Albert's research (1938) is reported in the article cited. Marcus Bell's book was published in Victoria, British Columbia in 1974.

*p. 39* The article in *World Wood* is by Poole.

## CHAPTER TWO: A REVOLUTION IN AGRICULTURE

*p. 71* Jim Hightower was quoted in *New Age Journal,* Sept.-Oct. 1986, p. 39.

*p. 74* Revelle made this remark at the 1985 AAAS Meeting in Los Angeles, May 26–31, in a talk on "The hydrological cycle." This might be a good place to mention that Roger Revelle is not primarily a climatologist at all, but an oceanographer. Yet he is probably the person most frequently asked for quotes about climate change.

*p. 79* The USDA study of dietary minerals is reported in Rodale Press' *Understanding Vitamins and Minerals.*

William Albrecht's seminal research on agriculture can be found in *The Albrecht Papers,* published by Acres USA (address in the *Access* section). I can no longer find the references for the NAS article or some of the other statements cited in this section.

*p. 90* Fukuoka's *One Straw Revolution* is, along with Hamaker and Weaver's book, and Max Gerson's *A Cancer Therapy,* one of the most important books of our time. Fukuoka recently published another book, *The Natural Way of Farming: The theory and practice of green philosophy.* Availability is mentioned in the *Access* section.

## CHAPTER THREE: THE POLITICAL CLIMATE

*p. 96* The 1972 meeting was described in Kukla (1980), the 1974 meeting in Bryson (1975), the 1975 meeting in Willard F. Libby (1976), and the 1979 meeting in Collins (1979).

*p. 97* Information about the 1976 NAS meeting comes from Irving Kaplan, in an interview with Barbara Logan and Alden Bryant of the Earth Regeneration Society, San Diego, January 18, 1984.

*p. 98* Transcripts of congressional hearings are available from the committee that held them, without charge.

*p. 99* The Hansen paper referred to is Hansen, Johnson, Lacis, Lebedeff, Lee, Rind, and Russell (1981) *p. 106* Jim Green is quoted in the *Guardian,* Jan. 9, 1985. The Environmental Protection Agency (EPA) has been pushing the warming theory unequivocably. (Hamaker calls it the Establishment Protection Agency.)

*p. 112* Ben Bagdikian's quote comes from his book *The Media Monopoly.* On a more humorous note, Ogden Nash said, "Progress was all right once, but it went on too long."

## CHAPTER FOUR: STOPPING THE COMING ICE AGE

*p. 121* Apolonildo Brito's story was written up in *The New York Times,* November 11, 1986.

*p. 123* Margarita de Botero's story was written up in the *San Francisco Chronicle,* November 4, 1986. Jon Carroll is also a columnist in the *Chronicle* (his quote was unrelated to the Botero story).

*p. 136* The full title of Lovins' book is *Soft Energy Paths: Toward a Durable Peace.* The information on Solar One and SolarPlant I came from *Popular Science,* February 1985.

*pp. 137–138* The information on generating electricity from ocean temperature differences came from an article in *Scientific American,* January 1987.

*p. 139* The information on methanol fuel came primarily from an article by M.D. Jackson et al., printed by the American Society of Mechanical Engineers, and one by C. Gray (1983) of the Environmental Protection Agency, published by, get this, the American Petroleum Institute. (They were trying to cover their bases and show how efficient methanol fuels derived from residual oil, residual gas, and coal could be. Pretty ironic.) Both articles were sent to me in a package on methanol fuels prepared by the California Energy Commission under Governor Jerry Brown. Also useful was Michael Cross (1984).

*p. 149* The idea of Public Energy Districts was proposed in an article by James Ridgeway and Bettina Conner (1979).

*pp. 177–181* The information on the prophecies came from a magazine article I have long since misplaced. I have since read or heard about some of the prophecies from other sources. Chief Seattle's speech has been reprinted a number of times by different organizations.

*p. 181 Akwesasne Notes* is available by subscription from Roosevelttown, New York, USA.

*p. 182* Lovelock's Gaia hypothesis is fully presented in his book (1979).

*p. 184* President Moi's remarks are from a speech given to the United Nations Environment Programme, and were reprinted in *Mazingira*, Vol. 6, 1982.

*pp. 188–189* The quotations from Patricia Ellsberg, Joanna Macy, John Steiner, and Helen Caldicott, M.D. were taken from the transcript of a television series, "How then shall we live?", produced by Original Face Video, Oakland, California. (415) 339-3126.

# Bibliography

Adam, David P. (1975) *Quaternary Research* 5:161.

Albert, R. (1938), "Investigation on the manner of improving impoverished soils with crushed rocks" (in German), *Forestarchiv* 14:237.

Andersen, Svend Th. (1966) *The Palaeobotanist* 15:117.

—— (1969), "Interglacial vegetation and soil development," *Medd. Dansk Geol. Foren, Kovenhavn,* Bind 19.

Anderson, R. F. (1960), *Forest and Shade Tree Entomology* (New York: Wiley).

Associated Press (1984), "Murres, kittiwakes puzzle scientists," *Juneau Empire,* December 26.

Bach, W., J. Pankrath, and J. Williams (1980), *Interactions of Energy and Climate* (Dordrecht, Boston, London: D. Reidel).

Barnett, Tim P. (1985), "Long-term climate change in observed physical properties of the oceans," in *Detecting the Climatic Effects of Increasing Carbon Dioxide* (U.S. Department of Energy).

Barnola, J. M., D. Raynaud, Y. S. Korotkevich, and C. Lorius, "Vostok ice core provides 160,000-year record of atmospheric $CO_2$," *Nature* 239:408 (1987).

Barry, Roger G. (1985), "The cryosphere and climate change," in *Detecting the Climatic Effects of Increasing Carbon Dioxide* (U.S. Department of Energy).

Bear, Firman E. (1948), in *Soil Science of America Proceedings.*

—— (1962), *Earth, The Stuff of Life* (University of Oklahoma Press).

Bell, Marcus (1974), *Influences of Fertilization on Forest Production and the Forest Environment* (Victoria, British Columbia).

Bentley, Charles, in Chicago Tribune article, "Greenhouse effect cuts no ice, expert says," May 29, 1986.

Berger, A., J. Imbrie, J. Hays, G. Kukla, and B. Saltzman (eds.) (1984), *Milankovitch and Climate* (Dordrecht/Boston/Lancaster: D. Reidel).

Bess, Henry A., Stephen H. Spurr, and E. W. Littlefield (1947), "Forest Site Conditions and the Gypsy Moth," *Harvard Forest Bulletin,* No. 22

Boyce, J. S. (1948), *Forest Pathology* (New York: McGraw-Hill).

Bradley, R. S., H. F. Diaz, J. K. Eischeid, P. D. Jones, P. M. Kelly, and C. M. Goodess, "Precipitation fluctuations over Northern Hemisphere land areas since the mid-19th century," *Science* 237:171 (1987).

Bradley, Raymond S., and P. D. Jones (1985), "Data bases for isolating the effects of the increasing carbon dioxide concentration," in *Detecting the Climatic Effects of Increasing Carbon Dioxide* (U.S. Department of Energy), p. 44.

Bradley, R. S., and G. H. Miller (1972), *Nature* 231:7.

Brewer, Peter G. (1978), "Carbon dioxide and climate," *Oceanus* 21:12.

Broecker, Wallace, and J. van Donk (1970), "Insolation changes, ice volumes, and the $O^{18}$ record in deep-sea cores," *Review of Geophysics and Space Physics* 8:169.

Bryson, Reid (1975), "The lessons of climatic history," *Environmental Conservation* 2:163

Bryson, Reid, and Brian M. Goodman (1980), "Volcanic activity and climatic changes," *Science* 207:1041.

Butzer, K. W. (1983), "Climatic change," in *Encyclopedia Brittanica.*

Campbell, Philip (1984), "New data upset ice age theories," *Nature* 293:12.

Caufield, Catherine (1985), *In the Rainforest* (New York: Knopf).

Choudhury, Bhashkar, and George Kukla (1979), "Impact of $CO_2$ on cooling of snow and water surfaces," *Nature* 280:668.

Collins, Peter (1979), "World climate conference turns to the weather," *Nature* 278:3.

Cross, Michael (ed.) (1984), *Grow Your Own Energy* (New York and London: Basil Blackwell, Ltd.).

Davis, Margaret (1976), "Pleistocene biogeography of temperate deciduous forests," in West and Haag (1976).

Davis, N.E. (1972), in *Quarterly Journal of the Royal Meteorological Society* 98:763.

Day, W. R. (1929), "Environment and disease," *Forestry* 3:1.

––––– (1938), "Root-rot of sweet chestnut and beech caused by species of phytophthora—I. Cause and symptoms of disease: Its relation to soil conditions," *Forestry* 12:2

––––– (1950), "The soil conditions which determine wind-throw in forests," *Forestry* 23:2.

Denton, George H., and Terence J. Hughes (1981), *The Last Great Ice Sheets* (New York: Wiley Interscience).

Dewey, Kenneth F., and Richard Heim, Jr. (1982), "A digital archive of Northern Hemisphere snow cover, November 1966 through December 1980," *Bulletin of the American Meteorological Society* 63:1132.

Diaz, H. F. and R. G. Quayle (1980), "An analysis of the recent extreme winters in the contiguous United States," *Monthly Weather Review* 108:687.

Dimbleby, G. W. (1962), "The development of British heathlands and their soils," *Oxford Forestry Memoirs* No. 23, Oxford University.

––––– (1964), "Post-glacial changes in soil profiles," *Proceedings of the Royal Society of Britain,* 161:355.

Editorial, "Towards a cold greenhouse," *New Scientist,* September 17, 1987.

Emiliani, Cesare (1955), "Pleistocene Temperatures," *Journal of Geology* 63:538.

Fink Julius, and George Kukla (1977), "Pleistocene climates in Central Europe: At least 17 interglacials after the Olduvai Event," *Quaternary Research* 7:363.

Gates, W. L. (1976), *Science* 191:1138.

Godwin, Sir Harry (1973), *The History of the British Flora* (Cambridge: Cambridge University Press).

Gordon, John E. (1981), "Glacier margin fluctuations during the 19th and 20th centuries in the Ikamiut Kangerdluarssuat area, West Greenland," *Arctic and Alpine Research* 13:47.

Graham, S. A. (1952), *Forest Entomology* (New York: McGraw-Hill).

Gray, C. (1983), "Methanol—the transportation fuel of the future," 48th Midyear Refining Meeting, American Petroleum Institute, May 11, 1983.

Green, Fitzhugh (1977), *A Change in the Weather* (New York: W.W. Norton).

Griffiths, J. F., and K. C. Vining (1984), in *International Journal of Environmental Studies* 22:103.

Hamaker, John D., and Donald A. Weaver (1982), *The Survival of Civilization* (Burlingame, CA: Hamaker-Weaver).

Hansen, James E., Andrew A. Lacis, David H. Rind, and Gary L. Russell (1984), "Climate sensitivity to increasing greenhouse gases," in M. Barth and J. Titus (eds.), *Greenhouse Effect and Sea Level Rise* (New York: Van Nostrand Reinhold).

Hansen, J., D. Johnson, A. Lacis, S. Lebedeff, P. Lee, D. Rind, and G. Russell (1981), "Climate impact of increasing atmospheric carbon dioxide," *Science* 213:957.

Hare, F. Kenneth (1982), *Impact of Science on Society* Vol. 32 No. 3.

Hensel, Julius (1894) *Bread from Stones* (Philadelphia: A.J. Tafel; reprinted by Health Research, Mokelumne Hill, CA, 1977).

Hollin, John T. (1980), "Climate and sea level in isotope state 5: an East Antarctic ice surge at about 95,000 BP?", *Nature* 283:629.

Howard, Sir Albert (1947), *The Soil and Health* (New York: Devin-Adair).

Imbrie, John, and John Z. Imbrie (1980), "Modeling the climatic response to orbital variations," *Science* 207:943.

Iverson, J. (1973), *"The Development of Denmark's Nature since the Last Glacial* (Copenhagen: Geological Survey of Denmark, V Series, No. 7-C).

Jackson, M. D., et al., "Methanol-fueled transit bus demonstration," American Society of Mechanical Engineers.

Jacoby, Gordon C., Jr., Edward R. Cook, and Linda D. Ulan (1985), "Reconstructed summer degree days in Central Alaska and Northwestern Canada since 1524," *Quaternary Research* 23:18.

Jones, P. D., T. M. L. Wigley, and P. M. Kelly (1982), "Variations in Surface Air Temperatures: Part 1. Northern Hemisphere, 1881–1980," *Monthly Weather Review,* 110:59.

——— (1986), "Global temperature variations between 1861 and 1984," *Nature* 322:430.

Kerr, Richard (1984), "Doubling of atmospheric methane supported," *Science* 226:954.

Kondrat'ev, K. Ya. (1986), *Changes in Global Climate* (Rotterdam: A. A. Balkema).

Kukla, George (1980), "End of the last interglacial: A predictive model of the future?" *Paleoecology of Africa.*

—— (1970), "Correlations between loesses and deep-sea sediments," *Geologiska Foreningen i Stockholm Forhandlingar* 92:148.

Kukla, George, and J. Gavin (1981), "Summer ice and carbon dioxide," *Science* 214:497.

Kukla, George, and Helena Kukla (1974), "Increased surface albedo in the Northern Hemisphere," *Science* 183:709.

Lachenbruch, Arthur H., and B. Vaughn Marshall (1986), "Changing climate: Geothermal evidence from permafrost in the Alaskan arctic," *Science* 234:689.

Lamb, Sir H. H. (1982), *Climate, History and the Modern World* (New York: Methuen).

Libby, Willard F. (1976), "Climatology conference," *Science,* May 28.

Likens, Gene, F. Herbert Bormann, Robert S. Pierce, John S. Eaton, and Noye M. Johnson (1977), *Biogeochemistry of a Forested Ecosystem* (New York: Springer-Verlag).

Lovelock, James E. (1979), *GAIA: A new look at life on Earth* (Oxford University Press).

Lovins, Amory (1977), *Soft Energy Paths: Toward a Durable Peace* (New York: Harper and Row).

Maddox, John (1986), "How to tell when the sea rises?" *Nature* 324:105.

Margolin, Malcolm (1985), *The Earth Manual: How to work on wild land without taming it* (Berkeley, California: Heyday Books).

Marland, Gregg, and Ralph M. Rotty (1979), *Reviews of Geophysics and Space Physics.*

Matson, M. and D. R. Wiesnet (1981), "New data base for climate studies," *Nature* 289:451.

Matson, M., C. P. Berg, and E. P. McClain (1979), "New data and new products: the NOAA/NESS continental snow cover data base," *Proceedings, Fourth Annual Climatic Diagnostics Workshop,* NOAA, Washington, D.C.

Matson, M. (1977), "Winter snow-cover maps of North America and Eurasia from satellite records, 1966–76," *NOAA Technical Memorandum NESS 84,* Washington, D.C.

McElroy, Michael B. (1983), discussed in C. Simon, "Marine Life: Effects on $CO_2$ and climate?" *Science News,* April 9.

Milankovitch, Milutin (1930), in W. Koppen and R. Geiger (eds.), *Handbuch der Klimatologie* (Berlin; Borntrager).

Mitchell, J. M., Jr. (1976), *Quaternary Research,* 6:481.

Montague, Jonathan (1986), "Eco-pagan militants defend the rain forest," *The Daily Californian,* December 1.

Myers, Dr. Norman (1984), *GAIA: An atlas of planet management* (New York: Anchor/Doubleday).

Peltier, W.R., R.A. Drummond, and A.M. Tushingham (1986), *Geophysical Journal of the Royal Astronomical Society* 87:79–116.

Perry, John (1984) *Nature* 311:681.

Pisias, Nicklas G., and Nicholas J. Shackleton (1984), "Modelling the global climatic response to orbital forcing and atmospheric carbon dioxide changes," *Nature* 310:757.

Pittock, A. Barrie (1983), "The carbon-dioxide problem and its impact," *Meteorology Australia*, February 1983.

Ponte, Lowell (1976), *The Cooling* (Englewood Cliffs, N.J.: Prentice-Hall).

Rampino, Michael, Stephen Self, and Rhodes Fairbridge (1979), "Can rapid climatic change cause volcanic eruptions?" *Science* 206:826.

Raphael, Ray (1981), *Tree Talk* (Covelo, California: Island Press, Star Route 1, Box 38, Covelo CA 95428 USA).

Revelle, R., and H.E. Seuss (1957), "Carbon dioxide exchange between the atmosphere and the ocean, and the question of an increase in atmospheric $CO_2$ during the past decades," *Tellus* 9:18.

Ridgeway, James and Bettina Connor (1979), "What can be done?" in Alexander Cockburn and James Ridgeway (eds.) *Political Ecology: An activist's reader on energy, land, food, technology, health, and the economics and politics of social change* (New York: Times Books).

Rodale, J.I. (1948), *The Healthy Hunzas* (Rodale Press).

Roeckner, E., U. Schlese, J. Biercamp, and P. Loewe (1987), "Cloud optical depth feedbacks and climate modelling," *Nature* 329:138.

Ruddiman, W.F., and A. McIntyre (1979), "Warmth of the subpolar North Atlantic ocean during Northern Hemisphere ice-sheet growth," *Science* 204:173.

—— (1981), *Quaternary Research* 16:125.

Schneider, Stephen, and Randi Londer (1984), *The Coevolution of Climate and Life* (San Francisco: Sierra Club Books).

Shackleton, N.J., M.A. Hall, J. Line, and Cang Shuxi (1983), "Carbon isotope data in core V19-30 confirm reduced carbon dioxide concentration in the ice age atmopshere," *Nature* 306:329.

Simkin, T., L. Siebert, L. McClelland, D. Bridge, C. Newhall, and J.H. Latter (1981), *Volcanoes of the World* (Stroudsburg: Hutchinson Ross Publishers).

Simpson, Sir George (1938), *Nature* 141:591; reprinted in the Annual Report of the Smithsonian Institution, 1938, 289–302.

Snoek, Helmut, and Horst Wulfrath (1983), *Das Buch von Steinmehl* (The book of stonemeal), (Orac Pietsch).

Turner, C., and R.G. West (1968), *The Subdivision and Zonation of Glacial Periods* (Cambridge University Press).

Volkov, N..A., and V.F. Zakharov (1977), "E'volutsiya ledyanogo pokrova v Artike v svyazi s izmeneniyami klimata" (Evolution of ice cover in the Arctic due to changes in climate), *Meteorologiya i Gidrologiya*, p. 47.

Watt, Kenneth E. F., "Tree mortality, acid rain, carbon dioxide and the green-house effect," University of California, Davis, unpublished.

—— "An alternative explanation of widespread tree mortality in Europe and North America," University of California, Davis, unpublished.

Watts, W. A. (1980), "The late quaternary vegetation history of the Southeastern United States," *Annual Review of Ecological Systems* 11:387.

Weisburg, Stefi, and Janet Raloff (1985), *Science News* 127:282.

West, R. C., and W. G. Haag (eds.) (1976), *Ecology of the Pleistocene,* Vol. 13 of Geoscience and Man (Louisiana State University School of Geoscience).

Wetherald, R. T. and S. Manabe (1986), *Climatic Change* 8:5.

White, Deborah (1977) *XV International Congress of Entomology* (College Park, Maryland: Entomological Society of America).

Williams, Larry D. (1978), "Ice-sheet initiation and climatic influences of expanded snow cover in Arctic Canada," *Quaternary Research* 10:141.

Woillard, Genevieve (1979), "Abrupt end of the last interglacial s.s. in northeast France," *Nature* 281:558.

Wood, Fred B. (1986), "Global climate/earth systems monitoring and modeling: An interdisciplinary evaluation," paper presented at the annual meetings of the Society for General Systems Research and the American Association for the Advancement of Science, May 26.

Woodwell, G. M., R. H. Whittaker, W. A. Reiners, G. E. Likens, C. C. Delwiche, and D. B. Botkin (1978), "The biota and the world carbon budget," *Science* 199:141.

# Expanded Contents